Practical Application Development with AppRun

Building Reliable, High-Performance Web Apps Using Elm-Inspired Architecture, Event Pub-Sub, and Components

Yiyi Sun

Apress®

Practical Application Development with AppRun

Yiyi Sun
Thornhill, ON, Canada

ISBN-13 (pbk): 978-1-4842-4068-7   ISBN-13 (electronic): 978-1-4842-4069-4
https://doi.org/10.1007/978-1-4842-4069-4

Library of Congress Control Number: 2018968420

Managing Director, Apress Media LLC: Welmoed Spahr
Acquisitions Editor: Jade Scard
Development Editor: Chris Nelson
Coordinating Editor: Nancy Chen

Cover designed by eStudioCalamar

Cover image designed by Freepik (www.freepik.com)

Distributed to the book trade worldwide by Springer Science+Business Media New York, 233 Spring Street, 6th Floor, New York, NY 10013. Phone 1-800-SPRINGER, fax (201) 348-4505, e-mail orders-ny@springer-sbm.com, or visit www.springeronline.com. Apress Media, LLC is a California LLC and the sole member (owner) is Springer Science + Business Media Finance Inc (SSBM Finance Inc). SSBM Finance Inc is a **Delaware** corporation.

For information on translations, please e-mail rights@apress.com, or visit www.apress.com/rights-permissions.

Apress titles may be purchased in bulk for academic, corporate, or promotional use. eBook versions and licenses are also available for most titles. For more information, reference our Print and eBook Bulk Sales web page at www.apress.com/bulk-sales.

Any source code or other supplementary material referenced by the author in this book is available to readers on GitHub via the book's product page, located at www.apress.com/9781484240687. For more detailed information, please visit www.apress.com/source-code.

Printed on acid-free paper

Table of Contents

About the Author

Yiyi Sun has an academic background in computer cartography and geographical information systems. He has more than 20 years of software development experience and more than 10 years of experience as a software architect. Currently, he works as the director of technology in a real estate company based in Toronto, Canada. Coding and fishing are his hobbies.

About the Technical Reviewer

Raed Alahmad has a bachelor's degree in computer engineering (Jordan) and a master's of business administration (United Kingdom). He has more than 19 years of professional experience working in application development. He has successfully led several development teams in Jordan, Dubai, and Toronto.

While experienced in enterprise web applications development, his boundaries expand far beyond; for more than ten years, Raed has led and successfully delivered several implementations of enterprise content management solutions such as Livelink and SharePoint, in addition to working on cloud solution architecture and developing for Office 365 and Azure. Furthermore, within the last few years, Raed has focused on web front-end JavaScript libraries and frameworks.

Currently, Raed works as a development manager and architect in a big firm in Toronto. He is also studying artificial intelligence and machine learning at the University of Toronto's School of Continuing Studies.

Acknowledgments

Thanks to everyone who participated and helped make this book possible. I will start with thanks to my wife, Juan Du, and my daughter, Yanting Sun. Your support and love are the greatest happiness in my life.

I also want to express my gratitude to the team at Apress for reaching out to me to propose a book for AppRun and working to create and publish quality content. It has been a great experience and a pleasure to work with the entire Apress team.

Many thanks also go out to my team and managers at work for using and testing AppRun and for providing feedback and support, including Mark Houghton, Jeff Colangelo, Amy Pickering, Carolyn Barratt, Edward Franolic, Miranda Amey, Saumiya Balasubramaniam, Raed Alahmad, Fred Curry, Andrew Cheung, Muhammed Ahmed, Blagoj Petrovski, Jeremy Li, Mohit Agastya, Rick Macfarlane, Allen Chen, Raymond Zhang, Peter Todorov, Nayyer Sultana, Monica Mera, Naren Ramanathan, Terri Dillon, Alla Fedotova, Louis Valongueiro, Nilo Laraya, Joby Chacko, Jamil Saeed, Mojtaba Shafiee, and Guesly St-Fleur.

Last but not least, a big thank-you to all the current and future sponsors, supporters, and followers of AppRun. I have learned a lot from you and hope AppRun brings value to your application development projects.

Introduction

Many web-based business applications built in the past several years are facing some challenges today: they are reaching the end of their lifecycles from the front-end technology point of view. For example, in one extreme case, I started developing an application with Angular 2. When the project was ready to be released into production, the Angular framework was being upgraded to Angular 5. Building a business application is a costly investment that takes a lot of time and resources. There was no business value in investing more time and resources to refresh the underlining technology, so I released the application to production to meet the project scope and budget. You are probably familiar with similar situations.

The result is that you can have an application in production that uses many different frameworks and versions, such as Backbone, jQuery, AngularJS, Angular, React, and Vue. As you can imagine, when the business requires further development to the existing application, it is a difficult decision whether to continue to work on the old technologies or refresh the old technology first and then build new features on top of it, which pretty much means rebuilding from scratch. Either way, it will be costly and difficult.

What we need in real-world business application development is a stable technology that developers can use not only to develop new applications but also to continue developing new features progressively for existing applications even when they are using different technologies.

After a couple of years of researching and developing, I developed such a new front-end framework, called AppRun. It has all the characteristics of being simple, flexible, and architecturally robust to meet real-world development requirements. I have used it to build new applications and to add new features to existing applications. I decided to release AppRun on GitHub as an open source project under the MIT license to share it with the development community.

Thankfully, Apress accepted the proposal of publishing a book for AppRun. This book aims to let more people know about AppRun, help people use it, and help developers contribute to the project.

In Chapter 1, "Getting Started," I will explain AppRun's overarching design goals and the many great ideas taken from other frameworks and libraries in order to help you learn the architectural concepts of AppRun.

Chapter 2, "AppRun Development Environment," introduces the tools recommended for complex applications and the AppRun CLI.

Chapters 3–6 contain in-depth discussions of the architectural concepts of AppRun as well as contain many easy-to-understand application examples.

Chapter 7, "Single-Page Applications," introduces the methods of building SPAs, including developing the components and the routing events.

Chapter 8, "Third-Party Library Integration," introduces the AppRun event lifecycle extension points for integrating third-party libraries, such as Bootstrap, jQuery plug-ins, chart.js, DataTable.js, D3, and FullCalendar, by implementing an administrative dashboard that has many data visualization widgets.

Chapter 9, "Server-Side Rendering," introduces the methods of turning an AppRun SPA into SSR. It also introduces the AppRun capability of turning existing traditional SSR (e.g., ASP.NET MVC applications or Express.js applications) into an SPA.

Chapter 10, "A Real-World SPA," demonstrates a full stack application, with features such as authentication, authorization, data CRUD, and user interaction and confirmations.

Chapter 11, "Unit Testing," introduces strategies for unit testing AppRun applications, such as mocking the back-end APIs, testing the events, and testing the views.

Chapter 12, "AppRun DevTools," introduces the developer tools for monitoring and verifying AppRun applications at runtime.

With many runnable example applications, this book will get you started developing AppRun applications. I strongly recommend you fork the source code of the examples of this book to run and tweak them. After all, the most effective way to learn coding is by coding.

I hope you find the value AppRun can provide to your development projects. You are welcome to provide feedback and comments about AppRun through its GitHub site. Please also contribute and send pull requests.

CHAPTER 1

Getting Started

AppRun (`https://apprunjs.org`) is a JavaScript library for developing applications using the Elm architecture, events, and components. It is an open source project released and published on GitHub (`https://github.com/yysun/apprun`) under the MIT license. The goal of introducing this library into the world, which already has many frameworks and libraries, is to make it simple for developers to build high-performance and reliable applications. The simplicity of AppRun brings many benefits. Developers can learn it easily and quickly develop product-ready applications. Developers also can maintain and improve the applications easily because they are architecturally simple. jQuery has ruled the development world for a long time because it is simple. However, jQuery lacks architectural rules for complex applications. Other frameworks and libraries have been invented for developing complex applications. However, then the development becomes more difficult, with more concepts to learn and more rules to follow.

In this chapter, you will learn about the technologies that other frameworks and libraries have introduced for developing complex applications that inspired AppRun. You will learn about the architecture concepts of AppRun using a counter application as an example; this is commonly used as an example with many other frameworks and libraries. Finally, you will take a look at how to make a static typed application using TypeScript if you prefer static typing to dynamic typing.

Background

Application development using JavaScript can be traced back to the 1990s when developers started to add dynamic content and interactions to static HTML web pages. Nowadays, JavaScript has evolved and become the ubiquitous language that powers not only web applications but also server applications, desktop applications, and mobile applications. Because of its widespread usage and its broad goal of serving the development needs of all platforms, we are now experiencing the phenomenon

© Yiyi Sun 2019
Y. Sun, *Practical Application Development with AppRun*, https://doi.org/10.1007/978-1-4842-4069-4_1

of JavaScript fatigue, which is the overwhelming situation of too many frameworks and libraries, too many tools, and too many APIs. Popular technologies are coming out so frequently that developers are finding it increasingly difficult to keep up with all the trends, and they worry that they will not able to leverage the latest and greatest technology. This book reveals the secret weapon to conquer the confusion and fear of JavaScript fatigue.

Keep it simple; always seek opportunities to simplify. Find out the real value of any new tools. These methods resulted in the birth of the new library AppRun.

Before getting into the technology, let me tell you about my personal experiences with the Disney theme park Epcot. Twenty years ago, when I visited Epcot for the first time, there was a hall that had a wall of machines to send e-mails. It was an amazing experience to send a couple of e-mails to China. It took two weeks to send a letter at that time. The funny sound that came from the modem was music to my ears. Ten years later, I revisited Epcot; the e-mail machines were replaced with digital photo-taking machines that could take and e-mail photos immediately. It was again an amazing experience. Fast-forward ten more years to today, and we now have high-resolution cameras on our mobile phones that can even remove wrinkles. And at Epcot, no new high-tech machines exist to excite us. In fact, the most interesting place to visit in Epcot is now the World Showcase, which contains scaled-down historical buildings, city streets, and restaurants of 11 countries. The traditional Africa streets, the Middle East market, and the French sweets are fantastic. All the ancient and old-fashioned stuff has beaten out the high-technology.

This story tells us that technology changes, but culture lasts. The real value of culture is buried in time. So, sticking to core concepts and finding out the true value of tools is the way to navigate through JavaScript fatigue.

Let's review the JavaScript development history. JavaScript started as a scripting language running inside web pages. It is lightweight and doesn't have a compiler. Everyone can code in JavaScript with or without a computer science degree or formal training. Developers would write functions in the web pages and refresh to see the result right away, and this ease of use significantly contributed the current success of JavaScript.

Despite that some senior developers, myself included, thought JavaScript was a toy or even a joke when compared with their estimated knowledge of enterprise architecture, layered approaches, and design patterns, the fact was that JavaScript spread widely quickly. jQuery and the jQuery plug-in ecosystem once ruled the JavaScript development world because jQuery made developing with JavaScript even easier by abstracting the details and differences of browser implementations. For example, handling button clicks just requires `$().click()`, and Ajax calls are handled with `$.ajax()`. Its ease of use and convenience are real values.

Of course, the concerns of senior developers were not nonsense. As soon as jQuery became successful, jQuery also became synonymous with spaghetti code. This is the direct result of it missing one of the core concepts of application development: *application architecture.* Application architecture is the discipline that guides application design, as defined in the *Gartner IT Glossary*. In the book *Patterns of Enterprise Application Architecture*, Martin Fowler explains *application architecture* as "The highest-level breakdown of a system into its parts." Application architecture is not only the structure of the application but also the discipline for breaking down the application logic.

jQuery has provided a great deal of convenience but not architecture. It does not tell you how to break down and organize the application logic. Since jQuery's release, the JavaScript community continues to improve not only the convenience but also the architecture. Continuous innovations have led to many new frameworks and libraries, such as Angular, React Vue, and Elm.

These successful frameworks and libraries have brought the following benefits in regard to architecture:

- *jQuery*: Abstraction, ease of use

- *Angular*: Components, modules, services, dependency injection, two-way data binding, strong typing, and template syntax

- *React*: Components, one-way data binding, virtual DOM, JSX

- *Vue*: Single-file components, two-way data binding, a particular compiler for temple syntax

- *Elm*: Elm architecture and functional programming

I like the architecture of Elm and the one-way data binding concept from Elm and React because they are simple yet brilliant solutions. Bruce Lee believes that "simplicity is the key to brilliance"[1] and so do I.

---

[1]Myrko Thum references this Bruce Lee maxim while describing his own simplicity ethos in "Simplicity Is Your Key to Brilliance." Accessed September 2018. `www.myrkothum.com/simple/`

However, I did not find a good answer to the architectural question of how to decouple code modules. *Coupling* is the degree of interdependence between software modules. When modules are dependent on each other, they are harder to change because changes in one module might break other modules. Coupled modules are also difficult to reuse because dependencies require more effort to manage and might even have conflicts that prevent us from assembling the modules. The decoupling of modules makes applications easy to modify, extend, and test. Well-structured applications have decoupled modules or loosely coupled modules.

Getting back to the jQuery era, to achieve better application architecture when building production business applications, I used a common design pattern called *event publication and subscription* (event pub-sub), also known as the event emitter pattern. Event pub-sub is the recognized and effective way of decoupling modules.[2] You will see how it is used in AppRun to archive the decoupling goal in the next section.

Continuing with the journey, these were the core concepts that I wanted to achieve with AppRun: an Elm-inspired architecture, the event pub-sub, and the concept of components. Also, it should be practical and flexible. It should give options for developers to choose.

- Developers can choose to include it as a `<script>` tag or use it with a build process.

- Developers can choose to use JavaScript or TypeScript.

- Developers can choose to apply the architecture globally or use components.

- Developers can choose to use HTML or use the virtual DOM/JSX to create the views.

- Developers can choose to use dynamic types or static types.

Following these design concepts and goals, I built AppRun. The overall result of the AppRun library is encouraging. AppRun applications have simpler project structure; more straightforward build script and process, which leads to better performance; and

---

[2]In his article "Mocking is a Code Smell," as part of the "Composing Software" series on learning functional programming and compositional software techniques, Eric Elliott identified event pub-sub as the solution for decoupling. Accessed September 2018. `https://medium.com/javascript-scene/mocking-is-a-code-smell-944a70c90a6a`

fewer lines of code when compared to many other popular frameworks and libraries (according to third-party research[3]). AppRun performance benchmarks are publicly published for comparison as well.[4]

Let's get started.

Introducing AppRun

AppRun is 3KB to 4KB when it is minified and zipped. The underlining AppRun architecture has adopted modern architectural concepts and functional programming techniques. It lets you focus on creating the application logic via an established architecture pattern without the distraction of the functional programming language syntax, types, and other nonbusiness logic concepts.

AppRun Architecture

Elm has inspired AppRun. Elm is a functional language that compiles into JavaScript and is said to have superior performance and no runtime exceptions as its advantages over other languages. Elm has introduced several concepts into web application development, such as static typing, functional programming, and a simple yet brilliant architecture. In the Elm architecture, the application logic breaks down into three parts.

- *Model*: The state of your application

- *View*: A way to view your state as HTML

- *Update*: A way to update your state

At first glance, it may look like the Model-View-Controller (MVC) architecture, which dates back to the 1970s. In the MVC architecture, the model, view, and controller are the three logical building blocks of the application front end. Although this model is an excellent logical and conceptual breakdown of the application logic, it has the problem

---

[3]Jacek Schae's "A Real-World Comparison of Front-End Frameworks with Benchmarks (2018 update)" gives AppRun high marks after comparing it with many other frameworks and libraries. Accessed March 2018. `https://medium.freecodecamp.org/a-real-world-comparison-of-front-end-frameworks-with-benchmarks-2018-update-e5760fb4a962`

[4]Stefan Krause created a project to compare the performance of JavaScript frameworks, including AppRun. `https://rawgit.com/krausest/js-framework-benchmark/master/webdriver-ts-results/table.html`

that the three blocks usually are coupled modules. They reference and manipulate each other. Because the code is coupled, it is difficult to test and maintain. There are many patterns derived from the MVC pattern aiming to solve the coupling problem, such as Model-View-Presenter, Presentation Model, and Model-View-ViewModel. Ultimately, they all attempt to either reduce the manipulations between the model, view, and controller or at least simplify the manipulations.

The Elm architecture solved the coupling problem brilliantly using the functional programming concept. For example, the `view` function is a pure function, which means it always returns the same result as long as the state is the same and it does not produce side effects, which means it does not change values outside the function or the passed parameters. The `view` function never changes the DOM. The `view` function returns the data that represents the HTML. The Elm runtime does the rendering to the Document Object Model (DOM). The update function is a pure function and returns the data that represents the operations. The Elm runtime performs the operations. If the operations have side effects, the Elm runtime handles them. This way, Elm claims that Elm applications have zero runtime exceptions. The Elm architecture has made Elm great for web application development.

However, Elm is a Haskell-style language. Compared to JavaScript's ease of use, the Elm language has a higher barrier for entry before developers can start developing. The Elm syntax is a burden for many developers.

Combining the Elm architecture and JavaScript leads to the AppRun library. AppRun allows the application developer to use the Elm architecture but with JavaScript. We can leverage the power of the Elm architecture but without going through the learning curve of the Elm language syntax.

Inspired by the Elm architecture, the AppRun architecture has the following three parts:

- *State*: The state of your application

- *View*: A function to display the state as HTML

- *Update*: A collection of event handlers to update the state

When developing an AppRun application, we break down the application logic into the state, view, and update parts, and we use the `app.start` function to tie them together and mount them to a web page element.

At a high level, Listing 1-1 shows the AppRun architecture.

Listing 1-1. The AppRun Architecture

```
1.    const state = {}
2.    const view = state => `<div>${state}</div>`;
3.    const update = {
4.        '#': state => state
5.    }
6.    app.start('my-app', state, view, update)
```

In the AppRun architecture, state is an object represents the application state. view is a function that creates HTML from the state. It does not change the DOM. AppRun renders the HTML to the web page. The view function is a function meant to be a pure function just like the correspondent view function in the Elm architecture. update is an object that contains a number of named event handlers. The event handlers process AppRun events and create and return new states. AppRun applications are event-driven.

Event Pub-Sub

As mentioned, AppRun uses the event publication and subscription pattern (event pub-sub). The event pub-sub pattern is fundamental to the web application programming model. The DOM-based web page development API is solely based on event pub-sub.

Let's break down event pub-sub.

- *Publishing* an event means to raise an event for some other code to handle. Publishing an event is also referred as *firing* an event or *triggering* an event.

- *Subscribing* an event means to register an event handler function to the event. The event handler function executes when the corresponding event is published.

AppRun has two functions to facilitate the event pub-sub pattern.

- app.on for registering event handlers (event subscription)

- app.run for firing events (event publication)

If module A provides a function to print some content, it subscribes.

```
app.on('print', e => console.log(e));
```

When module B wants to print something, it publishes the event.

```
app.run('print', 'Hello, print me');
```

The benefit of using events is that they can decouple modules. Module A and Module B do not know each other. They only need to know the global *app* object. Module B does not have reference to and is not dependent on Module A. Module A and Module B depend only on the global *app*. Therefore, Module A and Module B are decoupled. Event pub-sub is an effective method to decouple modules. By using event pub-sub, the building blocks or modules in the AppRun architecture are decoupled from each other. They communicate and invoke the functionalities through the events.

Leveraging event pub-sub, AppRun applications have an event lifecycle [1].

```
Web events => AppRun Events => (current state) => Update =>
(new state) => View => (HTML/Virtual DOM) => render DOM =>
(new state) => rendered                                        [1]
```

While developing AppRun applications, we convert web page events such as timer, user input, and button click events using the web event handlers for AppRun events. Therefore, the following steps take place:

1. AppRun dispatches the events to the event handlers in the update along with the current application state.

2. The event handlers create a new state based on the current state.

3. AppRun passes the new state to the `view` function.

4. The `view` function creates HTML or a virtual DOM.

5. AppRun renders the HTML to the screen and calls the optional rendered function to complete the AppRun event lifecycle (see Figure 1-1).

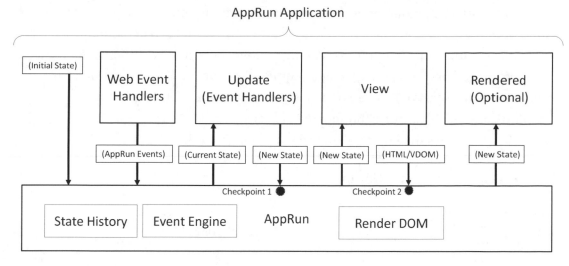

Figure 1-1. *AppRun event lifecycle*

There are two checkpoints in the AppRun event lifecycle where AppRun lets us stop the event lifecycle. They are also the points that AppRun publishes the built-in debug event to let us examine the state in the event lifecycle. There is also an optional callback function called rendered. If we create the rendered function, AppRun calls into the rendered function when it finishes rendering the DOM.

You will learn about all the types of the events, the checkpoints, and the asynchronous event handlers in Chapter 5 and Chapter 6. You will learn about integrating third-party libraries using the rendered function in Chapter 8.

Note   The app.run function publishes the events to drive the AppRun application logic ultimately. It is so important that the AppRun library is named after it.

Component

A *component* is a technique to decompose the large system into smaller, manageable, and reusable pieces. Usually, a component is an autonomous and reusable module that encapsulates a set of data and functions. A component is the basic building block in other popular frameworks and libraries such as Angular, React, and Vue. Elm does not have components. Elm has the concern that the relationship and communication between components might prevent or cause difficulties to ensure everything is done in the functional programming style.

AppRun solves the component relationship and communication problem by using event pub-sub. AppRun components are decoupled and isolated modules. Elm's concern is not an issue in AppRun. In AppRun applications, the component is a mini-application and has a component-scoped AppRun architecture, which includes the three architecture parts discussed previously: state, view, and update. Components communicate with each other through the events.

Listing 1-2 shows the AppRun component at a high level.

Listing 1-2. The AppRun Component

```
import app, {Component} from 'apprun';
export default class MyComponent extends Component {
  state = {};
  view = (state) => `<div>{state}</div>`;
  update = {
    '#Home': state => state,
  }
}
new MyComponent().start('my-app');
```

The component is suitable for developing single-page web applications (SPAs). An SPA is a modern and trendy style of web application. It loads the main web page once and switches the functionalities dynamically without a page refresh. Each functionality in an SPA is a mini-application. A famous SPA example is Gmail. You can search, read, compose, reply, and forward e-mails. You can also manage the calendar and even chat with your friends on a single page.

Using components to organize, modularize, and encapsulate the states makes your application code testable and maintainable. The SPAs developed in this book are business application development examples. In Chapter 7 of this book, you will learn how to build an SPA using AppRun components. You will also learn how to optimize the component modules such as code splitting, dynamic loading, and server-side rendering.

However, unlike other frameworks and libraries, which force us to make everything a component, AppRun is more flexible. AppRun does not force us always to use components. We can choose to develop applications using the AppRun architecture globally just like Elm.

A Counter App

To demonstrate the AppRun architecture, we will develop a counter application as an example. The counter application is also used in Elm, Vue and React/Redux. The counter application has two buttons. One of them increases the counter. The other one decreases the counter (see Figure 1-2).

Figure 1-2. *The AppRun counter application*

Following the AppRun architecture, the counter application has state, view, and update parts.

- The state is a number that represents the counter.

- The view function displays the counter and two buttons.

- The update has two event handlers for increasing and decreasing the counter.

Just like in the good old days of JavaScript development, we can include AppRun in a `<script>` tag and write the application inside the web page. Listing 1-3 shows the source code of the counter application.

Listing 1-3. Source Code of the Counter Application

```
1.    <!doctype html>
2.    <html>
3.    <head>
4.        <meta charset="utf-8">
5.        <title>Counter</title>
6.    </head>
7.    <body>
8.        <div id="my-app"></div>
9.        <script src="https://unpkg.com/apprun@latest/dist/apprun-html.js">
          </script>
10.       <script>
11.           const state = 0;
12.           const view = state => {
13.               return `<div>
14.                   <h1>${state}</h1>
15.                   <button onclick='app.run("-1")'>-1</button>
16.                   <button onclick='app.run("+1")'>+1</button>
17.               </div>`;
18.           };
19.           const update = {
20.               '+1': state => state + 1,
21.               '-1': state => state - 1
22.           };
23.       app.on('debug', p=>console.log(p));
24.       app.start('my-app', state, view, update);
25.   </script>
26.   </body>
27.   </html>
```

Let's review the code.

Event Lifecycle

The counter application starts with an initial state, the number 0 (line 11). You probably have noticed that the state uses the keyword `const` instead of `let`. This is because the initial state will not change after the application starts. AppRun takes the initial state value and manages the state internally. If you try to change the content of the state, it will not have any effect. The initial state is no longer useful after the first event handler creates a new state. The initial state is used only once to start the application. Using `const` can remind us not to change the state value. Once the application starts, AppRun saves the initial state and holds it as the current state.

- The buttons publish the -1 and +1 events (lines 15–16). The event names are strings. You can name them creatively.

- AppRun invokes the two event handlers (lines 20–21) with the current state as an event parameter.

- The two event handlers create a new state out of the current state.

- AppRun then invokes the `view` function with the new state.

- The `view` function creates HTML using the new state (line 12).

- AppRun renders the HTML to the element that has an ID of `my-app`.

In AppRun applications, the state access is only through the function parameter. There is no need to use `this.state`. Let AppRun manage the states for you.

Watch the State

AppRun has a built-in `debug` event to help us visualize the state at the two checkpoints in the AppRun event lifecycle (see Figure 1-3). When AppRun finishes invoking the event handlers, it publishes the `debug` event with the event name, event parameters, current state, and new state as event parameters. When AppRun finishes invoking the `view` function, AppRun publishes the `debug` event with the state and generates HTML as the event parameters.

We can subscribe to the `debug` event (line 23) to watch the events, states, and HTML in the browser's DevTool console (see Figure 1-3).

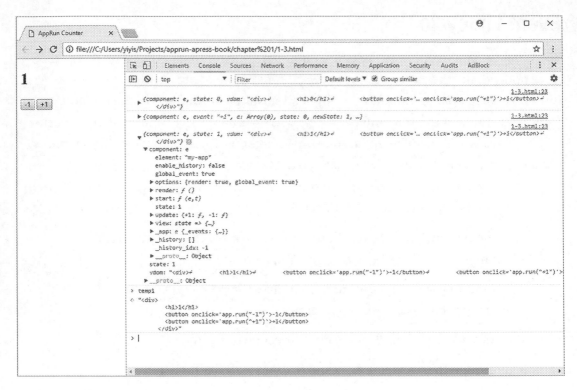

Figure 1-3. *AppRun debug event log*

Figure 1-3 shows the logged event parameters of the debug event. The initial state 0 is rendered into HTML as the h1 tag. It also renders the two buttons to publish the events. The event +1 changed the current state from 0 to the new state 1.

The debug event is the way for you to debug the applications by examining how AppRun manages the state internally. This is good for development. It makes the state transparent during the event lifecycle. There is no hidden or implicit magic. In production, we should not subscribe to the debug event.

Virtual DOM

AppRun uses the virtual DOM technology. The virtual DOM (VDOM) is the data representing a DOM structure. In the counter app, AppRun parses the HTML string into the VDOM and compares the VDOM with the real DOM. It updates only the changed elements and element properties. For example, you can click the two buttons of the counter application and see on the Elements tab of the DevTool only the h1 tag changes (see Figure 1-4).

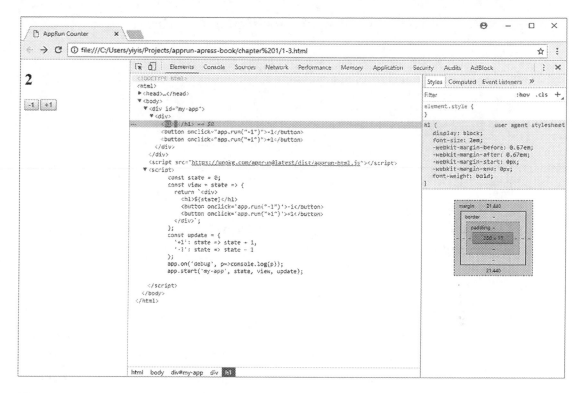

Figure 1-4. *AppRun virtual DOM*

Besides parsing the HTML string, AppRun supports using JSX in the `view` function. JSX is the syntactic sugar of function calls. We can compose the functions and apply dynamic and conditional rendering without the runtime cost of parsing the HTML string. You will learn about many view patterns of using JSX in Chapter 4.

State History

AppRun state management has built-in state history. To demonstrate the out-of-box AppRun state history, we will add two buttons to the counter application. The back button (<<) steps back in the state history and undoes the counter change. The forward button (>>) steps forward in the state history and redoes the counter change (see Listing 1-4).

Listing 1-4. Source Code of the Counter Application with History

```
1.    <!doctype html>
2.    <html>
3.    <head>
4.        <meta charset="utf-8">
5.        <title>AppRun Counter with History</title>
6.    </head>
7.    <body>
8.        <div id="my-app"></div>
9.        <script src="https://unpkg.com/apprun@latest/dist/apprun-html.js">
          </script>
10.       <script>
11.           const state = 0;
12.           const view = state => {
13.               return `<div>
14.                   <button onclick='app.run("history-prev")'> << </button>
15.                   <button onclick='app.run("history-next")'> >> </button>
16.                   <h1>${state}</h1>
17.                   <button onclick='app.run("-1")'>-1</button>
18.                   <button onclick='app.run("+1")'>+1</button>
19.               </div>`;
20.           };
21.           const update = {
22.               '+1': state => state + 1,
23.               '-1': state => state - 1
24.           };
25.           app.start('my-app', state, view, update, {history: true});
26.       </script>
27.   </body>
28.   </html>
```

To enable the state history, we set the history option to true in the app.start function call (line 25); then we can use the back button and the forward button to step back and forth, like undo and redo.

In the view function, the statement console.log (state) (line 13) prints the state to the browser's DevTool console (see Figure 1-5).

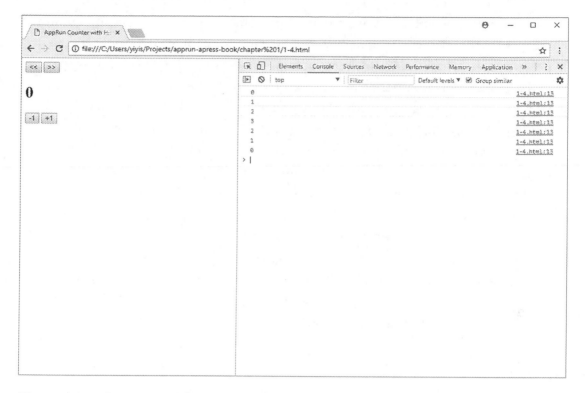

Figure 1-5. *Counter application with state history*

AppRun maintains internally a state history stack and a state history pointer. AppRun has two internal events for moving the history pointer: `history-prev` and `history-next`. The back button publishes the `history-prev` event to let AppRun set the current state to the state before the state history pointer. The forward button publishes the `history-next` event to let AppRun set the current state to the state after the state history pointer.

You will learn details about AppRun state management in Chapter 3.

Typed Architecture

The counter application uses JavaScript. JavaScript is dynamic typed/weak typed. Dynamic typing allows developers to focus on solving the application logic. It makes JavaScript easy to use. However, when modern web applications become complicated, a static typed/strong typed language compiler can identify code issues by checking the types at compile time instead of runtime.

We can use TypeScript for static typing. TypeScript is an open source programming language developed and maintained by Microsoft for developing large applications. Microsoft defines that TypeScript is a typed superset of JavaScript that compiles to plain JavaScript. Before exploring how to use the TypeScript type system, we need to understand the meaning of TypeScript as a superset of JavaScript. In other words, it means any valid JavaScript code is TypeScript code. For example, you can rename a JavaScript code file from `*.js` to a TypeScript code file (`*.ts`), which the TypeScript compiler compiles into the script file for running in the browser. The benefit of compiling is that it allows us to use the JavaScript language features that are not supported by the browsers such as JSX, async/await, class properties, and decorators. You will learn about using these features throughout the book.

We will take a first look at how to add types to the three parts of the AppRun architecture: state, view, and update. TypeScript has a type system that includes interfaces, classes, generics, and type aliases for static typing.[5] It is straightforward to define the AppRun architecture using TypeScript.

State

The state is the application state at any given time. It has a certain type, such as a number, an array, and an object, whatever best represents the application state. If you already have experience with other static typing programming languages like C# or Java, you might think to define the type first and then create an object out of the type. Whenever we change the data fields in the state, we had to modify the type first and then change the state object. However, TypeScript has the operator `typeof` to define the type alias based on an existing variable.

```
const state = {};
type State = typeof state;
```

This is an extremely helpful feature. We are able to add, remove, and change data fields in the state object freely and let TypeScript figure out the type. This allows us to focus on modeling the application state without manually synchronizing the object fields between the type definitions and the instant objects. It saves time and increases the developer productivity.

---

[5]For more information about TypeScript types, please visit the TypeScript Handbook. `https://www.typescriptlang.org/docs/handbook/generics.html`

View

View is a function to display the application state of a certain type as HTML or the virtual DOM. Given an abstract state type of T, we define the View type as follows:

```
type View<T> = (state: T) => string | VNODE | void;
```

The View type definition tells us that the view function is a function that takes in a certain type of state and outputs the HTML string, virtual DOM, or nothing. We can create the view function using the View type as follows:

```
const view = (state: State) => <div>{state}</div>;
```

Using the static type state parameter, we can check whether we are using the state parameter correctly. For example, if we try to access an object property that does not exist in the state type, the compiler can report the error (see Figure 1-6 in the following section).

You will notice the <div> tag in the view function. It looks like the HTML tags, but it is the JSX language extension to JavaScript supported by TypeScript.

Update

Update is a collection of named event handlers, or a dictionary of event handlers. Each event handler creates a new state from the current state.

```
type EventHandler<T> = (state: T) => T;
```

In JavaScript/TypeScript, we use the Object type for a collection or dictionary. The Update type is defined as follows:

```
type Update<T> = {[name: string]: EventHandler <T>};
```

The Update type definition tells us that the Update object is an object that names event handlers. We can create the update object using the Update type as follows:

```
const update: Update<State> = {
    '+1': state => state + 1
}
```

You will notice we use +1 as the event name. The event name is a string, not a variable name. We can be creative when naming the events. For example, we can group similar events by using namespaces in the event names such as auth:login, auth:login:success, and auth:login:failed, where we have multiple namespaces separated by colons.

Finally, the AppRun app object and its app.start and app.run functions have the type definition as well.

```
interface IApp {
  start<T>(element: string | HTMLElement,
          model: T,
          view: View<T>,
          update: Update<T>): void { }
  run(name: string, ...args: any[]): void { }
}
const app: IApp;
```

The View type definition (View<T>), the Update type definition (Update<T>), and the AppRun App type definition (IApp) are exposed from the AppRun library. We can import them from AppRun and change the counter application into the typed AppRun application shown in Listing 1-5.

Listing 1-5. Static Typed Counter Application

```
1.   import app, { View, Update } from 'apprun';
2.   const state: number = 0;
3.   type State = typeof state;
4.   const view = (state: State) => <div>
5.       <h1>{state}</h1>
6.       <button onclick={() => app.run('-1')}>-1</button>
7.       <button onclick={() => app.run('+1')}>+1</button>
8.   </div>;
9.   const update: Update<State> = {
10.      '-1': (state) => state + 1,
11.      '+1': (state) => state - 1
12.   };
13.  app.start<State>('my-app', state, view, update);
```

Notice that, in Listing 1-5, line 3 uses the TypeScript operator `typeof` to define the type alias from an existing variable. Because the `state` object is the number, the state type (`State`) is the type of number. Therefore, the `view` function must have the input parameter of the number type. The event handlers in the update object must also input parameters of the number type. If not, the TypeScript compiler reports compile-time errors, and this is known as *type checking*. The static typing helps type checking. Also, the TypeScript-aware code editor will gain knowledge of the application code based on the static types. The code editor can provide information such as the object member list, function signatures, and parameters. Microsoft offers code information through IntelliSense. We do not have to memorize the hundreds and thousands of standard JavaScript functions. IntelliSense helps us code against the functions correctly. The code editor can assist us in navigating through code, refactoring, and even formatting the code (see Figure 1-6).

```
1   import app, { View, Update } from 'apprun';
2
3   const state: number = 0;
    3 references
4   type State = typeof state;
5
6   const view = (state: State) => <div>
7     <h1>{state.counter}</h1>
8     <button onclick={() => app.run("-1")}>-1</button>
9     <button onclick={() => app.run("+1")}>+1</button>
10  </div>;
11
12  const update: Update<State> = {
13    '-1': (state='') => state - 1,
14    '+1': (state) => state + 1
15  };
16        (method) IApp.start<number>(element: Element, model: numbe
17        r, view: View<number>, update: Update<number>, options?: {
18            history: any;
19        }): void
20  app.start<State>('my-app', state, view, update);
```

Figure 1-6. *A TypeScript compile error in Visual Studio code*

In Figure 1-6, it shows that the Visual Studio code editor caught two type errors. One is at line 7 where the state should not have a `counter` property because the state is a number. The other error is at line 13 where the state cannot be a string.

TypeScript is not mandatory for developing applications with AppRun. You can start with JavaScript and add types gradually when you need them. When you choose to use TypeScript, however, the AppRun development environment enables the debugging of the TypeScript source code as well as the AppRun source code.

Summary

The key to winning the battle against JavaScript fatigue is simplicity. Always remember that less is more. We should keep challenging ourselves to simplify things as much as possible. The architectural elements irrelevant to the business logic are the architectural ceremony elements. The code irrelevant to the business logic is the code ceremony.[6] The ceremony has no business values. Can we simply remove the ceremony elements, such as dependency injection, custom templating language, artificial concepts such as actions, reducers and dispatchers, subscriptions and commands, and so forth?

AppRun's answer to the challenge is yes. These ceremonies are not needed and do not exist in AppRun applications. Pursuing simplicity has made AppRun a lightweight library. Not only it is just 3KB to 4KB when minimized and compressed, but it also has a tiny API with only three functions.

The AppRun architecture organizes the logic into the state, view, and update. AppRun does the heavy lifting to drive the application logic. Using AppRun, you capture the essence of the business logic and write less irrelevant code. Your application logic has the ultimate business value. AppRun adds no overhead or ceremony to your applications. AppRun also gives you options to choose what makes the most sense to your applications, such as choosing between vanilla JavaScript and TypeScript. AppRun plays well with other UI libraries, animation libraries, and visualization libraries, such as jQuery, D3, Electron, and Framework7. It can be used for web applications, desktop applications, and mobile applications.

In the next chapter, we will introduce a production-ready configuration that has development productivity in mind to prepare you for complex app development.

---

[6]Stuart Halloway's "Ending Legacy Code In Our Lifetime" from Code Freeze 2008 described essence versus ceremony and provided a number of examples of code ceremony. Accessed April 2008. http://thinkrelevance.com/blog/2008/04/01/ending-legacy-code-in-our-lifetime

CHAPTER 2

AppRun Development Environment

Using AppRun in a `<script>` tag and coding in plain JavaScript is perfect when developing small applications, prototyping, and trying ideas. However, in a complex AppRun application development scenario, we need a well-equipped development environment to achieve better code quality and better coding productivity.

In this chapter, we will introduce the AppRun development environment, which includes development tools such as a compiler, bundler, and testing framework. The compiler allows us to use advanced JavaScript/TypeScript language features. The bundler lets us transform, combine, optimize, and produce the code for production use. The testing framework enables a test-driven approach. The development environment also has automated scripts to invoke the development tools and to form a build process.

You will learn to use the AppRun command-line interface (CLI) to create the AppRun development environment that has all the tools configured to support the advanced technologies required in AppRun application development.

The AppRun CLI

The AppRun CLI is essentially a script tool to initialize projects, scaffold project folders and files, and configure the development tools. It runs in the terminal or in the command shell.

To use the AppRun CLI, we will need to have node.js, npm, and npx installed first. We can download node.js from its download page. Installing node.js also installs npm and npx. npm is the package manager of the world's largest JavaScript reusable package registry. npx is the tool to execute code in the npm package.

© Yiyi Sun 2019
Y. Sun, *Practical Application Development with AppRun*, https://doi.org/10.1007/978-1-4842-4069-4_2

AppRun is published and distributed as an npm package in the npm registry. We can use npx to execute the AppRun CLI to create an AppRun project. First, create the project folder; then run the AppRun CLI with the -i command (see Figure 2-1).

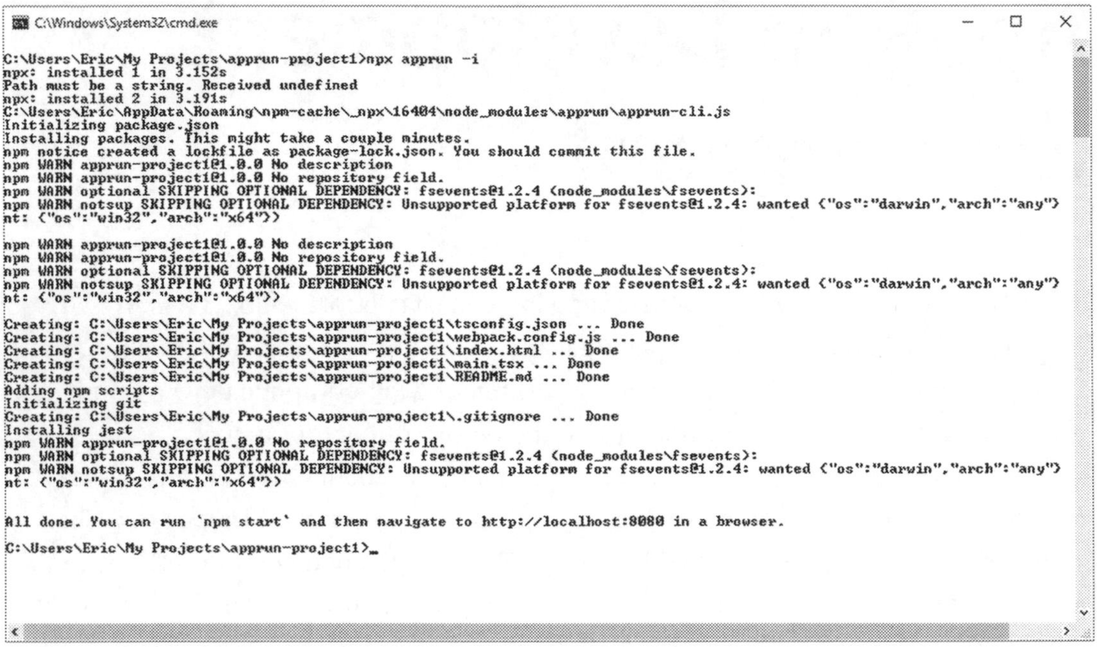

Figure 2-1. *AppRun CLI –i command*

After running the AppRun CLI -i command, the current folder has a local git repository, a Hello World application (index.html and main.tsx), and three configuration files (package.json, tsconfig.json, and webpack.config.js).

Project Boilerplate

The CLI-generated Hello World application is the boilerplate of an AppRun application. It has only two source files, index.html and main.tsx. The index.html file is the default HTML page of the application (Listing 2-1).

Listing 2-1. index.html

```
1.   <!doctype html>
2.   <html>
3.   <head>
4.       <meta charset="utf-8">
5.       <title>My App</title>
6.   </head>
7.   <body>
8.       <div id="my-app"></div>
9.       <script src="app.js"></script>
10.  </body>
11.  </html>
```

The <div> element (line 8) is the placeholder to render the application content. The app.js file (line 9) is the compiled code from the main.tsx file (Listing 2-2).

Listing 2-2. main.tsx

```
1.   import app from 'apprun';
2.   const model = 'Hello world!';
3.   const view = (state) => <div>
4.       <h1>{state}</h1>
5.   </div>;
6.   const update = {
7.   } ;
8.   app.start('my-app', model, view, update);
```

Listing 2-1 and Listing 2-2 are the starting points of AppRun application development. We are not just taking the JavaScript code from the HTML to compile and build. We can use many advanced development technologies available via the compiler and bundler that aren't available when embedding JavaScript in an HTML page.

Compiler

AppRun application development requires all the ECMAScript 2015 (ES 6) features plus a few other advanced syntax and language features provided by the TypeScript compiler discussed in this section.

JSX

JSX is a syntax extension to JavaScript. JSX is famous because of React. When React decided to use JSX, developers doubted whether JSX violated the *separation of concerns* (SoC) by putting HTML and JavaScript code together. The fact is that although JSX looks like HTML, it is actually a presentation of functions. For example, here's a `view` function written in JSX:

```
view = state => <div>{state}</div>
```

After compilation, the JSX tag becomes a function.

```
view = function (state) {
    return apprun_1.default.createElement("div", null, state);
};
```

In AppRun applications, the HTML-like `view` function is not a mix of HTML markup and JavaScript code. The TypeScript compiler compiles the JSX into JavaScript functions. You will learn how to compose the functions to make complex views in Chapter 4.

Class

The class syntax is defined in ECMAScript 2015 (ES 6), but it is missing an important concept, *class fields*. For example, if you have experience in C# or Java, you will naturally think of using fields in a class (Listing 2-3). However, ECMAScript 2015 does not support the class field. No browser can run Listing 2-3 yet.

Listing 2-3. A Class with Fields

```
1.   class Component {
2.       state = {};
3.       view = state => {};
4.       update = {};
5.   }
```

The TypeScript compiler can compile the classes that have fields to ES 5 to make the browsers happy; it also makes the developers happy because it is easier to understand and more familiar based on their knowledge of other languages.

async and await

async and `await` are standardized in ECMAScript 2017 (ES 8). They solved the asynchronous execution problem that many developers seem to struggle with. JavaScript is single-threaded, but the user interface in the browser is nonblocking, which means executions like network requests should not block and freeze the user interface. Those executions should be asynchronous. The JavaScript engine in browsers uses the event loop and the callback queue to manage asynchronous execution. It is difficult to write the callback functions in application development, especially when combining them with error handlings.

async and `await` make the asynchronous execution code look like synchronous execution to the degree that we almost do not have to understand any internal mechanism of the asynchronous execution.

In AppRun applications, we can use asynchronous event handlers with error handling that is easier to understand (Listing 2-4). The TypeScript compiler can compile code that uses async and `await` to ES 5.

Listing 2-4. Asynchronous Event Handler

```
1.    const fetch = async () => { ... }
2.    state = { data: " }
3.    view = state => <div>${state.error || state.data}</div>
4.    update = {
5.        '#': async (state) => {
6.            try{
7.                const data = await fetch();
8.                return {...state, data};
9.            } catch(error) {
10.               return {...state, error};
11.           }
12.       }
13.   }
```

Module Bundler

Large application code could grow into hundreds and thousands of lines. The best practice to manage the vast codebase is to divide it into modules. Although ECMAScript 2015 has defined a module format standard, modules are not supported in any browser.

The AppRun development environment includes webpack (`https://webpack.js.org`), a leading module bundler, to process the modules, resolve the module dependencies, and bundle the modules into the optimized code for browsers to run. webpack is the most feature-complete bundler. It has an ecosystem of many plug-ins. Through its plug-in ecosystem, webpack can minify and optimize the code for production. It can also integrate the TypeScript compiler into the build process.

When developing AppRun applications, we can use the ECMAScript 2015 module format freely to organize the codebase and let webpack bundle the modules, including bundling other third-party modules, which you will learn about in later chapters.

Development Server

The AppRun development environment includes the webpack development server to help the development workflow. The webpack development server compiles, bundles, and serves the application code from memory. During the development, there are no files saved to disk. The compiled code is in the memory. The webpack development server monitors the source code file changes and recompiles the source code automatically. It also injects a web-socket connection into the browser to let the browser refresh automatically when the source code is changed and recompiled.

A traditional web application workflow is that when the developers change the source code, they have to refresh the browser to verify the effects of the change. Although it sounds a really simple step to refresh the browser, the time adds up by the end of the day. The fact that the webpack development server makes the browser automatically refresh when the code changes is a significant time-savings for developers. It makes the development workflow more efficient.

A typical development setting is to have a split screen. In one part of the screen, developers edit the source code. In the other part of the screen, they verify the browser refreshes and run the application. If the developers have two monitors, they can use one monitor for editing code and the other monitor for running the application. This can save both time and effort.

Visual Studio Code

Visual Studio Code (`https://code.visualstudio.com`) is one of the best code editors for developing AppRun applications. It has detailed documentation that describes its features for development; it also has an ecosystem of many extensions. The extensions add many other features to Visual Studio Code.

An AppRun CLI–created project has everything configured to work with Visual Studio Code. Once the project is opened in the project folder in Visual Studio Code, it is ready for development right away (see Figure 2-2).

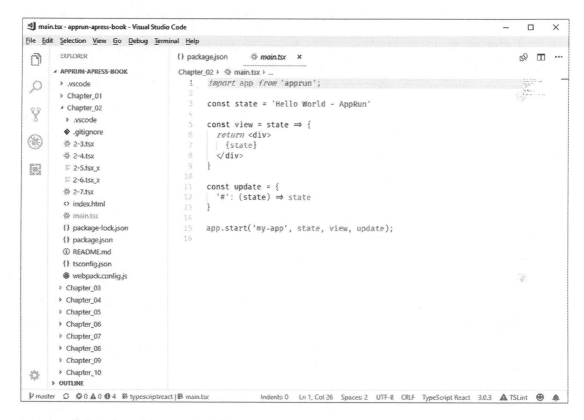

Figure 2-2. *Visual Studio Code*

When editing AppRun application code in Visual Studio Code, you will notice the TypeScript code is syntax highlighted. The code elements have different colors that are visually distinct according to their roles. You can quickly identify and distinguish keywords, variables, parameters, and string literals. You can install and switch to use different Visual Studio Code themes to make the background and color scheme best suitable to your preferences.

In addition, Visual Studio Code provides many other features to improve developer productivity. We will discuss the most relevant features related to AppRun application development next.

IntelliSense

AppRun publishes its type definition file `apprun.d.ts` within the AppRun packages located inside the `node_modules/apprun` folder. Visual Studio Code automatically detects the type definitions and then provides information via IntelliSense about the type, objects, and function information from AppRun (see Figure 2-3).

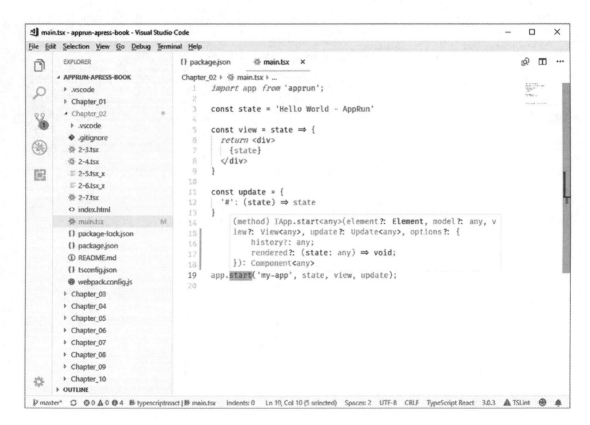

Figure 2-3. *IntelliSense*

Figure 2-3 shows that Visual Studio Code has detected and displays the signature of the `app.start` function. You can see the `app.start` function has a generic type of `any`.

Gradually Adding Types

We can add types to state, the view function, and the update object by importing View
and Update from AppRun (see Figure 2-4).

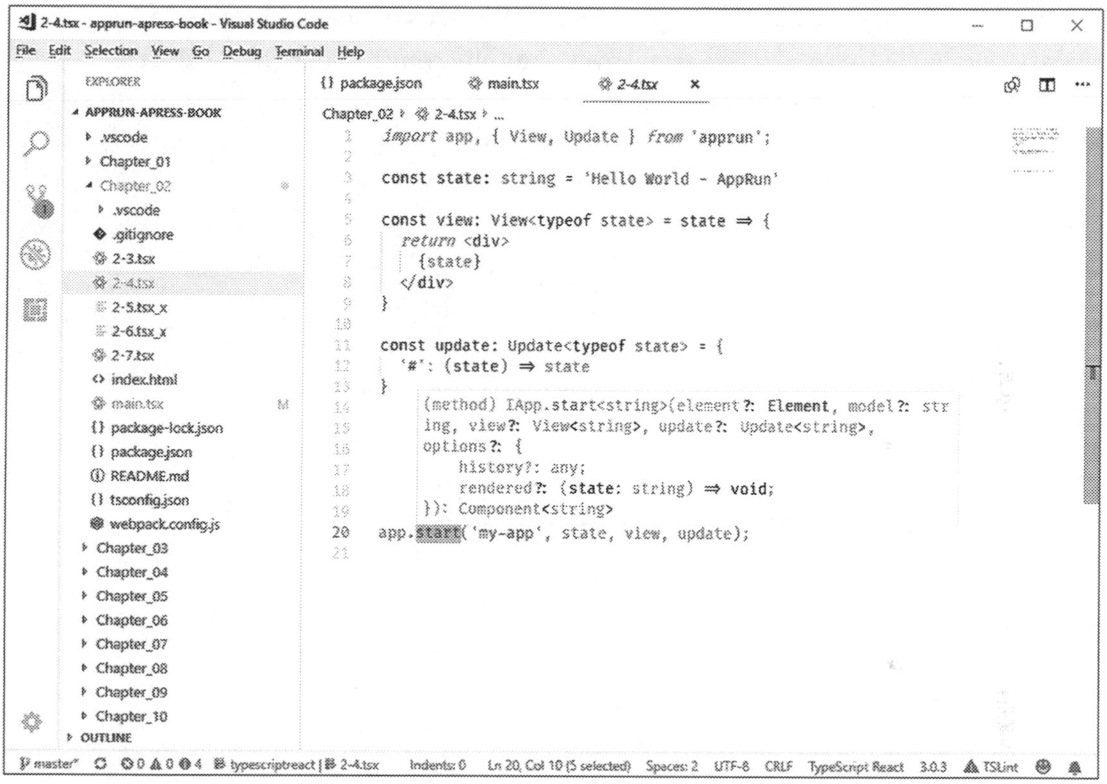

Figure 2-4. *Importing AppRun types*

We define the state to be a string (line 3). Then we apply View<typeof state> to the
view function (line 5) and apply <typeof state> to the update object (line 11). Visual
Studio Code uses the type inference feature of TypeScript to find out that app.start
should have the state parameter be a string, the view parameter be View<string>, and
the update parameter be Update<string>.

Type Checking

While we are writing the code, Visual Studio Code checks and verifies the types automatically behind the scenes. If we make a mistake, Visual Studio Code reports the type checking error.

The example in Figure 2-5 shows that when the update object is defined as Update<typeof state> and the actual event handler returns void (line 25), Visual Studio Code raises a TypeScript error (line 11).

Figure 2-5. *Type checking of the update object*

Figure 2-6 shows another example; if we mistakenly define the `update` object to be `Update<number>`, Visual Studio Code shows the type checking error when the `update` object is in the `app.start` function (line 26).

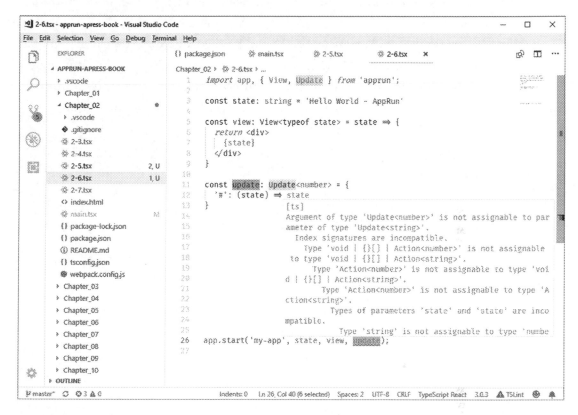

Figure 2-6. *Type checking of the app.start function*

Visual Studio Code uses TypeScript checks and reports the type checking error behind the scenes. Automated type checking is a great way to catch code mistakes.

Code Snippets

Code snippets are commonly used code blocks displayed in the IntelliSense suggestions. It can insert code blocks by using the Tab key, so it is also called *tab completion* or *auto code completion*.

AppRun has a code snippet extension for Visual Studio Code that you can download and install from the Visual Studio Marketplace. Once you've installed the AppRun code snippet extension, when typing apprun in Visual Studio Code, it suggests the AppRun application (see Figure 2-7). When you press Tab, the AppRun application template will be inserted into the editor (see Figure 2-8).

Figure 2-7. *Code snippet of AppRun*

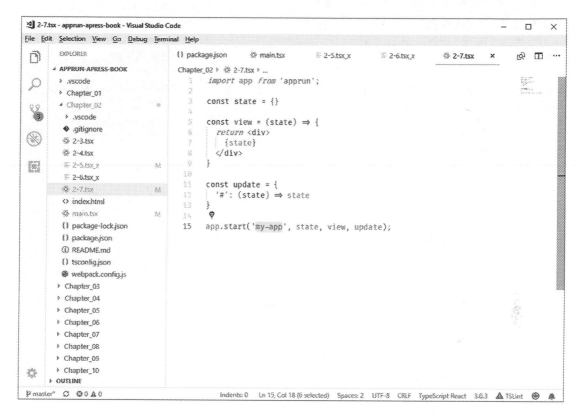

Figure 2-8. *Code snippet result*

The AppRun code snippet extension lists the commonly used code templates in Table 2-1.

Table 2-1. *AppRun Code Snippets*

Keyword	Code	Description

apprun	```import app from 'apprun';```
	```const state = {}```
	```const view = state => {```
	```return <div>```
	```{state}```
	```</div>```
	```}```
	```const update = {```
	```'#': (state) => state```
	```}```
	```app.start('my-app', state, view, update);```
		Inserts global application

component	```import app, { Component } from 'apprun';```
	```export default class MyComponent extends```
	```Component {```
	```state = {}```
	```view = state => {```
	```return <div>```
	```{state}```
	```</div>```
	```}```
	```update = {```
	```'#': (state) => state```
	```}```
	```}```
		Inserts component

on	```app.on(", () => {``` ```})```	Inserts event subscription
run	```{e => this.run(", e)}```	Inserts event publication

(continued)

Table 2-1. (*continued*)

Keyword	Code	Description

pfc	```const Tag = ({ prop }) => {```
	```return <div>```
	```</div>```
	```}```
		Inserts pure function component

@on	```@on(") fn = (state, e) => {```
	```return { ...state, e }```
	```}```
		Inserts update function in component using the @on decorator

@event	```@event('')```
	```function (state, e) {```
	```return { ...state, e }```
	```}```
		Inserts update function in component using the @event decorator

log	```console.log(state)```	Logs the state

These code snippets provide a quick way to enter the code. IntelliSense also supports the undo feature (Ctrl+Z or Command+Z).

Integrated Terminal

The other helpful feature of Visual Studio Code is that it has an integrated terminal. We can run AppRun CLI commands and other development commands right inside Visual Studio Code without switching between Visual Studio Code and the terminal windows.

There are three commands ready to use in the AppRun project folder.

- `npm test`: Starts unit testing

- `npm start`: Starts the development server

- `npm run build`: Builds the production-ready code

We use `npm start` in the Visual Studio Code integrated terminal to start the development server; we don't even have to leave Visual Studio Code to open the terminal or command shell (see Figure 2-9).

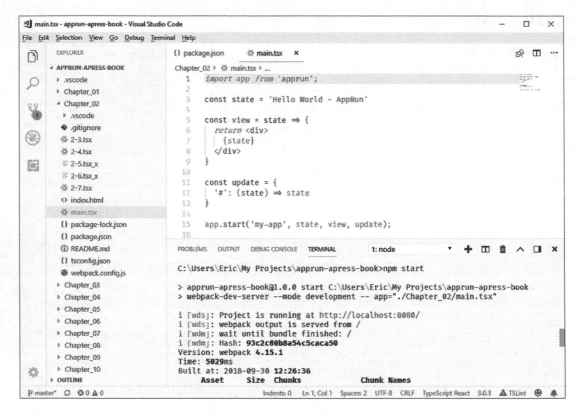

Figure 2-9. *Visual Studio integrated terminal*

Debugging

We can debug the AppRun applications right inside Visual Studio Code. To do so, we need to install the Debugger for Chrome extension from the marketplace. The steps are as follows:

1. Click the extension icon, shown here: 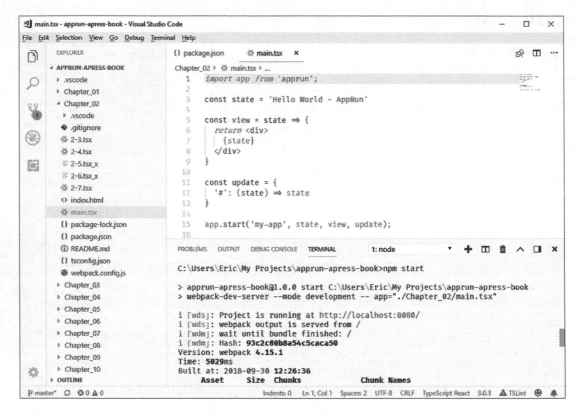.

2. Search for *Debugger for Chrome* (see Figure 2-10)

3. Click Install and reload Visual Studio Code.

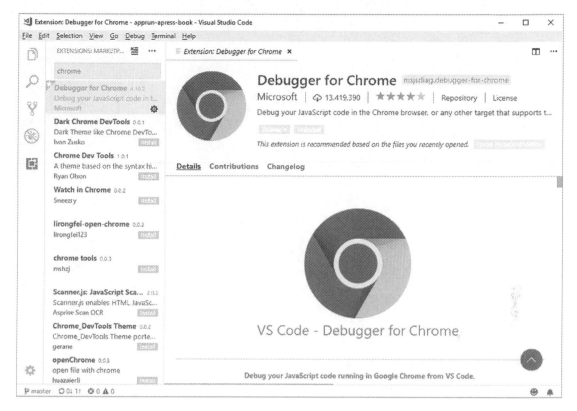

Figure 2-10. Debugger for Chrome

Once the Debugger for Chrome extension is active in Visual Studio Code, we can configure it for debugging AppRun applications. The steps are as follows:

1. Click the debug icon, shown here: .

2. Click the debug configuration icon, shown here: .

3. Set the environment to Chrome (see Figure 2-11).

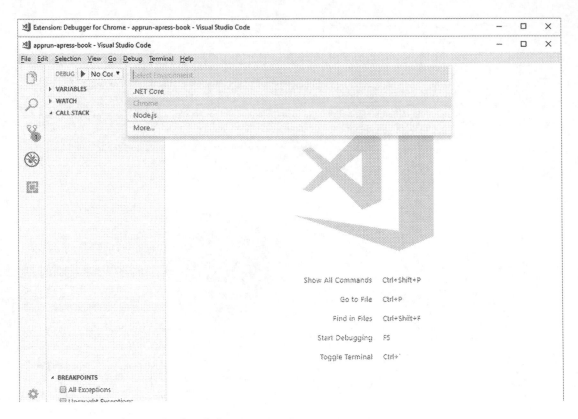

Figure 2-11. *Choosing the debugger environment*

Visual Studio creates the debugger configuration (`launch.json` file), as shown in Figure 2-12.

Figure 2-12. *Debugger configuration (launch.json)*

Once the Visual Studio Code debug configuration is complete, we can click the Debug button or press F5 to start the debugging session. We can set breakpoints, watch variables, and the call stack the same as it is in the browser DevTool (see Figure 2-13).

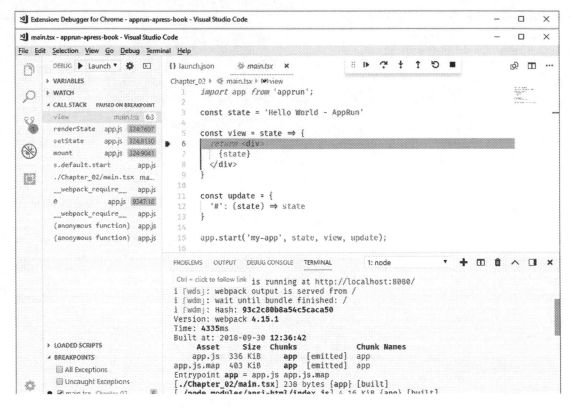

Figure 2-13.   *Visual Studio Code breakpoint*

So far, we have completed creating and exploring the AppRun development environment by using the AppRun CLI and Visual Studio Code. Now we have an AppRun development environment that has the development server and debugging enabled.

Summary

The AppRun development environment uses TypeScript as the compiler to compile advanced language features to the code that browsers can run. We can add types gradually. It is the recommended approach because we want to focus on the application logic instead of getting lost in defining data types. The AppRun development environment uses webpack as the bundler. We can develop AppRun applications utilizing the ECMAScript 2015 module format. Visual Studio Code is the recommended tool for developing AppRun applications. It provides features such as IntelliSense, type checking, code snippets, an integrated terminal, and the Debugger for Chrome extension.

With the AppRun CLI and Visual Studio Code, we are ready for some serious application development.

CHAPTER 3

Model the State

This chapter is a deep dive into the state concept of AppRun. The state is one of three main parts of the AppRun architecture. It plays an important role in the AppRun event lifecycle. It is equivalent to the mode of the Elm architecture. Elm defines the model as the application state. If fact, *model* and *state* are two names for the same thing. They are interchangeable in the AppRun architecture. Most of the time, we use the term *state* in AppRun.

In this chapter, you will learn about the concept of state, how to time-travel through the application state history to develop the undo and redo feature, how to save states locally and to the cloud, and how to sync states across multiple devices.

State Concept

The *state* is the application state at any given time of your application. As highlighted in Figure 3-1, the state is the data flow between the update and the view. It acts as the data transfer object (DTO) in a traditional multilayered application architecture, where the DTO is an object that carries data between the logical and physical layers.

© Yiyi Sun 2019
Y. Sun, *Practical Application Development with AppRun*, https://doi.org/10.1007/978-1-4842-4069-4_3

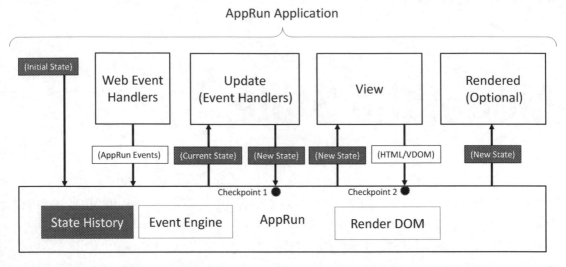

Figure 3-1. *State flow in the AppRun applications*

When AppRun applications are starting, the initial state is used to render the web page.

$$\text{Initial state} => \text{View} => (\text{HTML/Virtual DOM}) => \text{render DOM} \qquad [1]$$

When AppRun applications are running, AppRun manages the state flow through the event handlers and then through the view function and renders the web page during the event lifecycle.

Web events => AppRun events => (current state) => Update => (new state) =>
View => (HTML/Virtual DOM) => render DOM => (new state) => rendered   [2]

To demonstrate the state concept, we will develop the counter application introduced in Chapter 1 using the AppRun CLI and the AppRun development environment introduced in Chapter 2, which allows us to use the ECMAScript 2015 module format and JSX (Listing 3-1).

Listing 3-1. Source Code of the Counter Application (3-1.tsx)

```
1.   import app from 'apprun';
2.   const state = 0;
3.   const view = (state) => <div>
```

```
4.        <h1>{state}</h1>
5.        <button onclick={()=>app.run('-1')}>-1</button>
6.        <button onclick={()=>app.run('+1')}>+1</button>
7.    </div>;
8.    const update = {
9.        '+1': (state) => state + 1,
10.       '-1': (state) => state - 1
11.   };
12.   app.on('debug', p => console.log(p));
13.   app.start('my-app', state, view, update);
```

Initial State

The counter application starts with an initial state, the number 0 (line 2). It is used to start the application in the app.start function (line 13). The state uses the keyword const instead of let. It won't change after the application starts. The initial state is immutable. Sometimes we can pass the initial state into the app.start function without defining a state variable.

```
app.start('my-app', 0, view, update);
```

State History

AppRun has built-in state history and the state history pointer. In Chapter 1's example, we demonstrated the state history in the counter application. The back button (<<) steps back in the state history, or undoes the counter change. The forward button (>>) steps forward in the state history, or redoes the counter change. In Listing 3-2, we make a JSX version (Listing 3-2) and analyze the state history pointer movement.

Listing 3-2. Source Code of the Counter Application with History

```
1.    import app from 'apprun';
2.    const state = 0;
3.    const view = (state) => {
4.    console.log(state)
5.    return <div>
6.        <button onclick={() => app.run("history-prev")}> << </button>
```

```
7.        <button onclick={() => app.run("history-next")}> >> </button>
8.        <h1>{state}</h1>
9.        <button onclick={() => app.run('-1')}>-1</button>
10.       <button onclick={() => app.run('+1')}>+1</button>
11.   </div>;
12.   }
13.   const update = {
14.       '+1': (state) => state + 1,
15.       '-1': (state) => state - 1
16.   };
17.   app.start('my-app', state, view, update, {history: true});
```

We set the history option to true in the app.start function call (line 17) to enable the state history. The back (<<) button publishes the history-prev event to let AppRun set the current state to the state before the state history pointer (line 6). The forward (>>) button publishes the history-next event to let AppRun set the current state to the state after the state history pointer.

Let's visualize the state history and the state history pointer. First, we increase the number to 3; next, we click the back (<<) button three times; finally, we click the forward (>>) button three times. Table 3-1 shows the state history changes.

Table 3-1. *State History*

	State to View	**State History and Pointer**
The initial state.	0	0 <=
Increase the counter.	1	0
		1 <=
Increase the counter.	2	0
		1
		2 <=
Increase the counter.	3	0
		1
		2
		3 <=

(*continued*)

Table 3-1. (*continued*)

	State to View	State History and Pointer
Click the back (<<) button (take the state before the point).	2	0
		1
		2 <=
		3
Click the back (<<) button (take the state before the point).	1	0
		1 <=
		2
		3
Click the back (<<) button (take the state before the point).	0	0 <=
		1
		2
		3
Click the forward (>>) button (take the state after the point).	1	0
		1 <=
		2
		3
Click the forward (>>) button (take the state after the point).	2	0
		1
		2 <=
		3
Click the forward (>>) button (take the state after the point).	3	0
		1
		2
		3 <=

Although it is easy to enable the AppRun state history, the caveat is that it requires the state to be immutable. Because in the AppRun state history it stores the references to the states, if we have modified the state directly, each state stored in the state history refers the same state, which is always the value of last change. The time-travel back and forward will not work. The fundamental concept of using the state history is to make the state immutable.

Immutable State

Primitive data types in JavaScript, such as number, string, boolean, null, and undefined, are immutable already. The counter application has the state of type number, which is immutable out of the box. We can quickly enable the state history and the time-travel feature.

Nonprimitive data types such as array and object are mutable. When the state of an application is an array or an object, we need to leave the current state alone and always create a new state based on the current state.

Immutable Array

To demonstrate how to make the immutable state of the array, we will make a multiple-counter application. The multicounter application is a list of counters. It adds two buttons to the original back and forward buttons: one adds a new counter, and the other removes the last counter (see Figure 3-2). Each counter has three buttons: a button to increase the counter, a button to decrease the counter, and a new button to remove the counter from the counter list.

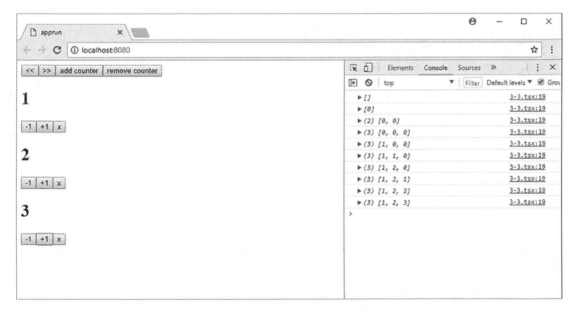

Figure 3-2. *Multicounter application*

The three application building blocks of the multicounter application are as follows:

- The state of the multicounter application is an array of numbers.

- The `view` function displays the buttons and the counter list.

- The `update` object has three event handlers for adding a counter, removing the counter, and updating the counters.

Let's dive deep into the state of the multicounter application. The state is an array of numbers. Each counter is a number within the array. The state is empty initially. We can add new counters, and we can remove counters. When a counter is added, a new number is added to the array. When a counter is removed, the correspondent number is removed from the array.

There are three events: `add-counter`, `remove-counter`, and `update-counter`. The `add-counter` and `remove-counter` events add and remove elements to and from the array, respectively. The `update-counter` event increases and decreases the element based on its index inside the array by the delta value.

Usually, we use the `array.push` function to add an element to the array and use the `array.splice` function to remove an element from the array. To update the counter in the array, we also usually just retrieve the element by index and update it directly. However, these functions mutate the array. In other words, they change the content in the array. We need different approaches.

Instead of using the `array.push` function to add an element to the array, we can use the spread operator defined in ECMAScript 2015. We create a new array, spread in old array elements, and add 0 to the end.

```
(state) => [...state, 0],
```

Instead of using the `array.splice` function to remove an element from the array by its index, we can use the spread operator twice. We create a new array and spread in elements before and after the index.

```
(state, idx) => [
  ...state.slice(0, idx),
  ...state.slice(idx + 1)
],
```

Instead of updating the element in the array directly, we can follow the same idea of composing the new array.

```
(state, idx, delta) => [
  ...state.slice(0, idx),
  state[idx] + delta,
  ...state.slice(idx + 1)
]
```

Based on previous immutable array operations, the technique to make immutable the state of an array is to break down the existing array and recompose it. The multicounter application implements the technique (Listing 3-3).

Listing 3-3. Source Code of the Multicounter Application

```
1.    import app from 'apprun';
2.    const state = [];
3.    const view = (state) => <div>
4.        <div>
5.            <button onclick={() => app.run("history-prev")}> << </button>
6.            <button onclick={() => app.run("history-next")}> >> </button>
7.            <button onclick={() => app.run("add-counter")}>add counter
              </button>
8.            <button onclick={() => app.run("remove-counter")}
              disabled={state.length <= 0}>remove counter</button>
9.        </div>
10.       { state.counters.map((num, idx) => <div>
11.           <h1>{num}</h1>
12.           <button onclick={() => app.run("update-counter", idx, -1)}>
              -1</button>
13.           <button onclick={() => app.run("update-counter", idx, 1)}>
              +1</button>
14.           <button onclick={() => app.run("remove-counter", idx)}>x
              </button>
15.       </div>
16.       )}
```

```
17.      </div>);
18.    };
19.    const update = {
20.        'add-counter': (state) => [...state, 0],
21.        'remove-counter': (state, idx = state.length - 1) => [
22.            ...state.slice(0, idx),
23.            ...state.slice(idx + 1)
24.        ],
25.        'update-counter': (state, idx, delta) => [
26.            ...state.slice(0, idx),
27.            state[idx] + delta,
28.            ...state.slice(idx + 1)
29.        ]
30.    };
31.    app.start('my-app', state, view, update, {history: true});
```

When running Listing 3-3, you can see that the back (<<) and forward (>>) buttons travel through the state change history just like the single-counter application (see the states printed in the console pane in Figure 3-2).

Immutable Object

The same technique of making immutable the array state applies to immutable object state. To demonstrate the immutable state of the object, we will build a to-do application (see Figure 3-3), similar to the ToDoMVC applications. The ToDoMVC website (http://todomvc.com) has a list of 60+ implementations of to-do applications for studying, comparing, and evaluating features, project structure, and application architecture using different frameworks and libraries. Modeled after the ToDoMVC projects, the functional specifications of our to-do application are as follows:

- Allow the user to add a new to-do item to the to-do list

- Allow the user to toggle the to-do item from active to complete

- Allow the user to delete the to-do items

- Allow the user to view the to-do items by category: all, active, and complete

- Allow the user to see the total number of active to-do items

- Allow undo and redo

- Save the to-do list locally on the computer

- Save the to-do list across multiple devices

Figure 3-3. *To-do application*

We will develop the to-do application's undo and redo features in this section. The last two requirements will be developed in the next two sections.

The state of the to-do application should cover all the requirements of the specification. We can build it piece by piece starting with the to-do item: TodoItem. A to-do item has a title and done flag. The done can be true or false to indicate whether the to-do item has been completed. A state is an object that has an array of to-do items and a filter that has three options: All, Active, and Complete (Listing 3-4).

Listing 3-4. The State of the To-Do Application

```
1.   type TodoItem = {
2.       title: string;
3.       done: boolean;
4.   }
5.   type State = {
6.       filter: 'All' | 'Active' | 'Complete',
7.       list: Array<TodoItem>
8.   };
9.   const state: State = {
10.      filter: 'All',
11.      list: []
12.  };
```

There are four event handlers (`add-item`, `delete-item`, `toggle-item`, and `filter-item`) for manipulating to-do items as well as an event handler for detecting the Return key press for adding new to-do items (Listing 3-5).

Listing 3-5. The Event Handlers of the To-Do Application

```
1.   const update = {
2.       'add-item': (state) => { },
3.       'delete-item': (state, idx) => { },
4.       'toggle-item': (state, idx) => { },
5.       'filter-item': (state, e) => { },
6.       'keyup': (state, e) => { }
7.   };
```

AppRun passes the current state into the event handlers. When the function parameter is an array or object, it is passed to the function as a reference. The `state` object can be changed inside the event handler. To create a new state based on the current state, we use the spread operator to break down the current state object properties, insert them into a new object, and then overwrite the properties with the new value according to the events. For example, the event handler of `toggle-item` overwrites the `filter` property of the new state object.

```
'filter-item': (state, e) => ({ ...state, filter: e.target.textContent })
```

55

The method applies to all simple property types. But the to-do item list in the state is an array. Adding, deleting, and changing the items inside the list should follow the technique of an immutable array (Listing 3-6).

Listing 3-6. Immutable State Update in the To-Do Application

```
1.    'add-item': (state, title) => ({
2.        ...state,
3.        list: [...state.list, { title, done: false }]
4.    }),
5.    'delete-item': (state, idx) => ({
6.        ...state,
7.        list: [
8.            ...state.list.slice(0, idx),
9.            ...state.list.slice(idx + 1)
10.        ]
11.    }),
12.    'toggle-item': (state, idx) => ({
13.        ...state,
14.        list: [
15.            ...state.list.slice(0, idx),
16.            { ...state.list[idx], done: !state.list[idx].done },
17.            ...state.list.slice(idx + 1)
18.        ]
19.    }),
```

The code snippets to add, delete, and change the list items within a state object (Listing 3-6) provide a reusable pattern that you can use in your applications. The complete source code of the preliminary to-do application without visual styling has 78 lines of code including static types (Listing 3-7).

Listing 3-7. Complete Source Code of the To-Do Application

```
1.    import app from 'apprun';
2.    type TodoItem = {
3.        title: string;
4.        done: boolean;
5.    }
```

```
6.    type State = {
7.        filter: 'All' | 'Active' | 'Complete';
8.        list: Array<TodoItem>;
9.    };

10.   const state: State = {
11.       filter: 'All',
12.       list: []
13.   };

14.   const view = (state: State) => {
15.       const countAll = state.list.length;
16.       const countActive = state.list.filter(todo => !todo.done).length || 0;
17.       const countComplete = state.list.filter(todo => todo.done).length || 0;
18.       return <div>
19.           <button onclick={() => app.run("history-prev")}> << </button>
20.           <button onclick={() => app.run("history-next")}> >> </button>
21.           <p><input onkeyup={e => app.run('keyup', e)} /></p>
22.           <ul> {
23.                   state.list
24.                       .map((todo, idx) => ({ ...todo, idx }))
25.                       .filter(todo => state.filter === 'All' ||
26.                               (state.filter === 'Active' && !todo.done) ||
27.                               (state.filter === 'Complete' && todo.done))
28.                       .map((todo) => <li>
29.                           <input type='checkbox' onclick={() =>
                            app.run('toggle-item', todo.idx)}
                            checked={todo.done} />
30.                           <span>{todo.title} {' '} (<a href='#' onclick=
                            {() => app.run('delete-item', todo.idx)}>&#9249;
                            </a>)</span>
31.                       </li>)
32.           }</ul>
```

```
33.          <div>
34.          <a href='#' onclick={e => app.run('filter-item', e)}>All</a>
             {` (${countAll}) | `}
35.          <a href='#' onclick={e => app.run('filter-item', e)}>Active</a>
             {`(${countActive}) | `}
36.          <a href='#' onclick={e => app.run('filter-item', e)}>
             Complete</a> {`(${countComplete})`}
37.      </div>
38.  </div>
39.  };
40.  const update = {
41.      'add-item': (state, title) => ({
42.          ...state,
43.          list: [...state.list, { title, done: false }]
44.      }),
45.      'delete-item': (state, idx) => ({
46.          ...state,
47.          list: [
48.              ...state.list.slice(0, idx),
49.              ...state.list.slice(idx + 1)
50.          ]
51.      }),
52.      'toggle-item': (state, idx) => ({
53.          ...state,
54.          list: [
55.              ...state.list.slice(0, idx),
56.              { ...state.list[idx], done: !state.list[idx].done },
57.              ...state.list.slice(idx + 1)
58.          ]
59.      }),
60.      'filter-item': (state, e) => ({ ...state, filter: e.target.
         textContent }),
61.      'keyup': (state, e) => {
62.          if (e.keyCode === 13 && e.target.value.trim()) {
```

```
63.                app.run('add-item', e.target.value);
64.                e.target.value = ";
65.            }
66.        }
67.    };
68.    app.start('my-app', state, view, update, { history: true });
```

We can conclude that the method to make the state immutable is to create a new state that replaces the current state. The AppRun architecture is designed to support the immutable state. If we implement the immutable state, AppRun provides the time-travel through the state history, which is useful for developing the undo and redo features. On the other hand, although making the state immutable is always a good practice, it does require extra attention and coding effort in JavaScript.

Note   The immutable state is not a mandatory requirement of AppRun. If you do not need the undo and redo feature in your application, you can mutate the current state. AppRun is flexible.

Persistent State

The state is like the soul of an AppRun application. We can save the state after the state change and load the state to resume the application. We can also share the state across browsers, platforms, and devices to run the applications simultaneously in different browsers and apps on various devices. We will demonstrate the local state and cloud state in the next two sections.

Local State

We will continue developing the to-do application by adding a new feature to store the to-do list on the local computer. The application saves the to-do list to the browser's local storage to preserve the state. When the application starts, it loads and renders the state automatically (see Figure 3-4).

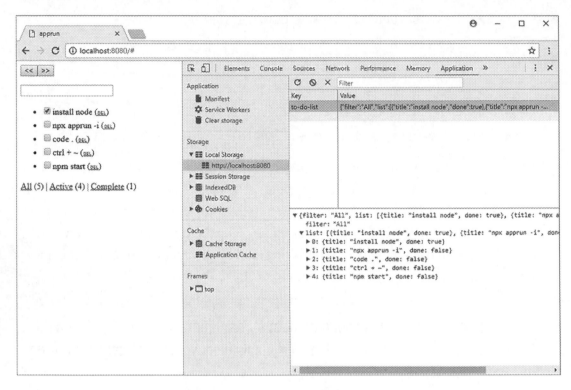

Figure 3-4. *Local storage of the to-do application*

Local storage is a browser feature to allow web applications to store data locally within the user's browser. It is secure, it is high performant, and it allows a large amount of data to be stored (at least 5MB). All pages, from the same origin (per domain and protocol), can save and load the data to and from the local storage. The Chrome browser DevTool displays the local storage content on the Application tab (see Figure 3-4).

Loading data and saving data are synchronous operations that can easily apply to AppRun applications (Listing 3-8).

Listing 3-8. Enable Local Storage in AppRun Applications

```
1.   import app from 'apprun';
2.   const state: State = {};
3.   const view = (state: State) => {};
4.   const update = {};
5.   const STORAGE_KEY = 'to-do-list';
```

```
6.   const rendered = state => localStorage.setItem(STORAGE_KEY, JSON.
     stringify(state));
7.   const stored = localStorage.getItem(STORAGE_KEY)
8.   app.start('my-app', stored ? JSON.parse(stored) : state, view, update,
     { rendered });
```

Loading the state from the local storage, we need to pay attention to a couple of details. The data stored in the local storage is always the string type. Therefore, it requires us to serialize and deserialize the state when saving to and loading from the local storage (line 7). When the first-time application runs, the state does not exist in the local storage. We fall back to using the default initial state (line 8).

To save the state to the local storage, we use the rendered callback function in the AppRun event lifecycle (see Figure 3-1). It is the last step before the event cycle ends. AppRun invokes the rendered callback function with the state parameter after it renders the HTML to the web page.

We create the rendered function for saving the state to local storage (line 6) and set the rendered callback function in the options parameter when we start the application (line 8).

By simply adding the logic of loading and saving the state (Listing 3-8, lines 6–8) to the to-do application, we have enabled local persistent storage to the application. Listing 3-8 is a reusable pattern that you can follow when developing other AppRun applications.

Cloud State

Although the local storage allows the data access across many browsers of the same type, by default the data is not accessible between different browser types. For example, Firefox browsers cannot access the local storage of the Chrome browsers. However, AppRun applications can run on multiple browsers and even various platforms and devices. We will finish this chapter by making the to-do application share the state across browsers, platforms, and devices.

We will save the state to Google Cloud Firestore and leverage Cloud Firestore to sync the data across multiple devices. Cloud Firestore is a cloud NoSQL database for developing mobile, web, and server applications from Firebase and Google Cloud

Platform. It keeps your data in sync across devices in real time and offers offline support for mobile and web applications. To add Google Cloud Firestore to the AppRun application, follow the steps:

1. Open the Firebase Console (`https://console.firebase.google.com/`), add a new project, and then enter your project name. If you have an existing Firebase project that you'd like to use, select that project from the console.

2. In the Database section, click the Get Started button for Cloud Firestore. Select the Test mode as the starting mode (remember to switch to Locked mode for production use later) and then click the Enable button.

3. From the project overview page, add Firebase to your web project.

4. Copy the configuration (Listing 3-9) and paste it into the store module (Listing 3-10).

5. Install Firebase in your AppRun project: `npm i firebase`.

Listing 3-9. Firebase Web Project Configuration

```
1.   var  config = {
2.       apiKey: "xxxxxxxxxxxxxxxxxxxxxxxxxxxxxxx",
3.       authDomain: "apprun-demo.firebaseapp.com",
4.       databaseURL: "https://apprun-demo.firebaseio.com",
5.       projectId: "apprun-demo",
6.       storageBucket: "apprun-demo.appspot.com",
7.       messagingSenderId: "--------------"
8.   };
```

We will use the configuration to create a store module that handles the events for saving and loading data to and from Firestore (Listing 3-10).

Listing 3-10. Module for Saving and Load Data to and from Firestore

```
1.   import app from 'apprun';
2.   import * as firebase from 'firebase';
3.   import 'firebase/firestore';
```

```
4.   const STORAGE_KEY = 'to-do-list';
5.   const config = {
6.       apiKey: "xxxxxxxxxxxxxxxxxxxxxxxxxxxxxx",  ,
7.       authDomain: "apprun-demo.firebaseapp.com",
8.       databaseURL: "https://apprun-demo.firebaseio.com",
9.       projectId: "apprun-demo",
10.      storageBucket: "apprun-demo.appspot.com",
11.      messagingSenderId: "-------------"
12.  };
13.  firebase.initializeApp(config);
14.  const db = firebase.firestore();
15.  const ref = db.collection(STORAGE_KEY).doc("state")

16.  app.on('save-state', state => ref.set(state));
17.  ref.onSnapshot(doc => {
18.      if (doc.exists) app.run('new-state', doc.data())
19.  });
```

Firestore access uses the event publication and subscription pattern just like AppRun. It is a natural fit for the AppRun applications. The store module (Listing 3-10) uses an AppRun event subscription for saving data to Firestore. Other AppRun application modules have no dependencies to the Firebase and Firestore library.

The store module subscribes to the save-state event (line 16). When the application needs to save the state, we can publish the save-state event with the state as event parameters to let the store module save that state to Firestore.

The store module also publishes the new-state event. When Firestore data is available in the Firestore onSnapshot event, it converts the Firestore onSnapshot event to the AppRun new-state event (lines 17–19).

The new-state and save-state events connect the to-do application with Firestore (Listing 3-11). The state and the view function are omitted to let you focus on the most relevant code that saves and loads the state in Listing 3-11.

Listing 3-11. Saving the State to the Cloud

```
1.   import app from 'apprun';
2.   import './store';
3.   const state = {...};
```

```
4.    const view = (state) => {... };
5.    const update = {
6.        'new-state': (_, state) => state,
7.        'add-item': (state, title) => app.run('save-state', {
8.              ...state,
9.          }),
10.       'delete-item': (state, idx) => app.run('save-state', {
11.             ...state,
12.         }),
13.       'toggle-item': (state, idx) => app.run('save-state', {
14.             ...state,
15.       })
16.   };
17.   app.start('my-app', state,  view, update, { history: true });
```

When the application connects to Firestore the first time, Firestore publishes the onSnapshot event. The store module publishes the AppRun new-state event. The new-state event handler returns the state to AppRun to render the web page (line 7).

When the users add, delete, and toggle to-do items, the corresponding event handlers of add-item, delete-item, and toggle-item publish the save-state event to let the store module save the state to Firestore.

When Firestore saves the state successfully, it publishes the onSnapshot event again. The onSnapshot event is converted to the new-state event again. AppRun renders the new state on the web page (see Figure 3-5).

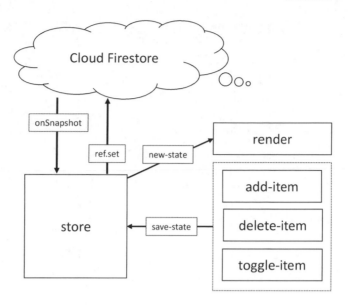

Figure 3-5. *Firestore events and AppRun events*

The event handlers of the add-item, delete-item, and toggle-item events call the app.run function only. They do not return any state (Lines 7-16). When the event handler returns a new state of the null or undefined object, the AppRun stops the AppRun event lifecycle at checkpoint 1 (see Figure 3-1). AppRun does not invoke the view function anymore. The event lifecycle stops. Nothing changes on the screen until the new-state event comes later.

We can open the to-do application in different browsers. Figure 3-6 shows the application, from left, in Chrome, Firefox, and Edge. The to-do list is automatically shared between them. When adding, toggling, and deleting the to-do items in one browser, the new to-do list is automatically displayed in the other browsers without a need to refresh the other browsers.

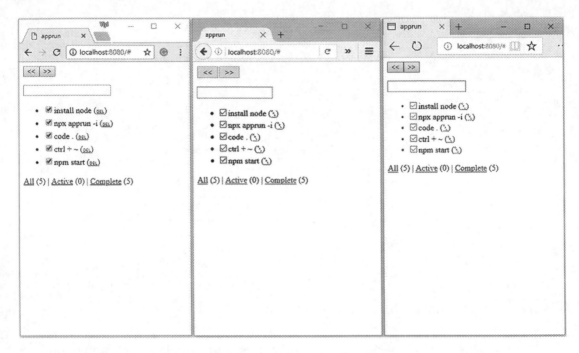

Figure 3-6. *Running the to-do application in multiple browsers*

Source Code of Examples

You can get the source code in this chapter by cloning the GitHub project from `https://github.com/yysun/apprun-apress-book`. You can run the six examples in this chapter using the npm scripts in Table 3-2.

Table 3-2. *npm Scripts of This Chapter*

Example	Script
The counter application (Listing 3-1)	`npm run jsx-counter`
The counter with history (Listing 3-2)	`npm run jsx-counter-history`
The multiple counter application (Listing 3-3)	`npm run counters`
The to-do application (Listing 3-8)	`npm run to-do`
The local to-do application (Listing 3-9)	`npm run to-do-local`
The cloud to-do application (Listing 3-11)	`npm run to-do-cloud`

Summary

In AppRun applications, the state is the DTO between the event handlers and the `view` function. AppRun manages the state flow. It takes an initial state and keeps tracks of the state and manages the state history. You can travel through the state history if you keep the state immutable by always creating a new state to replace the current state.

The state is the soul of the AppRun application. Persisting the state in the local storage allows the user to exit the applications without losing data. Sharing the state into the cloud makes the applications run across browsers, platforms, and devices.

When the applications become complicated, the states of the applications become complicated. They can have the data fields and visual flag fields. The data fields are the dynamic content to render the web pages. The visual flag fields are to control the visual presentation of web page elements such as the visibility, color, open and collapse status, class, and styles of the web page elements. In the next chapter, we will introduce the various strategies, patterns, and techniques of rendering the state to the web pages in the `view` function.

CHAPTER 4

View Patterns

This chapter is a deep dive into the view concept of AppRun, an important part of the AppRun architecture. In the AppRun event lifecycle, the *view* is responsible for displaying the web pages according to the application states.

The Document Object Model (DOM) is the programming API for web development. It allows us to manipulate the elements, styles, and content of the elements on the web pages. However, the view does not update the DOM directly. The view creates the data structure representation of the DOM, called the virtual DOM. AppRun renders the virtual DOM to the actual DOM. It can also create the HTML string. AppRun converts the HTML string into the virtual DOM. Before rendering the virtual DOM to the actual DOM, AppRun compares them to each other. It only updates the changed elements and element properties.

This chapter will introduce the role that the view plays in the AppRun event lifecycle, JSX, and the virtual DOM. You will learn about many JSX patterns commonly used when developing the `view` function. This chapter also introduces AppRun components and web components as they are important to learning the view patterns. You will also be able to develop web components for modern browsers after reading this chapter.

View Concept

We will start with reviewing the role of the view in the AppRun event lifecycle.

The View Function

In AppRun applications, the view is a function often named `view`. During the AppRun event lifecycle, AppRun invokes the `view` function after the event handlers have created the new states (see Figure 4-1).

© Yiyi Sun 2019
Y. Sun, *Practical Application Development with AppRun*, https://doi.org/10.1007/978-1-4842-4069-4_4

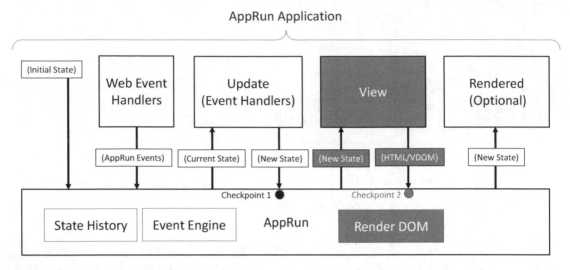

Figure 4-1. *View function in AppRun event lifecycle*

The position of the view in the AppRun event lifecycle is highlighted in [1].

Web events => AppRun Events => (current state) => Update =>
(new state) => **View** => (HTML/Virtual DOM) => render DOM   [1]

The AppRun event lifecycle in [1] is a full and happy path. There are other scenarios where the event lifecycle ends differently.

Notice in Figure 4-1 that there are two checkpoints. At the first checkpoint, AppRun checks whether the event handlers return null or undefined. If they do return null or undefined, AppRun skips calling the view function. The flow looks like [2].

Web events => AppRun Events => (current state) => Update =>
(null or undefined) => [**No View**]   [2]

At the second checkpoint, AppRun checks whether the view function returns null or undefined, and if so, AppRun skips rendering the DOM. The flow looks like [3].

Web events => AppRun Events => (current state) => Update =>
(new state) => **View** => (null or undefined) => [**No render DOM**]   [3]

Also, there is an optional rendered function in the AppRun event lifecycle. AppRun calls the rendered function after it renders the DOM if it is present. The flow is shown in [4].

Web events => AppRun Events => (current state) => Update => (new state) =>
View => (HTML/Virtual DOM) => render DOM => (new state) => rendered   [4]

The extended flow with the `rendered` function is the way to integrate with other libraries. For example, we can use libraries such as jQuery to change the DOM after AppRun renders the DOM. You will learn how to use it in Chapter 8.

HTML vs. JSX

After learning when the `view` function is invoked in the event lifecycle, we will focus on how to create HTML elements.

First, we can use the `view` function to create an HTML string. For example, to create a `<div>` element, we can use JavaScript string template literals to create an HTML string.

```
const view = state => `<div id='main' class='page'>${state}</div>`;
```

AppRun parses the HTML string into the virtual DOM. You will learn about the data structure of the virtual DOM in the "Virtual DOM" section later in this chapter.

Although sometimes the HTML string is easy to understand and useful for trying ideas, it takes time to parse it into the virtual DOM at runtime, which may cause performance issues. It also has some problems that have been documented by the Facebook React team.[1] We recommend using JSX.

```
const view = state => <div id='main' class='page'>{state}</div>;
```

The JSX looks like the HTML, but it is indeed the syntactic sugar of function calls. The TypeScript compiler compiles the previous JSX into the following function call:

```
view = state => app.createElement("div", {id:'main', className:'page'}, state);
```

Using JSX, it is easier to understand the intention of the `view` function, which is to create HTML elements. Using JSX can also prevent missing tags or mismatches of the closing tags because the syntax is enforced and checked at compile time. For example, we can write the `view` function using an HTML string that has an error without notice.

```
const view = state => `<div id='main' class='page'>${state}<div>`;
```

The `view` function has no compile error and can run in the browser. The browser might be able to close the `<div>` tag by itself. There are two `<div>` elements in DOM, which might change the screen layout and design.

---

[1]See "Why not Template Literals?" at http://facebook.github.io/jsx/#why-not-template-literals.

However, the `view` function won't pass the JSX complication when using JSX. The compiler will catch the error of the unclosed tag and remind us to fix it.

```
const view = state => <div id='main' class='page'>{state}<div>;
                                                          ^^^^
```

Because of the compile-time validation, we can say using JSX is better, especially for applications that are not demos or prototypes.

The AppRun CLI-initialized development environment has everything configured to use JSX. If you want to code the scripts directly without a build process, you can use the `app.createElement` function. You can also alias the `app.createElement` function as the h function and use it the way you would use HyperScript.[2]

```
const h = app.createElement;
const view = state => h("div", {id:'main', className:'page'}, state);
```

Custom JSX Tag

A useful convention in JSX is that when the JSX tag name is capitalized, it calls a custom function instead of calling `app.createElement`. For example, we can define a function named as `MyDiv`, as shown here:

```
const MyDiv = ({content})=><div>{ content }</div>;
```

Then, we can use the `MyDiv` function as the custom JSX tag in JSX.

```
const view = state => <MyDiv content='Hello' />;
```

A custom JSX tag can have properties. When calling custom functions, the JSX tags properties are passed into the functions as function parameters. The `content` property in the previous example is passed to the `MyDiv` function.

Because the custom JSX tags are function calls, we can break down and organize the application codebase by function. You will learn more about this in the "JSX Patterns" section later in this chapter.

Also, the custom JSX tag is used to create components. You will learn about this in the "Components" section later in this chapter.

---

[2]For more information about HyperScript, please visit its GitHub page at `https://github.com/hyperhype/hyperscript`.

Virtual DOM

The Virtual DOM is the in-memory data structure representation of the DOM. AppRun defines the virtual DOM as follows:

```
type VNode = {
  tag: string,
  props: {},
  children: Array<VNode | string>
}
```

Say we have the following example view function:

```
const view = state => `<div id='main' class='page'>${state}<div>`;
```

Run the view function called view() to get the following virtual DOM:

```
{ "tag": "div",
  "props": { "id": "main", "className": "page" },
  "children": [""]
}
```

We can use the app.render function to render the virtual DOM to a web page element, such as to the body element, as shown here:

```
app.render(document.body, { "tag": "div",
  "props": { "id": "main", "className": "page" },
  "children": ["Hello"]
})
```

AppRun renders the virtual DOM to a web page element as the first child. The body element will have a <div> element.

```
<body><div id="main" class="page">Hello</div><body>
```

The app.render function is the function used by AppRun internally for rendering the virtual DOM. In AppRun application development, we usually don't use the app.render function directly. We will be focusing on creating the view function and let AppRun connect the state, view, and update for us through the event lifecycle.

Now that we understand the role of the `view` function and the virtual DOM, we will move on to discuss some common patterns of using JSX for creating web page elements dynamically based on the application states.

JSX Patterns

We will use the to-do application from Chapter 3 to explore the patterns and techniques for developing `view` functions. We'll apply the styles from the ToDoMVC project (`http://todomvc.com/`) to our to-do application.

The ToDoMVC web site is the place for studying, comparing, and evaluating the features, project structure, and application architecture of different frameworks and libraries. It has a standard style guide that includes the HTML and CSS.

The ToDoMVC to-do list style guide defines the following UI features:

- The to-do items should be rendered as an unordered list, where each to-do item is a `<li>` element.

- The to-do items should be able to be filtered into three categories: all, active, and complete.

- The three filter buttons should be highlighted when they are clicked by using the `selected` CSS class.

- The completed to-do item should be grayed out and crossed out by using the `complete` CSS class.

- The complete to-do item should be rendered by using the `view` CSS class.

- The check box in front of each to-do item should be selected for the completed to-do items.

- The "Clear completed" button should be visible only if there are completed to-do items.

The good news is we can leverage the CSS published by the ToDoMVC project. Once we create the right HTML elements and apply the right CSS classes to the elements, the to-do application looks like Figure 4-2.

Figure 4-2. *The ToDoMVC-styled to-do application*

We will create the elements dynamically and apply the CSS classes dynamically for the to-do application. Let's start with the HTML structure.

Custom JSX Tags

The ToDoMVC HTML template has the structure shown in Listing 4-1.

Listing 4-1. ToDoMVC HTML Structure

```
1.    <html lang="en">
2.    <head></head>
3.    <body>
4.        <section class="todoapp">
5.            <header class="header"></header>
6.            <section class="main">
7.                <ul class="todo-list"></ul>
8.            </section>
```

```
9.                  <footer class="footer"></footer>
10.         </section>
11.         <footer class="info"></footer>
12.         <script src="app.js"></script>
13.   </body>
14.   </html>
```

There will be many elements created and filled in to the HTML structure dynamically when the application runs.

We create custom functions for each section of the HTML structure and use the custom JSX tags to integrate them into the main HTML structure (Listing 4-2).

Listing 4-2. The View Function Structure

```
1.    import app from 'apprun';
2.    const state = { list: [] };
3.    const Header = () => <header className="header"></header>;
4.    const Footer = () => <footer className="info"></footer>;
5.    const Todo = ({ todo, idx }) => <li className="completed"></li>;
6.    const Main = ({ state }) => <>
7.        <section className="main">
8.            <ul className="todo-list"> {
9.                state.list.map((todo, idx) => <Todo todo={todo} idx={idx} />)
10.           } </ul>
11.       </section>
12.       <footer className="footer"></footer>
13.   </>;
14.   const view = (state) => <>
15.       <section className="todoapp">
16.           <Header />
17.           <Main state={state} />
18.       </section>
19.       <Footer />
20.   </>;
21.   const update = {};
22.   app.start(document.body, state, view, update, { history: true });
```

Using the custom JSX tags is an effective way to break down a complicated HTML structure into smaller and more manageable functions. The custom JSX tags are also known as *stateless functional* components or *pure function* components. Therefore, in Listing 4-2, <Header/>, <Footer/>, and <Todo/> are all stateless functional components.

The custom JSX tags can also be used to create another type of component, called *stateful components*, that you will learn about in the "Components" section later in the chapter.

JSX Fragments

Usually JSX returns a root element that includes some child elements. But the designer of the ToDoMVC template has created the HTML template with two parallel elements: <section class="todoapp" /> and <footer class="info" /> (Listing 4-1, lines 4 and 11). To create the parallel elements, we can use a JSX fragment. A fragment lets us group multiple elements and components into an array without a root element. A JSX fragment wraps child elements using <> and </> (Listing 4-3).

Listing 4-3. JSX Fragments

```
1.    const view = (state) => <>
2.        <section className="todoapp">
3.            <Header />
4.            <Main state={state} />
5.        </section>
6.        <Footer />
7.    </>;
```

Create a List

To render the dynamic to-do item list stored in the state object as an array called state. list, we first create a Todo function for one to-do item. The Todo function turns the individual to-do item into a <li> element. Then, we call the ToDo function by using the custom JSX tag in the array.map function to build a list of <li> elements (Listing 4-4).

Listing 4-4. Rendering the List

```
1.   <ul className="todo-list"> {
2.       state.list.map((todo, idx) => <Todo todo={todo} idx={idx} />)
3.   } </ul>
```

Create a List Item

The ToDo function creates the to-do item. It has two input parameters: todo and idx. The custom JSX tag also has two properties, todo and idx. These are passed into the ToDo function as parameters.

To retrieve the two parameters from the JSX properties in the Todo function, we use the parameter destructuring feature of ECMAScript 2015 (ES6). The ToDo function creates the <li> element using these parameters:

```
const Todo = ({ todo, idx }) => <li><label>{todo.title}</label></li>;
```

Filter a List

There are three filters to display the to-do items in three categories: all, active, and complete. The current filter is stored in the state object as state.filter. The state. list has to be filtered using state.filter before building the list of <li> elements. We use the array.filter function before using the array.map function to achieve the filtering (Listing 4-5).

Listing 4-5. Filtering a List

```
1.   <ul className="todo-list"> {
2.       state.list
3.           .filter(todo => state.filter === 'All' ||
                       (state.filter === 'Active' && !todo.done) ||
                       (state.filter === 'Complete' && todo.done))
4.           .map((todo, idx) => <Todo todo={todo} idx={idx} />)
5.   }
6.   </ul>
```

So far, we have filtered and created the elements for the to-do item list based on the state object. We will continue to apply the CSS classes to the elements based on the properties of the to-do items.

Apply a Class

Each <li> element should have the CSS class view for active items and the CSS class completed for completed items. We use the ternary operator to apply different classes to the element.

```
const Todo = ({ todo, idx }) => <li className={todo.done ? "completed" : "view"}>
    <label>{todo.title}</label>
</li>
```

Notice that we use className to represent the class property in JSX instead of class. This is because class is a JavaScript reserved keyword.

The CSS class of the <li> element can be changed back and forth based on the done property of the todo object. We also refer to it as *toggling* the class.

Set the Element Property

In front of each to-do item, there is a check box indicating whether the to-do item is completed. The checked property of the check box is also set according to the done property of the todo object (todo.done). Since todo.done is the boolean type, it can be set to the checked property of the check box directly.

```
const Todo = ({ todo, idx }) => <li className={todo.done ? "completed" : "view"}>
  <div>
    <input className="toggle" type="checkbox" checked={todo.done}/>
    <label>{todo.title}</label>
  </div>
</li>
```

Set Active Classes

There are three filters for users to choose. They are displayed as <a> elements. The filter elements need to be highlighted to indicate which one is the currently chosen filter. The highlight is done by attaching the selected CSS class to the chosen filter. We use the ternary operator to toggle between the selected class and an empty string that cleans the class properties (Listing 4-6).

Listing 4-6. Set Active Classes

```
1.   <ul className="filters">
2.       <li><a className={state.filter === 'All' ? 'selected' : ''} >
         All</a></li>
3.       <li><a className={state.filter === 'Active' ? 'selected' : ''}>
         Active</a></li>
4.       <li><a className={state.filter === 'Complete' ? selected' : ''} >
         Complete</a></li>
5.   </ul>
```

When state.filter is All, the <a> elements to All have the CSS class selected applied. The other two <a> elements have the CSS class selected applied when state.filter is All or Complete, respectively.

Show and Hide Elements

Dynamically showing and hiding elements are the commonly used scenarios of web applications. For example, in the to-do application, the "Clear completed" button is displayed or hidden dynamically based on the count of the completed to-do items. We need to calculate the content first and then use the ternary operator to show or hide the <button> element (Listing 4-7).

Listing 4-7. Showing and Hiding Elements Using the Ternary Operator

```
1.   const countComplete = state.list.filter(todo => todo.done).length || 0;
2.   { countComplete > 0 ? <button>Clear completed</button> : ''}
```

Or we can to show or hide the <button> element use the && operator (Listing 4-8).

Listing 4-8. Showing and Hiding Elements Using the && Operator

```
1.   const countComplete = state.list.filter(todo => todo.done).length || 0;
2.   { countComplete > 0 && <button>Clear completed</button> }
```

To conclude, using custom tags, using JSX fragments, creating lists, creating list items, filtering lists, applying CSS classes, toggling CSS classes, and showing/hiding elements using JSX are the commonly used tasks in AppRun applications. You can use all these tasks when developing your applications.

Components

So far, we have been developing AppRun applications by using the AppRun architecture globally. The state, view, and update are all global variables. This is a straightforward and effective way of developing AppRun applications. However, there is only one state, one view, and one update globally. Even by using the custom JSX tags and custom functions to help break down an application's codebase, this technique is still not scalable for complex applications. For complex applications, AppRun supports building applications using components just like in many other frameworks.

Component Class

AppRun components are like mini-AppRun applications. Each component has the AppRun architecture, which means each component has the state, view, and update. It is quite easy to create AppRun components. They are derived classes from the AppRun Component class. We can take a global AppRun application and add the Component class syntax around it to make it a component (see Table 4-1).

Table 4-1. *Global Application and Component Application*

Global Application	Component Application
| ```
import app from 'apprun';
const state = {}
const view = state => {state}
const update = {
 '#': state => state
}
app.start('my-app', state, view, update);
``` | ```
import app, {Component} from 'apprun';
class MyComponent extends Component {
  state = {};
  view = (state) => <div>{state}</div>
  update = {
     '#': state => state
  }
}
new MyComponent().start('my-app');
``` |

We can develop the components as TypeScript classes. As mentioned in Chapter 2, the TypeScript compiler supports classes and class fields. We can define state, view, and update as the class fields in the TypeScript Component class (Listing 4-9).

Listing 4-9. TypeScript Component Class

```
1.   class MyComponent extends Component {
2.       state = {};
3.       view = (state) => <div>{state}</div>
4.       update = {
5.       }
6.   }
```

If you want to use an ECMAScript 2015 (ES6) class without TypeScript, you will need to define the state, view, and update properties in the class constructor (Listing 4-10).

Listing 4-10. ES6 Component Class

```
1.   class MyComponent extends Component {
2.       constructor() {
3.           super();
4.           this.state = {}
5.           this.view = state => `<div></div>`;
```

```
6.          this.update = {
7.          };
8.      }
9.  }
```

You will see an example of using the ES6 class in the "Web Components" section later in the chapter.

Once we have created AppRun components, there are two ways of using them: use them in code or use them in JSX.

Create Components in Code

Because components are classes, it is straightforward to use them in code. We first create an object of the component. Optionally, we can initialize state when calling the constructor (Listing 4-11).

Listing 4-11. Initializing Component State in Constructors

```
1.  import app, {Component} from 'apprun';
2.  class MyComponent extends Component {
3.      view = (state) => <div>{state}</div>
4.      update = { };
5.  }
6.  const  state = { };
7.  new MyComponent(state).start('my-app');
```

The AppRun Component class has a start function similar to the app.start function, which we can use to run the component inside a web page element (Listing 4-12).

Listing 4-12. Starting a Component

```
1.  import app, {Component} from 'apprun';
2.  class MyComponent extends Component {
3.  }
4.  new MyComponent().start('my-app');
```

The start function is inherited from the AppRun Component class. It displays the component inside the element and activates the event handlers of the component.

Sometimes we want to associate the component with an element without displaying it. In this case, we can use the mount function inherited from the Component class. It only activates the event handlers without displaying the component. These types of components are *lazy* components (Listing 4-13).

Listing 4-13. Lazy Components

```
1.    import app, {Component} from 'apprun';
2.    class MyLazyComponent extends Component {
3.    }
4.    new MyLazyComponent().mount('my-app');
```

The component is mounted to the web page element or element ID. When the component is mounted to an element ID, it retrieves the element by using the document. getElementID function at the time it needs to render the element. It will not render the element if it cannot find it. The *lazy* components are useful for single-page applications (SPAs), where we can mount multiple components to a single element. The components are hidden until the events that wake them up and display them. You will learn about developing SPAs using components in Chapter 7.

Create Components in JSX

In addition to using components in code, we can use custom JSX tags to create AppRun components (Listing 4-14).

Listing 4-14. Components in JSX

```
1.    class App extends Component {
2.        state = {};
3.        view = <div></div>;
4.        update = {
5.        };
6.    }
7.    app.render(document.body, <App />);
```

In Listing 4-14, we use a custom JSX tag called <App /> to create the App component. Then we use the app.render function to display the App component in the body element.

We have used custom JSX tags to call custom functions, which are called *stateless functional components*. The AppRun components created using the custom JSX tags are called the *stateful components*.

When using custom JSX tags to create components, the JSX tag properties are set into the state field of the components (Listing 4-15).

Listing 4-15. JSX Properties as Component States

```
1.    class Child extends Component {
2.        view = (state) => <div>{state.n}</div>;   // state.n is expected to
                                                        be '8'
3.    }
4.    class Parent extends Component {
5.        view = (state) => <div>
6.            <Child n='8'/>
7.        </div>;
8.    }
9.    new Main().start();
```

In Listing 4-15, we use the custom JSX tag <Child n='8'/> to create the Child component (line 9). Notice that the Child component class has no state field. The component object created by the custom JSX tag has values of the JSX tag properties. If you define a state field in the component, your state field overwrites the JSX properties.

Custom JSX tags can have child tags. AppRun passes the child tags as the children property to the state field of the component so that the component can render the child tags (Listing 4-16).

Listing 4-16. Component Children

```
1.    class Child extends Component {
2.        view = (state) => {state.children}</div>;
3.    }
4.    class Main extends Component {
5.        view = (state) => <div>
6.            <Child>
7.                <p>child</p>
8.            </Child>
```

```
9.        </div>;
10.  }
11.  const element = document.createElement('div');
12.  new Main().start(element);
```

The end result from Listing 4-16 is as follows:

```
<div>
    <div>
        <p>child</p>
    <div>
<div>
```

Let's put AppRun components into action.

Two To-Do Lists

To demonstrate the AppRun component, we will make the to-do application have two to-do lists, called *my todos* and *team todos*. The two lists have the same functions and two different states (Figure 4-3).

Figure 4-3. *The two todo lists*

We convert the to-do application into the Todo component. Then, we modify main.tsx to use the Todo component twice (Listing 4-17).

Listing 4-17. Two To-Do Components

```
1.    import app from 'apprun';
2.    import TodoComponent from './to-do-component';
3.    const view = state => <div className="main">
4.        <TodoComponent type="my" title="my todos" />
5.        <TodoComponent type="team" title="team todos" />
6.    </div>;
7.    app.start(document.body, null, view);
```

This is different from the global to-do application, which had only a global state and events. The Todo component has its own scope of state and events (Listing 4-18).

Listing 4-18. To-Do Components

```
1.    import app, { Component } from 'apprun';
2.    const STORAGE_KEY = 'to-do-list-';
3.    export default class TodoComponent extends Component {
4.        state: State = {
5.            filter: 'All',
6.            list: [],
7.            type: "my",
8.            title: "my todos"
9.        };
10.       Header = ({ title }) => <header className="header">
11.           ......
12.       </header>;
13.       Footer = () => <footer className="info">
14.           ......
15.       </footer>
16.       Todo = ({ todo, idx }) => <li className={todo.done ? "completed" :
          "view"}>
17.           ......
18.       </li>;
```

```
19.     Main = ({ state }) => {...};
20.     view = (state: State) => <>
21.         <section className="todoapp">
22.         <this.Header title={state.title}/>
23.         <this.Main state={state} />
24.         </section>
25.         <this.Footer />
26.     </>;
27.     update = {....};
28.     constructor(props) {
29.         super();
30.         const storageKey = STORAGE_KEY + props['type'];
31.         const stored = localStorage.getItem(storageKey);
32.         this.state = stored ? JSON.parse(stored) : { ...this.state,
                ...props, storageKey };
33.     }
34.     rendered = state => localStorage.setItem(this.state['storageKey'],
            JSON.stringify(state));
35.     }
```

The Todo component has a local scoped state, which identifies the type and title of the to-do list (Listing 4-18, lines 4–9). It initializes the local state based on the JSX properties in the constructor (Listing 4-18, lines 28–34).

The Todo component is a mini-application. We have reused it twice to create two to-do lists.

Web Components

The component concept is so important that the web community wanted it to be standardized and supported by browsers out of the box. Component support is currently being added to the HTML and DOM specs through the Web Components specifications. The Web Components specifications are a set of API standards that the W3C has been working on to bring components to browsers.[3] Web components allow us to extend HTML with custom elements. Custom elements are reusable. Their styling, behavior, and functionality are *encapsulated*,[4] in other words, scoped.

Web components and AppRun components follow the same concepts. Both are reusable and scoped. In addition, they share a similar structure. In fact, AppRun components can be converted to web components.

Web components require ECMAScript 2015 (ES6). AppRun has two versions. One is for ES5, and the other one is for ES6. The ES5 version is published on `npm` as the default package. To use the ES6 version, you need to install the AppRun package tagged as `apprun@es6` in your project.

```
npm i apprun@es6
```

Also, you need to set the TypeScript compilation option in your project's `tsconfig.json` file so that it is `target=es2015` or `target=es6`.

After configuring the project for ES6, we can start to create AppRun components as web components. First, we define a component class. Then, we use the `app.webComponent` function to convert the component to be a web component. Finally, we can use the custom element `<my-app />` directly in HTML.

We will demonstrate the process by making a counter component and converting it into a web component (Listing 4-19).

Listing 4-19. Converting an AppRun Component to a Web Component

```
1.    import app, { Component } from 'apprun';
2.    class CounterComponent extends Component {
3.        state = 0;
4.        view = (state) => <div>
5.            <h1>{state}</h1>
6.            <button onclick={() => this.run("-1")}>-1</button>
7.            <button onclick={() => this.run("+1")}>+1</button>
8.        </div>;
```

---

[3]https://github.com/w3c/webcomponents/
[4]https://developer.mozilla.org/en-US/docs/Web/Web_Components

```
9.        update = {
10.          '+1': (state) => state + 1,
11.          '-1': (state) => state - 1
12.        };
13.    }
14.    app.webComponent('my-app', CounterComponent)
```

We can then use the counter component just like the standard elements in HTML (Listing 4-20).

Listing 4-20. Counter as Web Component

```
1.    <!doctype html>
2.    <html>
3.    <head>
4.        <meta charset="utf-8">
5.        <title>Counter web component</title>
6.    </head>
7.    <body>
8.        <my-app id="counter"></my-app>
9.        <script src="app.js"></script>
10.   </body>
11.   </html>
```

The counter web component example (Listing 4-19 and Listing 4-20) is the pattern for developing web components using AppRun. You can use the pattern to develop your web components.

Listing 4-19 is written in TypeScript. We can develop web components without TypeScript because ES6 and the Web Components standard is now supported in almost all modern browsers. We can include the ES6 version of AppRun in a <script> tag and create web components in plain HTML and JavaScript (Listing 4-21).

Listing 4-21. Using AppRun in a Script Tag for a Web Component

```
1.    <!doctype html>
2.    <html>
3.    <head>
```

```
4.          <meta charset="utf-8">
5.          <title>Counter web component</title>
6.      </head>
7.      <body>
8.          <my-app id="counter"></my-app>
9.          <script src="https://unpkg.com/apprun@es6/dist/apprun-html.js">
            </script>
10.         <script>
11.             class Counter extends Component {
12.                 constructor() {
13.                     super();
14.                     this.state = 0;
15.                     this.view = state => `<div>
16.                         <h1>${state}</h1>
17.                         <button onclick='counter.run("-1")'>-1</button>
18.                         <button onclick='counter.run("+1")'>+1</button>
19.                     </div>`;
20.                     this.update = {
21.                         '+1': state => state + 1,
22.                         '-1': state => state - 1
23.                     };
24.                 }
25.             }
26.             app.webComponent('my-app', Counter, { shadow: true });
27.         </script>
28.     </body>
29. </html>
```

Because AppRun components are mini-AppRun applications that have the AppRun architecture, the web components converted from the AppRun components are powered by the AppRun architecture and the event publication and subscription. AppRun is useful for building web components.

Source Code of Examples

You can get the source code of this chapter by cloning the GitHub project from
`https://github.com/yysun/apprun-apress-book`. You can run the three examples
from this chapter using the npm scripts in Table 4-2.

Table 4-2. *npm Scripts of This Chapter*

Example	Script
The styled to-do application (Listings 4-1 and 4-2)	`npm run to-do-mvc`
The two to-do lists application (Listings 4-17 and 4-18)	`npm run to-do-mvc-2`
The web component counter (Listings 4-19 and 4-20)	`npm counter-web-component`

Summary

The view is one of the three parts of the AppRun architecture, and it plays a key role in
the AppRun event lifecycle. The view, or the `view` function, outputs the virtual DOM and
is solely dependent on the `state` parameter. The `view` function does not change the state
and does not have any other side effects because it does not change the DOM. AppRun
takes care of the side effects to render the virtual DOM to the real DOM.

There are benefits to using JSX compared to an HTML string. You have seen
many view patterns for creating HTML elements and applying CSS classes using
JSX. The patterns described in this chapter are useful references for your application
development.

We can develop AppRun applications with or without using components.
A component has two benefits: scope and reuse. AppRun components are mini-
AppRun applications. AppRun components can be easily converted to standard web
components.

Web components developed from AppRun components are self-contained, scoped/
encapsulated, full-featured, and reusable DOM custom elements. They can be used
directly or along with other frameworks and libraries.

In this chapter, we have focused on the view and have not discussed event handling
in the example applications. AppRun applications are event-driven. In the next chapter,
we will deep dive into AppRun events.

CHAPTER 5

Event Patterns

When the JavaScript runtime in a browser executes application code written in JavaScript, it uses the techniques of events and event handling. When the browser accesses web pages from back-end servers and when the users interact with the browser, the JavaScript runtime publishes the DOM events. The application code handles the DOM events in the event handlers. The DOM event handlers are the entry points to developing web applications.[1] Events and event handling are part of the programming model of JavaScript web application development.

AppRun application development uses the event publication and subscription (event pub-sub) pattern as the primary programming model. The AppRun programming model matches perfectly with the event-driven programming model of JavaScript. To develop AppRun applications, we need to connect the DOM events to the AppRun events. The AppRun events have two categories: global and local events. The global events are the events that are broadcast to all modules and components. The local events are the events that are broadcast and scoped only within the components.

This chapter demonstrates some of the commonly used DOM events, including a button click event, an input event, keyboard events, mouse events, a browser history event, and web workers. You will learn all the event-handling techniques necessary for your application development projects.

We will start with reviewing the concept of events.

Event Concept

There are two types of events: DOM events and AppRun events.

---

[1]For more information about web event handling, visit https://developer.mozilla.org/en-US/docs/Web/Guide/Events/Overview_of_Events_and_Handlers.

© Yiyi Sun 2019
Y. Sun, *Practical Application Development with AppRun*, https://doi.org/10.1007/978-1-4842-4069-4_5

DOM Events

The JavaScript runtime in browsers uses DOM events. Browsers are multithreaded themselves. The browser code is running on multiple threads to interact with the operating system and the hardware to capture events. An event is a signal that something has happened.[2] Examples include the user clicking a button, pressing a key, and moving the mouse; a system time ticker; network I/O; and so forth. The browser adds a message into the message queue of the JavaScript runtime. The message queue is like a to-do list. Therefore, it allows the JavaScript runtime to run on a single thread. The JavaScript runtime continually monitors the message queue. It picks up the messages one by one from the message queue and invokes the functions that are associated with the messages. It repeats the loop until the message queue is empty. The functions that the JavaScript runtime invokes upon events are the *event listeners* or *event handlers*. JavaScript programming mostly is creating DOM event handlers and registering them with DOM events.

AppRun Events

AppRun has a built-in event engine. It follows the event pub-sub pattern. It also has unique features. First, it connects to the AppRun state history. When invoking AppRun event handlers, it passes the current application state along with other event parameters. Second, the event lifecycle includes a few unique steps. It checks whether there is any data returned from the event handlers. If there are, it invokes the `view` function. It then checks whether the view returns the virtual DOM. If it does, AppRun renders the virtual DOM to the actual DOM. It also checks whether there is an optional `rendered` callback function defined. If there is, it invokes the `rendered` function before it ends the event lifecycle (see Figure 5-1).

---

[2]See this online tutorial that defines events as signals that something has happened:
`https://javascript.info/introduction-browser-events`.

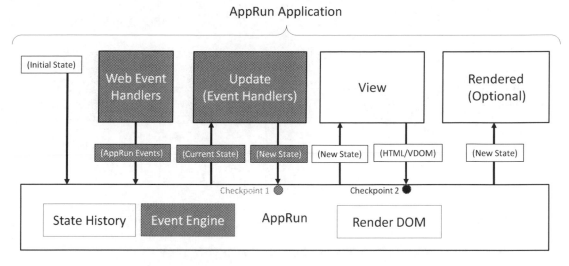

Figure 5-1. *AppRun event engine*

Figure 5-1 shows the AppRun architecture and breaks down the application logic. It also shows the interaction between the application code and AppRun. The application code is developed as event handlers and the view function piece by piece. There is no direct relationship between the event handlers and the view function. We rely on AppRun events to trigger the AppRun event lifecycle, which means we can publish an AppRun event and expect the DOM to be updated.

Connect the Events

After learning about DOM event handling and AppRun event handling, you can easily understand that developing AppRun applications is mostly making connections from the DOM events to the AppRun events, as summarized in Figure 5-2.

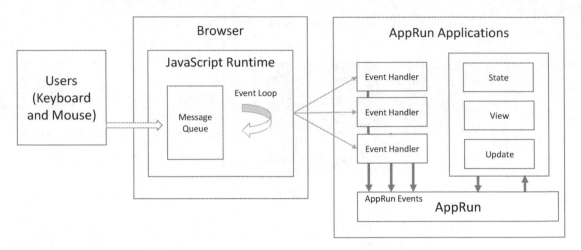

Figure 5-2. *Connecting DOM events to AppRun events*

To connect DOM events to AppRun events, first we create a DOM event handler and subscribe to the DOM event. Then we publish the AppRun events in the DOM event handlers. For example, to subscribe to the onclick event of an existing button and publish an AppRun foo event, we can use the addEventListener function, as shown here:

```
document.getElementById('foo').addEventListener('click',  () => app.
run('foo'));
```

We can also subscribe to the DOM event while creating the button using JSX in the view function, as shown here:

```
<button onclick={ ()=>app.run('foo') }>foo</button>
```

Notice that using JSX, we assign an anonymous function as the event handler to the onclick attribute of the button. We can also publish the DOM event parameter as the AppRun event parameter.

```
<button onclick={ (e)=>app.run('foo', e) }>foo</button>
```

Publishing the AppRun events in the DOM event handlers is a commonly used pattern in AppRun application development.

Global and Local Events

In Chapter 4, you learned that we can develop AppRun applications using a global architecture, which has a global state and uses global events. For example, Listing 5-1 shows a global architecture and a global event named foo.

Listing 5-1. The AppRun Global Architecture and Global Event

```
1.   const state = {};
2.   const view = state => <button onclick={ ()=>app.run('foo') }>foo
     </button>;
3.   const update = {
4.       'foo': state => state
5.   };
6.   app.start('my-app', state, view, update);
```

The foo event in Listing 5-1 is a global event. We publish the foo event from the button's onclick event handler by calling the app.run function (line 2 of Listing 5-1). The event is broadcast globally to all code modules.

You also learned that we can develop AppRun applications using the component architecture. Each component has its event engine. Events inside components are limited inside the components as local events. The local events are broadcast only within the components. Listing 5-2 shows the component architecture and a local event named bar.

Listing 5-2. The AppRun Component Architecture and Local Event

```
1.   import app, { Component } from 'apprun';
2.   export default class MyComponent extends Component {
3.       state = {};
4.       view = state => <button onclick={ ()=>this.run('bar') }>foo
         </button>;
5.       update = {
6.           'bar': state => state
7.       };
8.   }
```

The bar event is a local event that is only scoped in the component in Listing 5-2. We publish the bar event from the button's onclick event handler by calling the this.run function (line 4 of Listing 5-2).

The general rule is that we use the app.run function to publish the global events and use the this.run function to publish the local events. However, AppRun has a convention that if the event has a special name that starts with # or /, the event is a global event. Global events with special names can be published using the this.run function inside components. The components can also subscribe to and handle the global events with the special names (Listing 5-3).

Listing 5-3. Global Events in a Component

```
1.   import app, {Component} from 'apprun';
2.   class MyComponent extends Component {
3.       state = {};
4.       view = (state) => <div>
5.           <button onclick={()=>this.run('event')}>{state}</button>
             // publish local event
6.           <button onclick={()=>this.run('#event')}>{state}</button>
             // publish global event
7.           <button onclick={()=>app.run('event')}>{state}</button>
             // publish global event
8.       </div>
9.       update = {
10.          'event': state => state // local event handler
11.          '#event': state => state // global event handler
12.       }
13.  }
```

To demonstrate how to handle the global events with special names, we will develop a clock application (see Figure 5-3).

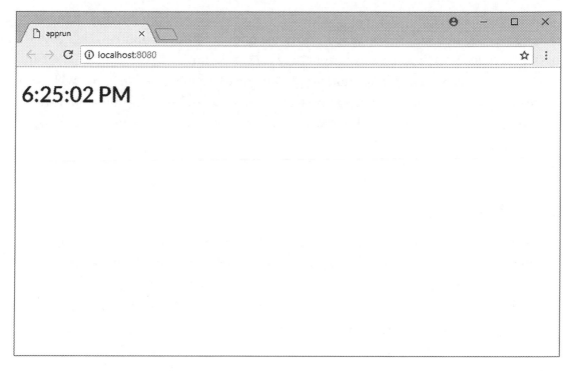

Figure 5-3. *The clock application*

The clock application uses the window.setInterval function to publish the #tick event using the app.run function every second. The clock component of the clock application subscribes to and handles the #tick event (Listing 5-4).

Listing 5-4. Clock Application

```
1.   import app, { Component } from 'apprun';
2.   class ClockComponent extends Component {
3.       state = new Date();
4.       view = state => <h1>{state.toLocaleTimeString()}</h1>;
5.       update = {
6.           '#tick': state => new Date()
7.       };
8.   }
9.   window.setInterval(() => { app.run('#tick') }, 1000);
10.  new ClockComponent().start('my-app');
```

In the clock application (Listing 5-4), we use the system timer to publish an AppRun global event named #tick (line 9). The #tick event triggers the AppRun event lifecycle of ClockComponent to display the current time every second.

So far, you learned about AppRun events and the event lifecycle. Next, you will learn more about the various DOM events and learn how to use them in AppRun applications. All the example applications in the next sections are developed using the component architecture.

User Input

User input starts with the keyboard and mouse. Modern web browsers also support advanced technologies such as drag and drop and touch. They all follow the same event-driven programming model: when user input happens, the browsers publish DOM events. Our general approach to handle user input is to publish the AppRun events in the DOM event handlers to trigger the AppRun event lifecycle.

Click Events

We will first develop a Hello World application that takes user input and displays it on the screen. The Hello World application has a text input box for the user to type into and a button to display the user input (see Figure 5-4 and Listing 5-5).

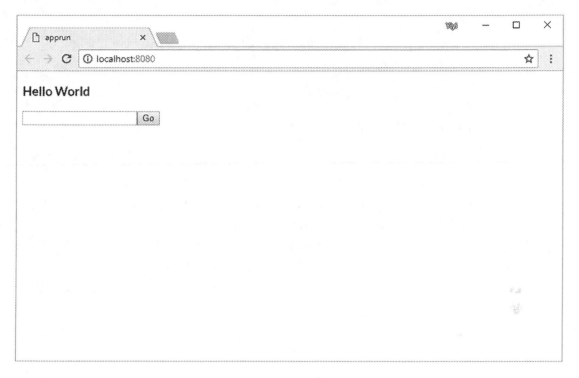

Figure 5-4. *Hello World application*

We will handle the onclick event of the Go button by assigning an anonymous function as the DOM event handler, as mentioned earlier in the section "Connect the Events." Listing 5-5 shows the source code of the Hello World application.

Listing 5-5. The Click Event

```
1.   import app, { Component } from 'apprun';
2.   class HelloComponent extends Component {
3.       state = 'World';
4.       view = (state) => <div>
5.           <h3>Hello {state}</h3>
6.           <input id="text"/>
7.           <button onclick={() => this.run("input")}>Go</button>
8.       </div>;
```

```
9.        update = {
10.            'input': (state) => (document.getElementById('text') as
               HTMLInputElement).value
11.        }
12.    }
13.  new HelloComponent().start('my-app');
```

The Hello World application shown in Listing 5-5 publishes the AppRun event input in the button's onclick event handler (line 7). The AppRun event handler of the input event creates a new state using the value of the input box (line 10). The view function creates the virtual DOM using the new state (lines 4–8).

There is one more detail that is worth mentioning. When AppRun renders the DOM, it encodes the user input to prevent cross-site scripting attacks. For example, if the user types a script, the application displays it as text, not as a runnable script (see Figure 5-5).

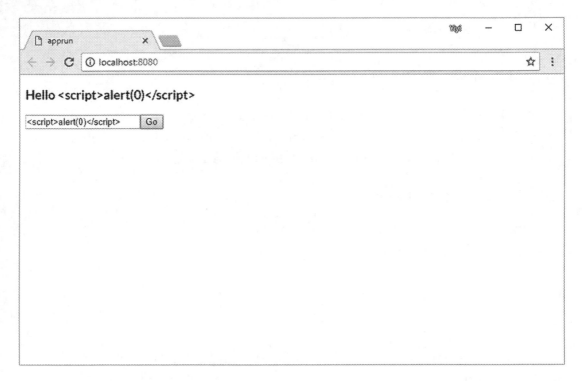

Figure 5-5. *User input encoding*

Input Event

In the previous Hello World application, the application displays the user's input after a button click. Sometimes we want to process user input while users are typing such as for a live update to the web page content and input validation. The next application, an echo application, will update the <h3> element to include the user's input (see Figure 5-6).

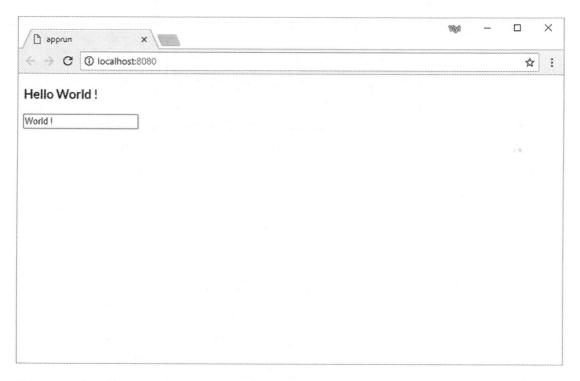

Figure 5-6. *Live update application*

To get users' input while they are typing, we can subscribe to the DOM `input` event of the text input and then publish the AppRun `input` event and use the DOM event as the AppRun event parameter (Listing 5-6).

Listing 5-6. The Input Event

```
1.    import app, { Component } from 'apprun';
2.    class EchoComponent extends Component {
3.        state = 'World';
4.        view = (state) => <div>
```

```
5.              <h3>Hello {state}</h3>
6.              <input oninput={ e => this.run("input", e)}/>
7.          </div>;
8.          update = {
9.              'input': (state, e) => e.target.value
10.         }
11.     }
12.     new EchoComponent().start('my-app');
```

The AppRun event handler in Listing 5-6 receives the DOM event as the function parameter. We can get the value of the input box from `event.target` (line 9). The value of the input box is synchronized with the state.

In some cases, we want to postpone publishing the AppRun events until after a certain period has elapsed. Delaying the event handling is a useful feature. It is also called *debouncing*. Often this is used in a type-ahead scenario. AppRun supports delaying the event handling. To use the feature, we use a tuple in the `update` object. The tuple includes the event handler function and an `options` object where we can define a `delay` value in milliseconds. For example, the following tuple delays the event handling for 1,000 milliseconds, or one second:

```
'input': [(state, e) => e.target.value, {delay: 1000}]
```

We can modify the echo application to delay the display of the user's input for a second, in which the user can continue to type. The `<h3>` element updates only every second. It is like throttling the user input. Listing 5-7 shows the delayed echo application.

Listing 5-7. The Delayed Input Event

```
1.   import app, { Component } from 'apprun';
2.   class DelayedEchoComponent extends Component {
3.       state = 'World';
4.       view = (state) => <div>
5.           <h3>Hello {state}</h3>
6.           <input oninput={ e => this.run("input", e)}/>
7.       </div>;
```

```
8.       update = {
9.           'input': [(state, e) => e.target.value, {delay: 1000}]
10.      }
11.  }
12.  new DelayedEchoComponent().start('my-app');
```

Next, we will develop a type-ahead application to demonstrate the delayed event handling along with the keyboard events.

Keyboard Events

Type-ahead is also known as *auto-complete suggestions*. It can help the user to find out what they want. Like the live update example, the type-ahead example needs to get a user's input while typing to search and retrieve a list of options. The main difference is that type-ahead also needs to handle a few special keys, such as the Enter key to select an item from a list of options, the up and down arrows for moving the selection within the options, and the Esc key to cancel the search. We can develop a simple type-ahead experience that allows users to type and search the U.S. states (see Figure 5-7).

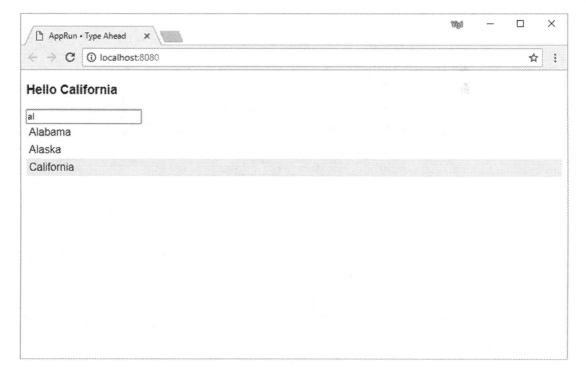

Figure 5-7. Type-ahead

First, we will develop a generic type-ahead component, the TypeAhead component. We want it to be generic, which means that it mainly handles user interaction with the keyboard and shows or hides the data options in a drop-down list. It does not search for data or handle the selected data. It requires two callback functions for searching the data and for processing the selected data passed in from the main program as JSX properties.

```
<TypeAhead  onSearch={search}  onSelect={text => this.run('input', text)}/>
```

The onSearch property is a function that searches a data source. The onSelect property is a function that processes the selected data. By using the two JSX properties, it makes the TypeAhead component focus on handling the keyboard events (Listing 5-8).

Listing 5-8. TypeAhead Component

```
1.    import app, { Component } from 'apprun';
2.    export default class TypeAheadComponent extends Component {
3.        view = state => {
4.        return (
5.            <div className="typeahead">
6.                <input
7.                    type="text"
8.                    placeholder=" Search:"
9.                    autocomplete="off"
10.                   value={state.selected || "}
11.                   oninput={e => this.run('search', e)}
12.                   onkeydown={e => this.run(`keydown`, e)}
13.               />
14.               <ul>{state.show && state.options.length ?
15.                   state.options.map(option => (
16.                       <li className={option === state.selected ?
                        'selected' : "}
                    onclick={() => this.run('select', option)}>{option} </li>
17.                       )) : "}</ul>
18.               </div>
19.           );
20.       };
```

```
21.     update = {
22.         search: [(state, e) => {
23.             const options = this.state.onSearch(e.target.value);
24.             return {
25.                 ...state,
26.                 show: true,
27.                 selected: e.target.value,
28.                 options
29.             };
30.         }, { delay:200}],
31.         popup: (state, show) => (state.show === show ? null : {
            ...state, show }),
32.         keydown: (state, e) => {
33.             if (!state.options) return;
34.             let selectedIdx = state.options.indexOf(state.selected);
35.             switch (e.keyCode) {
36.             case 27: // ESC key to hide the popup
37.                 return { ...state, show: false };
38.             case 38: // Up key to move the selection up
39.                 selectedIdx--;
40.                 if (selectedIdx < 0) selectedIdx = 0;
41.                 return { ...state, selected: state.options[selectedIdx] };
42.             case 40: // Down key to move the selection up
43.                 selectedIdx++;
44.                 if (selectedIdx>=state.options.length) selectedIdx =
                    state.options.length - 1;
45.                 return { ...state, selected: state.options[selectedIdx] };
46.             case 13: // Enter key to select the data
47.                 e.preventDefault();
48.                 this.run('select', state.selected);
49.             }
50.         },
```

```
51.          select: (state, selected) => {
52.              this.state.onSelect(selected);
53.              return { ...state, selected, show: false };
54.          }
55.      };
56.  }
```

The TypeAhead component shown in Listing 5-8 has the majority of code to handle the DOM keyboard events of the text input control.

The search event is for taking the user's input when the user is typing (lines 22–30). It has a delay of 200 milliseconds. The keydown event is for handling the Esc key, the up and down arrow keys, and the Enter key (lines 32–49).

While the user is typing, the TypeAhead component calls the onSearch function to let the main program decide how to search and retrieve the options. When the user has selected one item, the TypeAhead component calls the onSelect function to let the main program decide what to do with the selected item. We will use it in the main program (Listing 5-9).

Listing 5-9. Type-Ahead Application

```
1.   import app, { Component } from 'apprun';
2.   import TypeAhead from './typeahead';
3.   const states = ['Alabama', 'Alaska', 'Arizona', 'Arkansas', 'California',
4.       'Colorado', 'Connecticut', 'Delaware', 'Florida', 'Georgia', 'Hawaii',
5.       'Idaho', 'Illinois', 'Indiana', 'Iowa', 'Kansas', 'Kentucky',
         'Louisiana',
6.       'Maine', 'Maryland', 'Massachusetts', 'Michigan', 'Minnesota',
7.       'Mississippi', 'Missouri', 'Montana', 'Nebraska', 'Nevada',
         'New Hampshire',
8.       'New Jersey', 'New Mexico', 'New York', 'North Carolina', 'North
         Dakota',
9.       'Ohio', 'Oklahoma', 'Oregon', 'Pennsylvania', 'Rhode Island',
10.      'South Carolina', 'South Dakota', 'Tennessee', 'Texas', 'Utah',
         'Vermont',
11.      'Virginia', 'Washington', 'West Virginia', 'Wisconsin', 'Wyoming'
12.  ];
```

```
13.  const search = text => states.filter(s => s.toLowerCase().
     indexOf(text.toLowerCase()) >= 0);
14.
15.  class HelloComponent extends Component {
16.    state = ";
17.    view = (state) => <div>
18.      <h3>Hello {state}</h3>
19.      <TypeAhead
20.        onSearch={search}
21.        onSelect={text => this.run('input', text)}/>
22.    </div>;
23.    update = {
24.      'input': (state, text) => text
25.    }
26.  }
27.  new TypeAheadApp().start('my-app');
```

The type-ahead application in Listing 5-9 has the U.S. states in an array (lines 3–12) and the search function for searching the states (lines 13–14). It also has an AppRun event input for updating the state (line 24). The main program uses the TypeAhead component (Listing 5-9) by setting the two callback functions for searching the options and for handling the selected item (lines 19–21).

So far, we have developed the TypeAhead component as a generic component and used it in an application for selecting U.S. states. You can use the application as an example to reuse the TypeAhead component in other applications.

Mouse Events

The mouse is one of the most used interaction tools. We will develop an application that connects the DOM mouse events to AppRun events to implement a draggable button, also known as *float action* button (see Figure 5-8). The float action button can be dragged around on the web page.

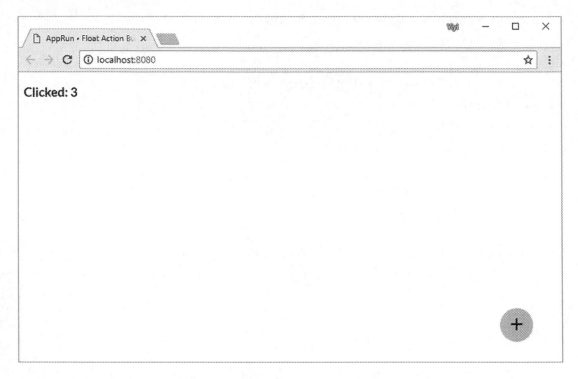

Figure 5-8. *Float action button*

The float action button is also a reusable component. We use it in the main program (Listing 5-10).

Listing 5-10. Float Action Button Application

```
1.    import app, { Component } from 'apprun';
2.    import Fab from './fab';
3.    class FabApp extends Component {
4.        state = 0;
5.        view = (state) => <div>
6.            <h3>Clicked: {state}</h3>
7.            <Fab id='fab' position={{x: 500, y:300}}
8.                    onClick={text => this.run('action')} />
9.        </div>;
```

```
10.      update = {
11.          'action': state => state + 1
12.      }
13.  }
14.  new FabApp().start('my-app');
```

The main program sets the initial location of the float action button (line 7). It also sets the callback function to publish the AppRun event, called action (line 8), which will record the number of times the button is clicked.

The float action button is also developed as a reusable component (Listing 5-11).

Listing 5-11. Float Action Button Component

```
1.   import app, { Component } from 'apprun';
2.   export default class FabComponent extends Component {
3.       view = (state) => {
4.           const style = {
5.               'left': `${state.position.x}px`,
6.               'top': `${state.position.y}px`,
7.           };
8.           return <div className='fab-btn' style={style}
9.               onpointerdown={e => this.run('drag', e)}
10.              onpointermove={e => this.run('move', e)}
11.              onpointerup={e => this.run('drop', e)}> + </div>
12.      };
13.      update = {
14.          drag: (state, e) => ({
15.              ...state,
16.              dragging: true,
17.              start: { x: e.pageX, y: e.pageY },
18.              last: { x: e.pageX, y: e.pageY }
19.          }),
20.          move: (state, e) => {
21.              if (!state.dragging) return;
22.              e.target.setPointerCapture(e.pointerId);
23.              const last = { x: e.pageX, y: e.pageY }
```

```
24.              const position = {
25.                  x: state.position.x + e.pageX - state.last.x,
26.                  y: state.position.y + e.pageY - state.last.y
27.              }
28.              return ({ ...state, position, last });
29.          },
30.        drop: (state, e) => {
31.            if (state.last.x - state.start.x === 0 &&
32.                state.last.y - state.start.y === 0) state.onClick();
33.            e.target.releasePointerCapture(e.pointerId);
34.            return { ...state, dragging: false };
35.          }
36.      }
37.  }
```

The float action button component shown in Listing 5-11 tracks the button position in its state (lines 4–7). The position is applied to the button in the `view` function (line 8). It creates a `<div>` element and subscribes to its three DOM pointer events: `pointerdown`, `pointermove`, and `pointerup`. It is the same as using the DOM events: `mousedown`, `mousemove`, and `mouseup`. The DOM Pointer API is the unified API that incorporates more forms of input, including mouse, touchscreens, and pen input.

Brower History Event

Web browsers record and keep a history of the URLs that users visit. When the user enters a URL in the browser's address bar, clicks a hyperlink in a web page, or clicks the back/forward button, the browser saves the corresponding URL in the browser history and publishes a DOM event: the `popstate` event.

A URL is the web address of web resources, such as web pages. Also, the URL can identify a specific location within the web pages. The location within the web pages is identified by a *fragment identifier*, which is anything in the URL after the # sign. We can navigate to different locations of web pages by changing this fragment identifier. Changing the fragment identifier does not make the browser navigate to other web pages, but it does create browser history entries and publish the `popstate` events. We can subscribe to the `popstate` event and use `window.location.hash` to retrieve the fragment identifier.

AppRun has built-in code that subscribes to the popstate event. AppRun parses the URL into the event parameters and publishes the # event. For example, if the browser address URL is http://.../#/a/b/c, AppRun publishes the # event as app.run('#', ['a', 'b', 'c']).

To demonstrate the AppRun # event, we will modify the echo application to subscribe to the # event and manipulate the browser history. Every time a user enters a new word in the input box, the application pushes the user input into the history; therefore, the # event is also published (see Figure 5-9).

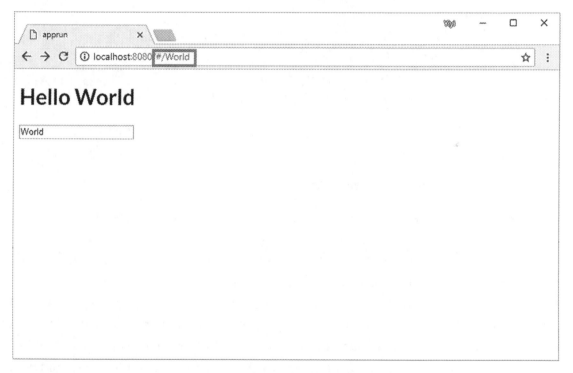

Figure 5-9. *Saving user input as the fragment identifier*

Running the application, the user can type into the input box. When a user presses the Enter key or moves the input focus away from the input box, what the user typed is shown in the browser address with the # sign. The <h1> element is also updated accordingly. Listing 5-12 shows the source code of the application.

Listing 5-12. Handling Browser History

```
1.   import app, { Component } from 'apprun';
2.   class HelloComponent extends Component {
3.       state = 'World';
4.       view = state => <div>
5.           <h1>Hello {state}</h1>
6.           <input onchange={e => this.run('change', e)} value={state} />
7.       </div>;
8.       update = {
9.           '#': (state, hash) => hash || state,
10.          "change": (_, e) => {
11.              const text = e.target.value;
12.              history.pushState(null, text, '#/' + text);
13.          }
14.      };
15.  }
16.  new HelloComponent().start('my-app');
```

There are a few interesting points to explain in Listing 5-12. The view function displays the state to the <h1> element (line 5). The <input> element's DOM event, the change event, is converted to the AppRun change event (line 6). The event handler for the # event sets the location hash as the current state (line 9). In the event handler of the change event, we take the user's input and push it into the browser history as a new fragment identifier (lines 11–12). Notice the change event handler does not return anything. Therefore, the event lifecycle ends. However, because we pushed data into the browser history, the browser publishes the DOM popstate event. AppRun then converts it to the # event. We have another event lifecycle. The event handler for the # event returns the new state, which is displayed in the <h1> element.

The AppRun # event often is used as the main entry point of AppRun applications. It is also commonly used in single-page applications, which you will learn more about in Chapter 7.

Web Workers

Because the main JavaScript runtime inside web browsers executes application code in a single thread, it could slow down the user interface or even make it become unresponsive when the application code is computationally heavy and time-consuming. A web worker is a new JavaScript runtime with which we can spawn web workers to execute application code in the background. Web workers provide a way to create a multithreaded architecture in which the browser can execute multiple tasks at once. Web workers are often able to utilize multicore CPUs more effectively.

To allow multithreaded execution, the web workers do not have direct access to the DOM. The web page and the web workers communicate with each other by passing messages. The process of sending and processing messages again falls into the AppRun sweet spot. AppRun is an event engine that abstracts away the complexity of dispatching events and messages.

Using AppRun, we can publish events from the web page to a web worker.

```
worker.run('+1', state);  // in web page
```

The web worker subscribes to and handles the event.

```
app.on('+1', state => value = state + 1);  // in web worker
```

We can also publish events from a web worker to a web page.

```
page.run('#', value);  // in web worker
```

AppRun dispatches the # event from the web worker into the AppRun application's event handler (see Figure 5-10).

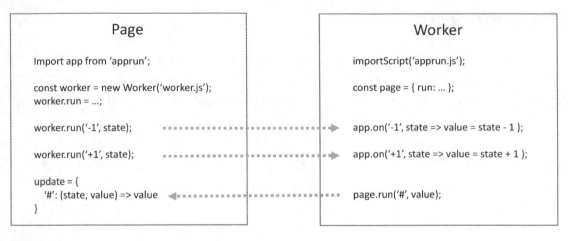

Figure 5-10. *AppRun events between web page and web worker*

We will change the counter application from Chapter 3 (see Listing 3-1) to use a web worker to do the calculation in a separate thread. Listing 5-13 shows the web page code, and Listing 5-14 shows the web worker code.

Listing 5-13. Web Page Using Web Worker

```
1.    import app, { Component } from 'apprun';
2.    const worker = new Worker("worker.js") as any;
3.    worker.onmessage = e => {
4.        const { name, parameters } = JSON.parse(e.data);
5.        app.run(name, ...parameters);
6.    }
7.    worker.run = (name, ...parameters) =>
8.        worker.postMessage(JSON.stringify({ name, parameters }));
9.    class CounterComponent extends Component {
10.       state = 0;
11.       view = (state) => <div>
12.           <h1>{state}</h1>
13.           <button onclick={() => worker.run("-1", state)}>-1</button>
14.           <button onclick={() => worker.run("+1", state)}>+1</button>
15.       </div>;
```

```
16.     update = {
17.         '#': (state, val) => val
18.     };
19.  }
20.  new CounterComponent().start('my-app');
```

Listing 5-14. Web Worker

```
1.   importScripts('//unpkg.com/apprun@latest/dist/apprun.js');
2.   onmessage = function (e) {
3.       const { name, parameters } = JSON.parse(e.data);
4.       app.run(name, ...parameters);
5.   };
6.   const page = {
7.       run: (name, ...parameters) => postMessage (
8.           JSON.stringify({ name, parameters }))
9.   };
10.  app.on('+1', n => page.run('#', n + 1));
11.  app.on('-1', n => page.run('#', n - 1));
```

Although the counter calculation is not heavy-computational code, it demonstrates the architecture of using a web worker with AppRun.

Source Code and Examples

You can get the source code of this chapter by cloning the GitHub project at https://github.com/yysun/apprun-apress-book. You can run the seven examples in this chapter using the npm scripts in Table 5-1.

Table 5-1. *npm Scripts of This Chapter*

Example	Script
The button click event (Listing 5-5)	`npm run hello`
The input event (Listing 5-6)	`npm run echo`
The delayed input event (Listing 5-7)	`npm run echo-delayed`
The keyboard event (Listings 5-8 and 5-9)	`npm run typeahead`
The mouse events (Listings 5-10 and 5-11)	`npm run fab`
The browser history events (Listing 5-12)	`npm run echo-hash`
The web worker event (Listings 5-13 and 5-14)	`npm run worker`

Summary

JavaScript programming on the web platform is event-driven. From the system timer and user input to the browser history and web workers, we respond to various events, attach callbacks, and send messages. When developing AppRun applications, we mainly connect the DOM events to the AppRun events.

AppRun has an event engine that supports event publication and subscription. Associated with the event engine, it has state management and a DOM rendering engine. When AppRun events are published, AppRun not only invokes the event handlers but also manages the states and renders the DOM. We can publish an AppRun event and expect the web page to be updated.

By using AppRun events, code is well organized, modularized, and decoupled. It solves the problem that code is like spaghetti in the event-driven world.

The events discussed in this chapter are all synchronous events. We will introduce the asynchronous events in the next chapter.

CHAPTER 6

Asynchronous Events

The JavaScript runtime executes event handlers one at a time in the event loop. If an event handler takes a long time to execute, the user interface appears to be unresponsive or frozen. This is because the JavaScript runtime must wait for the event handler to finish. The code execution is blocked while waiting. To avoid blocking the code execution, JavaScript uses a technique called *asynchronous operations*.

For example, getting data from a back-end server over the Internet requires a comparatively long-running code execution. It requires us to define a function as the callback function when it begins sending requests to the back-end server. The underlining browser code interacts with the operating system to send and receive data from the back-end server while the other JavaScript code continues to execute. When the server has returned the data, the JavaScript runtime invokes the callback function.

The asynchronous operations are implemented not only by using callback functions but also by using the `Promise` object and the `async/await` syntax. The AppRun architecture supports `async/await` with the AppRun `async` event handlers. It makes the asynchronous operations feel logical and natural.

This chapter explains the three methods of asynchronous operation and the AppRun asynchronous event handlers. It has example applications of pulling and pushing data from the back-end servers. You can learn all the techniques you'll need for your application development projects.

Asynchronous Operations

As mentioned, asynchronous operations in JavaScript have evolved from the callback functions to the `Promise` object and to the `async/await` syntax. We will first review the evolution and then learn how to use them in AppRun application development.

© Yiyi Sun 2019
Y. Sun, *Practical Application Development with AppRun*, https://doi.org/10.1007/978-1-4842-4069-4_6

Callbacks

Callback functions are the first method of asynchronous operations that we'll discuss. Assume we want to schedule a function execution, `console.log`, in ten seconds but don't want to freeze the user interface. We use the `window.setTimout` function to schedule a callback function.

```
window.setTimout(()=>{console.log(0)}, 10000);
```

This adds a message into the message queue. Ten seconds later, the message will be picked up by the event loop. The callback function will be invoked then.

The callback function is the foundation of asynchronous operations. All other asynchronous operations use the callback function. It is easy to understand, but it is not scalable. For example, if we want to schedule three functions one after another, the callback functions are nested, as in the following example, and they become difficult to manage:

```
window.setTimeout(()=>{
    console.log(1);
  window.setTimeout(()=>{
      console.log(2);
      window.setTimeout(()=>{
          console.log(3);
      }, 10000);
  }, 10000);
}, 10000);
```

Again, the code becomes difficult to manage. Also, it is difficult to handle errors in the nested callback functions. The `Promise` object comes to rescue.

Promise

The `Promise` object was standardized in ECMAScript 2015 (ES6) to improve callbacks. The `Promise` object represents the operation completion (or failure) of an asynchronous operation and its resulting value.[1]

---

[1]For more information about the `Promise` object, please visit `https://developer.mozilla.org/en-US/docs/Web/JavaScript/Reference/Global_Objects/Promise`.

We can create a `Promise` object for the `window.setTimout` function, as shown here:

```
const delay = (f, t) => new Promise((resolve) =>
setTimeout(()=>resolve(f()), t));
```

In the `then` function of `Promise`, we provide a callback function for handling the success of the operations.

```
delay(()=>console.log(1), 10000).then(()=>{});
```

We can return another `Promise` in the `then` function. Then we can chain all the `Promise` executions.

```
delay(()=>console.log(1), 10000)
    .then(() => delay(()=>console.log(2), 10000))
    .then(() => delay(()=>console.log(3), 10000));
```

In case of a failed operation, the `catch` function of the `Promise` object is where we can handle the errors. Any error from all `Promise` objects will fall into one `catch` function.

```
delay(()=>console.log(1), 10000)
    .then(() => delay(()=>console.log(2), 10000))
    .then(() => delay(()=>console.log(3), 10000))
    .catch(error=>{});
```

The `Promise` object is an improvement to the callback functions. Using the `Promise` object, we flatten the nested callback structure and can handle the errors using the `catch` function. But using `Promise` still feels verbose. The new `async/await` syntax is designed to further improve the asynchronous operation code.

async/await

`async/await` is a special syntax to work with `Promise` objects.[2] It was originally intended to be in ECMAScript 2015 but kept getting pushed back and finally landed in ECMAScript 2017. The `async/await` syntax makes the use of `Promise` objects straightforward.

---

[2]For more information about `async/await`, please visit `https://javascript.info/async-await`.

```
await delay(()=>console.log(1), 10000);
await delay(()=>console.log(2), 10000);
await delay(()=>console.log(3), 10000);
```

The error handling with the `async/await` syntax is also simpler.

```
try {
    await delay(()=>console.log(1), 10000);
    await delay(()=>console.log(2), 10000);
    await delay(()=>console.log(3), 10000);
} catch (err) {
}
```

To summarize asynchronous operations, the callback function is the foundation. The `Promise` object can wrap the callback functions. The `async/await` syntax is built on top of the `Promise` objects. Any function that returns `Promise` objects can be used with `async/await`. Using the `async/await` syntax, the asynchronous code looks like synchronous code and feels natural.

AppRun async Event Handlers

The AppRun architecture supports asynchronous operations in the AppRun event handlers. We only need to add the `async` keyword in front of the event handler and call the functions to return a `Promise` object with the `await` keyword (Listing 6-1).

Listing 6-1. Asynchronous Event Handler

```
1.   import app from 'apprun';
2.   const get = async (url) => { };
3.   const state = {};
4.   const view = (state) => <div>{state}</div>;
5.   const update = {
6.       '#': async (state) => {
7.           try {
8.               const data = await get('https://...');
9.               return { ...state, data }
10.          } catch (err) {
```

```
11.                return { ...state, err }
12.            }
13.        }
14.   };
15.   app.start('my-app', state, view, update);
```

In Listing 6-1, adding the keyword async to the event handler (line 6) makes it an asynchronous event handler. We then can call the other async functions (line 8). It also can have the error-handling structure using the try and catch statements (lines 10–12).

When the AppRun event handlers are defined as async functions, they return promises of new application states to AppRun, which resolves them to get the new states and then passes them to the view function (see Figure 6-1).

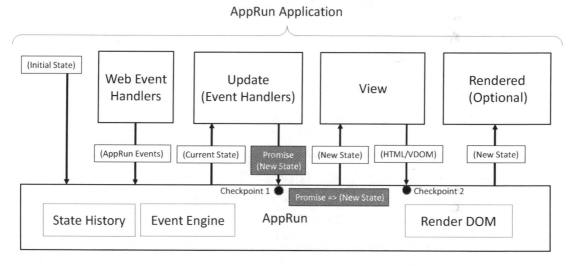

Figure 6-1. *Async event handlers return promises*

Server Requests

Sending data to and receiving data from the back-end servers are typical asynchronous operations for which we can use callbacks, Promise objects, and the async/await syntax. Usually, we have two scenarios: getting JSON data from the servers or posting JSON data to the servers.

```
export const get = (url) => {}
export const post = (url, data) => {}
```

JavaScript has two ways to make the server requests, using XMLHttpRequest or using the Fetch API. We will implement the get function and the post function using XMLHttpRequest and the Fetch API.

XMLHttpRequest

XMLHttpRequest (XHR) is the underlying technology designed to support the concept of Ajax, which originally stood for Asynchronous JavaScript and XML. Originally Ajax was for getting XML data from servers asynchronously. Nowadays, the back-end servers favor the JavaScript Object Notation (JSON) format and REST-style web services to serve the data.

XHR is callback-based. It has two callback functions, onload and onerror. We can wrap the XHR callback functions with a Promise object and then implement the get function and the post function (Listing 6-2).

Listing 6-2. XHR Promise Wrapper

```
1.    export interface IRequest {
2.        method?: 'GET' | 'POST',
3.        headers?: {}
4.        body?
5.    }
6.    export default function getJSON(url: string, request: IRequest = {}) {
7.        return new Promise(function (resolve, reject) {
8.            const req = new XMLHttpRequest();
9.            req.open(request.method || 'GET', url);
10.           if (request.headers) {
11.               for (let name in request.headers) {
12.                   req.setRequestHeader(name, request.headers[name]);
13.               }
14.           }
15.           req.onload = () => {
16.               if (req.status == 200) {
17.                   resolve(JSON.parse(req.response));
18.               } else {
19.                   reject(JSON.parse(req.response));
20.               }
21.           };
```

```
22.          req.onerror = (err) => {
23.              reject(Error("Network Error"));
24.          };
25.          req.send(JSON.stringify(request.body));
26.      });
27.  }
28.  export const get = (url, headers?) => getJSON(url, { headers });
29.  export const post = (url, data, headers?) => getJSON(url, {
30.      method: 'POST',
31.      headers,
32.      body: JSON.stringify(data)
33.  });
```

The getJSON function wraps XHR and returns a Promise object (Listing 6-2, line 6). The get function (line 28) and the post function (lines 29–33) call into the getJSON function.

The Fetch API

JavaScript also has a relatively new API, called the Fetch API, which is a better alternative to the XHR.[3] It is Promise-based. We can create the get function and the post function directly using the fetch function without a wrapper (Listing 6-3).

Listing 6-3. Using the Fetch API

```
1.  export const fetchJSON = async (url: string, request?: RequestInit) => {
2.      const response = await fetch(url,
3.      );
4.      if (!response.ok) {
5.          const data = await response.text();
6.          throw data;
7.      }
8.      return response.json();
9.  }
```

---

[3]For more information about the Fetch API, please visit https://developer.mozilla.org/en-US/docs/Web/API/Fetch_API/Using_Fetch.

```
10.  export const get = (url, headers?) => fetchJSON(url, { headers });
11.  export const post = (url, data, headers?) => fetchJSON(url, {
12.      method: 'POST',
13.      headers,
14.      body: JSON.stringify(data)
15.  });
```

Notice that there are two promises when using the fetch function. One is for creating the response (line 2). The other one is for getting data from the response (line 7). We can check the ok property of the fetch response object to see whether there is an error (lines 3–6).

Comparing the Fetch API with XHR, the Fetch API provides functionalities that we have to write ourselves when using XHR. For example, the Fetch API can add HTTP request headers, whereas when using XHR, we need to write the code for it (Listing 6-3, lines 10–14).

On the other hand, XHR sends the cookies to the servers, but the Fetch API does not send cookies to the server. You can choose based on the authentication requirements of the back-end servers.

So far we have created the get function and the post function to support GET or POST data to the server, respectively. They have identical function signatures with either XHR or the Fetch API underneath. You have the option to choose from the two underlying technologies to develop your AppRun applications.

Pulling Data

To demonstrate the data access, we will develop an application that retrieves and displays the current weather and forecast.

Weather Application

The weather application displays the current weather and forecast of Toronto, Canada, by default (see Figure 6-2).

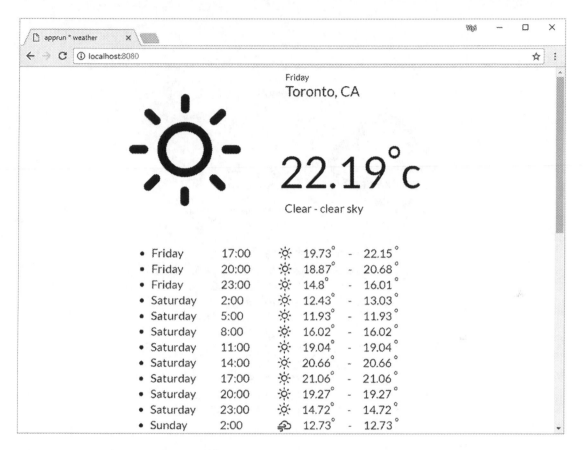

Figure 6-2. *The weather application*

The weather application accepts the city from the URL fragment. For example, the URL `http://localhost:8080/#/new york,` us displays the weather and forecast for New York in the United States (see Figure 6-3).

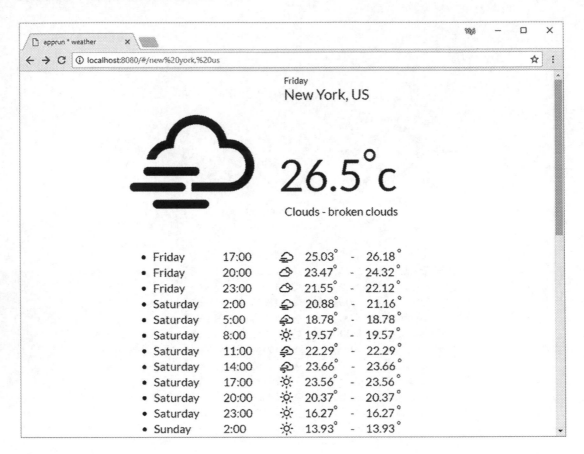

Figure 6-3. *The weather application displaying the weather for New York*

The weather application displays an error message when the city is not found (see Figure 6-4).

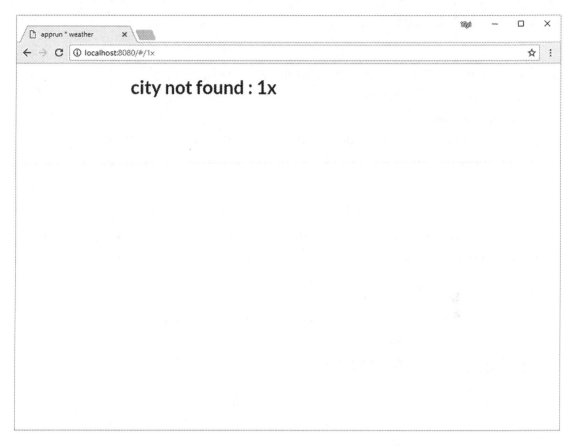

Figure 6-4. *Error handling in the weather application*

The Data API

We will use the Open Weather Map API.[4] It is easy to use the JSON Data API that returns the current weather, forecast, historical weather information, and weather station data. We can sign up to get an API key (app ID) to get started using the API for free. Each API call requires the API key to be sent along with other parameters.

We will use two APIs, one for getting the current weather data and the other for getting the forecast data for a city. We wrap the two APIs as the async functions within an object (Listing 6-4). The object serves as the API layer.

---

[4]https://www.openweathermap.org/api

Listing 6-4. API Layer

```
1.   import { get } from './xhr;
2.   const url = 'http://api.openweathermap.org/data/2.5/';
3.   const appid = 'xxxxxxxxxx';
4.   export default {
5.       current: q => get(`${url}weather?q=${q}&appid=${appid}&units=metric`),
6.       forecast: q => get(`${url}forecast?q=${q}&appid=${appid}&units=metric`)
7.   }
```

The weather object has two functions for retrieving the current weather data and the forecast data (lines 5–6). It uses the get function built on top of XHR (line 1). You can switch it to test the Fetch API.

```
import { get } from './xhr;
```

The application runs identically using either XHR or the Fetch API.

Data Access Architecture

The data access architecture of the weather application has several layers: the AppRun async event handlers, an API layer, the get function and the post function, and the XHR or Fetch API (see Figure 6-5).

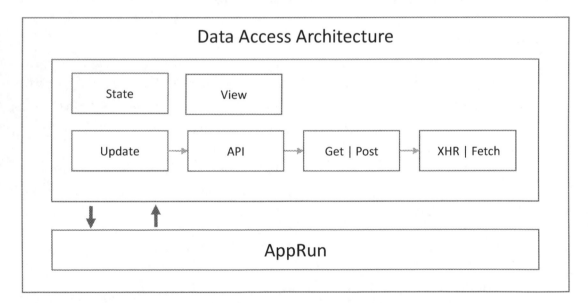

Figure 6-5. *Data access architecture*

The API layer is an object that provides `async` functions to call the back-end server. It serves as a namespace for the server access functions. Using an API layer is the pattern for larger applications because namespaces can help organize the APIs. Also, by using an API layer, the data access code is separate from the event handler, which makes it is easy to unit test.

The weather application is a global AppRun application (Listing 6-5).

Listing 6-5. The Weather Application

```
1.    import app from 'apprun';
2.    import weather from './weather';
3.    const state = { /* omitted state code */ };
4.    const view = (state) => <>/* omitted view code */</>;
5.    const update = {
6.        '#': async (_, city) => {
7.            try {
8.                city = city || 'Toronto,CA';
9.                const current = await weather.current(city);
10.               const forecast = await weather.forecast(city) as any;
11.               return { ...current, list: forecast.list };
12.           } catch (err) {
13.               return { err: err.message, city };
14.           }
15.       }
16.   };
17.   app.start('my-app', state, view, update);
```

We have omitted the state and the `view` function of the weather application to let us focus on the `async` event handler (Listing 6-5). The `async` event handler (line 6) calls the `weather` object twice with the `await` keyword to retrieve data from the back-end server (lines 9–10). By using the `await` syntax, the first API call, `await weather.current()`, fires first. Only when the first call's results are returned by the server does the second API call, `await weather.forecast()`, fire. The API calls are sequential.

When the `async` event handler returns the `Promise` object to AppRun, AppRun waits until the `Promise` object resolves before it calls the `view` function and renders the screen. It is safe and convenient to mark the event handlers with the `async` keyword for asynchronous operations.

To conclude, the weather application implements the AppRun `async` event handler pattern (Listing 6-1) and has the data access architecture (see Figure 6-4).

Pushing Data

The weather application demonstrates pulling data from the back-end server. Sometimes it would be nice to have the back-end server push data into our applications. We will develop a Hacker News reader application to demonstrate getting the data pushed from the back-end server.

Hacker News Reader

Hacker News (`https://news.ycombinator.com`) is a social news web site focusing on computer science and entrepreneurship. Hacker News is a fascinating and fun website to visit and share information.[5]

Hacker News partners with Firebase and publishes a public API that provides Hacker News data in near real time.[6] The Firebase Realtime Database is a cloud-hosted database. It can push data to every connected client. Applications built with Firebase automatically receive updates with the newest data.

By developing a Hacker News reader application, we'll explore how to handle the data pushed from Firebase using AppRun. The Hacker News reader application has two screens. One screen is a list screen that displays the Hacker New stories in categories: Top, New, Best, Show, Ask, and Jobs (see Figure 6-6). The other screen displays the story and its comments (see Figure 6-7).

---

[5]The Hacker News submission guidelines define the content type for the site. In general, content that can be "anything that gratifies one's intellectual curiosity." `https://news.ycombinator.com/newsguidelines.html`

[6]For more information about the Hacker News API, please visit its GitHub project at `https://github.com/HackerNews/API`.

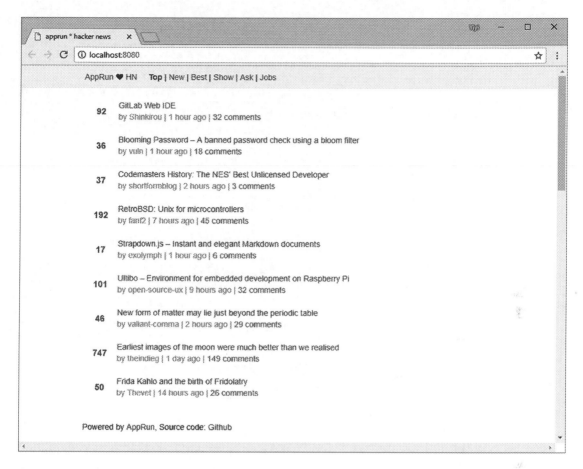

Figure 6-6. *Hacker News reader, story list*

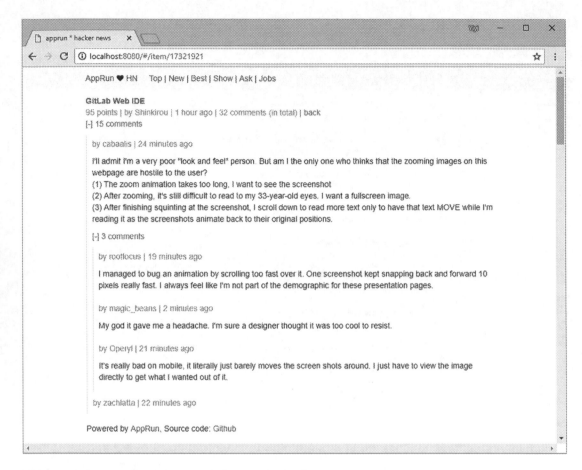

Figure 6-7. *Hacker News reader, story and comments*

The Hacker News API

There are two ways to use the Firebase Hacker News API: use the JSON API or use the Firebase API. The JSON API can be used to pull the data from the server. The Firebase API can be used to let the server push the data to the application.

The JSON API has the URL endpoint `https://hacker-news.firebaseio.com/v0/item/{story id}`. For example, the URL to a story at `https://hacker-news.firebaseio.com/v0/item/8863.json` returns the JSON data of the story.

To use the Firebase API, we use the Firebase database reference. First we create the Firebase database, and then we get the Firebase database reference of the story list and story detail (Listing 6-6).

Listing 6-6. Firebase Database References

```
1.    import * as firebase from 'firebase/app';
2.    import 'firebase/database';
3.    firebase.initializeApp({ databaseURL: 'https://hacker-news.
      firebaseio.com' });
4.    const db = firebase.database().ref('/v0');
5.    const list_ref = db.child(`${category}stories`);
6.    const item_ref = db.child(`item/${id}`);
```

The stories posted to Hacker News are categorized as Top, New, Best, Show, Ask, and Jobs. The story list of each category has the Firebase database reference. We can get the Firebase database reference of the story list (line 5). Also, we can get the Firebase database reference of the story detail (line 6).

The Story List

The Firebase story list reference publishes the value event with an array of at most 500 story IDs when the application connects to Firebase; in addition, the story list has updates at the server side. We can create the getList function to subscribe to the value event to get the story IDs (Listing 6-7).

Listing 6-7. Getting the Story List

```
1.    export const getList = (category, min, max) => {
2.        const ref = db.child(`${category}stories`);
3.        ref.on('value', async snapshot => {
4.            const items = await Promise.all(snapshot.val().map((id, idx) =>
5.                (idx >= min && idx < max && (typeof id === 'number')) ?
6.                    fetchJSON(`item/${id}`) : id
7.                ));
8.            app.run('refresh', category, { min, max, items });
9.        });
10.   };
```

Since the story list is just an array of story IDs, we then retrieve the story details of each story ID (line 4). We use the fetchJSON function to retrieve story details within the index range between min and max. The fetchJSON function is an async function that returns a Promise object. We use Promise.all to wait until all fetchJSON function calls are completed.

The fetchJSON function is a wrapper of the Fetch API that handles the JSON data format (Listing 6-8).

Listing 6-8. fetchJSON

```
1.   const fetchJSON = async (url: string) => {
2.       url = `https://hacker-news.firebaseio.com/v0/${url}.json`;
3.       const response = await fetch(url);
4.       if (!response.ok) {
5.           const data = await response.text();
6.           throw data;
7.       }
8.       return response.json();
9.   }
```

The Story Detail

Like the story list, the Firebase story reference publishes the value event with the story detail. We can create the getItem function to subscribe to the value event to get story IDs (Listing 6-9).

Listing 6-9. Getting the Story

```
1.   export const getItem = (id) => {
2.       const ref = db.child(`item/${id}`);
3.       ref.on('value', async snapshot => {
4.           const item = await fetchItem(snapshot.val());
5.           app.run('refresh', id, item);
6.       })
7.   };
```

The story detail object has a `kids` property, which is an array of IDs of the child stories. A child story can also have its own child stories. This makes the story a hierarchical structure. We need to use the `fetchItem` function to retrieve all the child stories using the story IDs recursively (Listing 6-10).

Listing 6-10. Getting a Story and Its Children

```
1.    const cache = {};
2.    const fetchItem = async ({ id }) => {
3.        const item = cache[id] || await fetchJSON(`item/${id}`);
4.        if (item && item.kids) item.kids =
5.            await Promise.all(item.kids.map((kid) =>
6.                typeof kid === 'number' ? fetchItem({id: kid}) : kid
7.        ));
8.        return item;
9.    }
```

Both the `fetchList` function and the `getItem` function share a common pattern. They both subscribe to the Firebase event. In the Firebase event handler, they use the `async` functions to download more data. Once all the `async` functions are completed, they publish the AppRun `refresh` event to the main application to render the screen.

The Application

The main application has a global AppRun application architecture (Listing 6-11).

Listing 6-11. The Hacker News Reader Main Program

```
1.    import app from 'apprun';
2.    import { getList, getItem } from './hn';
3.    const page_size = 30;
4.    type State = {
5.        id: 'top' | 'new' | 'best' | 'ask' | 'show' | 'job' | number
6.    }
7.    const state: State = {
8.        id: 'top'
9.    }
```

```
10.  //#region view functions
11.  /* Omitted the view code*/
12.  //#endregion
13.  const update = {
14.      '#': (state, mode, id) => {
15.          id = id || mode || 'top';
16.          if (!state[id]) {
17.              mode === 'item' ?
18.                  getItem(id) :
19.                  getList(id, 0, page_size);
20.          }
21.          return { ...state, mode, id };
22.      },
23.      'refresh': (state, id, data) => {
24.          state[id] = data;
25.          if (id === state.id) return state;
26.      }
27.  };
28.  app.start('my-app', state, view, update);
```

We have omitted the view functions to focus on analyzing the application architecture. In the application, a state is an object. It has an id property that is the story list ID or story detail ID of the screen (line 7). The story list ID is the story category (Top, New, Best, Show, Ask, and Jobs). The story detail ID is a number. The state object caches the story list and story detail using the id value as the cache key.

The application has two event handlers for event # and event refresh. The # event handler is the routing event hander (line 14). It accepts the following URL fragments:

- /#/{category}

- /#/item/{story id}

When the story list or story detail has already been cached, the event handler returns the current state to render the screen. Otherwise, it uses the fetchList function and the getItem function to subscribe to the Firebase event (lines 17–19).

The refresh event handler is called when Firebase has pushed data to the application (line 23). It stores the data into the state and returns the state for screen rendering only when the ID matches the current screen ID (lines 24–25). For example, when the screen is displaying the new story list and the new story list has the update pushed down, it refreshes the screen to show an updated story list. However, when the screen is displaying a story and the new story list has the update pushed down, it only stores the updates but does not refresh the screen.

Now we can enjoy reading the stories and let the application update the stories automatically behind the scenes.

To conclude, the Hacker News reader application uses both the Firebase API and the JSON API. It leverages AppRun pub-sub to connect the Firebase events to the AppRun events.

Source Code and Examples

You can get the source code of this chapter by cloning the GitHub project from `https://github.com/yysun/apprun-apress-book`. You can run the two examples of this chapter using the `npm` scripts in Table 6-1.

Table 6-1. npm Scripts of This Chapter

Example	Script
The weather application (Listings 6-4 and 6-5)	`npm run weather`
The Hacker News reader (Listings 6-6 and 6-11)	`npm run hn`

Summary

JavaScript uses an asynchronous operation to handle long-running code execution using only a single thread. The asynchronous operation uses callback functions. The `Promise` object and the `async/await` syntax make the code easier to read and write.

AppRun supports asynchronous event handlers using the `async/await` syntax. We only need to add the `async` keyword in front of the event handler to allow calling the `async` functions in the event handlers. AppRun manages and resolves the promises.

Data access is an asynchronous operation. Calling to the `async` functions of data access in AppRun `async` event handlers feels like synchronous code. The error handling using the `try` and `catch` structure also feels just like synchronous code.

Furthermore, we can bind the asynchronous data access with real-time database update events to the development of push-based applications.

From Chapter 3 up to this chapter, we have covered the three parts of the AppRun architecture and shown examples of small applications. Starting in the next chapter, we will discuss how to use AppRun in real application development scenarios, such as single-page applications, administrative dashboards, and line-of-business applications.

CHAPTER 7

Single-Page Applications

The Web started as static web sites that served static HTML documents. The HTML documents contained hyperlinks to other documents distributed on web servers all over the world. Later, the web sites became web applications when web servers could generate dynamic content based on the user navigation and input. These web servers use a server-side technology, such as ASP, JSP, or PHP, to retrieve and update data from and to databases and generate HTML dynamically. This is called traditional *server-side rendering* (SSR).

Traditional SSR has the problem that every user interaction requires a full-page reload. User interactions such as button clicks and form submissions trigger either a GET or a POST on the web server, and the web server always generates the entire HTML page. The full-page reload causes a white page flicker, which impacts the smoothness of the user experience. It also makes more server load when rendering the whole page. The server has to know the application state in the browser such as the logged-in user's ID, page number, and form content to render a whole page. Synchronizing the state between the browser and the server is difficult.

The Web application programming interface (API) and Asynchronous JavaScript and XML (Ajax) were created to solve the SSR problems, which eventually led to the single-page application (SPA). SPAs are the technology that manages application state and logic mainly in the browser. When the applications require dynamic data, they send requests to the Web API. The Web API retrieves the data from the database and sends back the data in JSON format. The web application then renders the page in the browser. There is no more full-page reload. The pages can be updated partially, which provides a smooth user experience more like a desktop application installed on a computer.

The state of an SPA stays in the browser, and JavaScript frameworks such as AppRun manage the state in the browser and update the screen partially and dynamically. When applications are complicated, AppRun supports using components as the building blocks of the SPA. The components are organized and managed using ECMAScript modules. Components communicate with each other through AppRun events.

© Yiyi Sun 2019
Y. Sun, *Practical Application Development with AppRun*, https://doi.org/10.1007/978-1-4842-4069-4_7

This chapter introduces the architecture of SPAs, the routing events that activate components, and the techniques to manage the modules such as dynamic import and native module import.

SPA Architecture

AppRun comes with a command-line interface (CLI) that can create an SPA project's boilerplate. You can create a project folder and run the following command in your application project folder to initialize an AppRun SPA project:

```
npx apprun -i  --spa
```

The AppRun CLI has the following files in the project folder:

- `index.html`: The default HTML file

- `main.tsx`: The main program

- `Home.tsx`: The Home page component

- `About.tsx`: The About page component

- `Contact.tsx`: The Contact page component

The AppRun CLI also configures the development environment, including the project file (`package.json`), TypeScript configuration(`ts.config`), and webpack configuration (`webpack.config.js`). The convention to compile and bundle the application is to use these `npm` scripts:

- `npm start`: Starts the webpack development server

- `npm run build`: Creates the application code for production use

Run the command `npm start`, and you will see a new browser open with the SPA running inside it (see Figure 7-1).

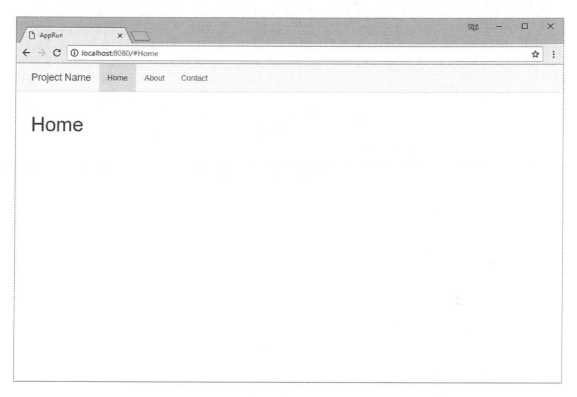

Figure 7-1. *AppRun SPA*

To summarize, the AppRun CLI–generated SPA project boilerplate includes an HTML file, the main program, and three components for three pages (Figure 7-2).

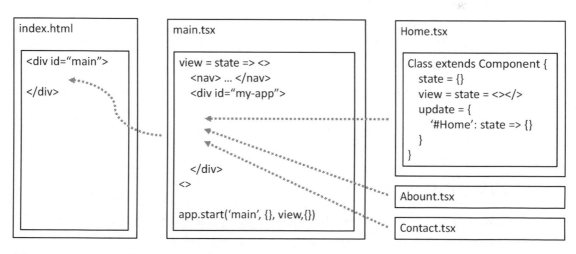

Figure 7-2. *AppRun SPA architecture*

The HTML is the starting point of the SPA. The main program renders the SPA screen layout. The components render the SPA pages. To develop the AppRun SPA, we create the HTML file, the main program, and the components. Or we can modify the AppRun CLI–generated files.

HTML

index.html is the default application start page (Listing 7-1).

Listing 7-1. AppRun SPA index.html

```
1.    <!doctype html>
2.    <html>
3.    <head>
4.        <meta charset="utf-8">
5.        <meta name="viewport" content="width=device-width,
          initial-scale=1, maximum-scale=1">
6.    <title>AppRun</title>
7.        <link rel="stylesheet" href="https://maxcdn.bootstrapcdn.com/
          bootstrap/3.3.7/css/bootstrap.min.css">
8.    </head>
9.    <body>
10.       <div id="main"></div>
11.       <script src="app.js"></script>
12.   </body>
13.   </html>
```

The index.html file has an empty <div> tag with an id value of main (line 10) and a script tag for the bundled application code, app.js (line 11). The index.html file also references the Bootstrap styles (line 7).

Main Program

The main program (app.js) renders the screen layout project. app.js is the result of compiling and bundling the main program, main.tsx (Listing 7-2).

Listing 7-2. AppRun SPA Main Program

```
1.    import app from 'apprun';
2.    app.on('#', _ => app.run('#Home'))
3.    app.on('//', route => {
4.        const menus = document.querySelectorAll('.navbar-nav li');
5.        for (let i = 0; i < menus.length; ++i) menus[i].classList.
          remove('active');
6.        const item = document.querySelector(`[href='${route}']`);
7.        item && item.parentElement.classList.add('active');
8.    })
9.    const view = state => <div>
10.       <nav className="navbar navbar-default">
11.           <div className="container">
12.               <div className="navbar-header">
13.                   <button type="button" className="navbar-
                      toggle collapsed" data-toggle="collapse" data-
                      target="#navbar" aria-expanded="false"
14.                   aria-controls="navbar">
15.                       <span className="sr-only">Toggle navigation</span>
16.                       <span className="icon-bar"></span>
17.                       <span className="icon-bar"></span>
18.                       <span className="icon-bar"></span>
19.                   </button>
20.                   <a className="navbar-brand" href="/">Project Name</a>
21.               </div>
22.               <div id="navbar" className="navbar-collapse collapse">
23.                   <ul className="nav navbar-nav">
24.                       <li className="active"><a href="#Home">Home</a></li>
25.                       <li><a href="#About">About</a></li>
26.                       <li><a href="#Contact">Contact</a></li>
27.                   </ul>
28.               </div>
29.           </div>
30.       </nav>
```

```
31.     <div className="container" id="my-app"></div>
32.   </div>
33.   app.start('main', {}, view, {})
34.   import Home from './Home';
35.   import About from './About';
36.   import Contact from './Contact';
37.   const element = 'my-app';
38.   new Home().mount(element);
39.   new About().mount(element);
40.   new Contact().mount(element);
```

The SPA main program is an AppRun global application. It renders the web page layout using the Bootstrap styles, which includes the top menu bar (lines 9–30) and the main content area, which is a `<div>` tag with an `id` value of `"my-app"` (line 31). SPA pages will be rendered into the `my-app div`.

The SPA has three pages: Home, About, and Contact. Each page is an AppRun component. The components are implemented and exported from modules. The SPA main program imports the three components from the modules (lines 34–36). It then creates the components and mounts them to the `my-app div` (lines 37–40). We do not need to embed the components into the HTML structure.

Components

An SPA's codebase contains all the features and functionalities of the applications. The codebase could be large and complex to manage. To develop SPAs, we use components to divide the application code into smaller and manageable units. As the building blocks of the SPA, components are developed and tested independently. They are combined to form the complete application code.

An SPA component is a subclass of the AppRun `Component` class. For example, the Home page component is a class that extends the AppRun `Component` class (Listing 7-3).

Listing 7-3. Home Page Component

```
1.   import app, {Component} from 'apprun';
2.   export default class extends Component {
3.       state = 'Home';
4.       view = (state) => {
```

146

```
5.            return <div>
6.                <h1>{state}</h1>
7.            </div>
8.        };
9.        update = {
10.            '#Home': state => state,
11.        };
12.    };
```

The component consists of the state, view, and update (event handlers), which form the AppRun architecture (Listing 7-3).

To use the AppRun components, we mount them to a web page element or element ID. When the components are mounted to a page element, they are sitting there doing nothing until the related events are published. The events cause the component to render its state to the page element. In the Home page component example, the event is #Home (line 10). If someone publishes the #Home event, the Home page renders to the screen.

Routing Events

In the SPA when users navigate around, the application renders the relevant pages onto the screen. The mechanism to load, execute, and render the pages is called *routing*. Routing sends users' interactions to the component code. In AppRun, SPA routing is simple. It is based on the AppRun event pub-sub and requires no routing code. It is not too much different from button clicks.

Location Hash Change Event

The three pages (Home, About, and Contact) of the example SPA are linked from the top navigation menu (Listing 7-4).

Listing 7-4. SPA Top Navigation Menu

```
1.    <div id="navbar" className="navbar-collapse collapse">
2.        <ul className="nav navbar-nav">
3.            <li><a href="#Home">Home</a></li>
```

```
4.              <li><a href="#About">About</a></li>
5.              <li><a href="#Contact">Contact</a></li>
6.          </ul>
7.      </div>
```

When the URL fragment in the address of the browser changes, the browser window publishes the onpopstate event. AppRun applications just need to convert the onpopstate event into the AppRun events. It's business as usual; the event drives the application logic through the event lifecycle.

AppRun automatically converts the onpopstate event to an AppRun event. For example, when the anchor element <a href="#Home">Home</a> is clicked, AppRun publishes the global event #Home. The event is handled by the event handler of the Home page component.

```
update = {'#Home': state => state };
```

The Home page then is activated and rendered to the screen. The same mechanism applies to the About and Contact pages.

Generic Routing Events

To automatically convert the onpopstate event to an AppRun event, AppRun publishes three built-in events, named #, /, and //.

AppRun publishes the # event and the / event after the web page has loaded and is ready to run the scripts. We can subscribe to the # event and publish the #Home event to activate the Home page once the application starts (Listing 7-2, line 2).

```
app.on('#', _ => app.run('#Home'));
```

Upon each of the onpopstate events, AppRun also publishes to the // event. AppRun parses the web address path. It breaks the URL fragments into an easily consumable data array as the event parameter. Here are some examples:

- http://...../# => app.on('//', '#', [])

- http://...../#Home => app.on('//', '#Home', [])

- http://...../#/Home => app.on('//', '#', ['Home'])

- `http://...../#Home/1/2/3 => app.on('//', '#Home', ['1', '2', '3'])`

- `http://...../#/Home/1/2/3 => app.on('//', '#', ['Home', '1', '2', '3'])`

SPAs could have different routing URL requirements. Some applications require us to use the hash sign only, as in `http://....../#Home`. Some other applications require us to use the hash sign and the slash sign, as in `http://....../#/Home`. The `//` event lets us handle either routing URL requirement.

The `//` event also provides us with the opportunity to update the navigation menu to have the menu of the current page highlighted. We can subscribe to the # event directly (Listing 7-5).

Listing 7-5. Update Navigation Menu

```
1.   app.on('//', route => {
2.       const menus = document.querySelectorAll('.navbar-nav li');
3.       for (let i = 0; i < menus.length; ++i) menus[i].classList.
         remove('active');
4.       const item = document.querySelector(`[href='${route}']`);
5.       item && item.parentElement.classList.add('active');
6.   })
```

Listing 7-5 is used in the main program of the SPA example (Listing 7-2, lines 3–8).

Using the hash sign or the URL fragments is the default routing mechanism supported by AppRun. The benefit of using the hash sign is that AppRun publishes the routing events out of the box. We can subscribe to the routing events in the components and wait for the user interaction. When the back and forward buttons of the browsers and even the refresh button are clicked, the application works properly.

History API

By default, AppRun SPAs use URL fragments. Sometimes, we might have the application requirements ask us not to use URL fragments, in which case the navigation menu has no hash signs. AppRun supports this scenario too. Listing 7-6 shows the menu structure.

Listing 7-6. SPA Top Navigation Menu: No Hash

```
1.    <div id="navbar" className="navbar-collapse collapse">
2.        <ul className="nav navbar-nav">
3.            <li><a href="/Home">Home</a></li>
4.            <li><a href="/About">About</a></li>
5.            <li><a href="/Contact">Contact</a></li>
6.        </ul>
7.    </div>
```

Without the hash sign, the hyperlinks make the web browser redirect to new pages. The browser window will still publish the onpopstate event, but the event is not cancelable, which means we cannot stop the page redirection in the onpopstate event handler. To handle this situation, we need to change the anchor's behavior and handle the browser history API (Listing 7-7).

Listing 7-7. Changing the Anchors

```
1.    const rendered = () => {
2.        const menus = document.querySelectorAll('.navbar-nav li a');
3.        for (let i = 0; i < menus.length; ++i) {
4.            const menu = menus[i] as HTMLAnchorElement;
5.            menu.onclick = event => {
6.                event.preventDefault();
7.                history.pushState(null, ", menu.href);
8.                app.run('route', menu.pathname);
9.            };
10.        }
11.    }
```

In Listing 7-7, we attached the onclick event handler to all the navigation menus that will stop the click event (line 6). Then, the event handler will continue with calling the History API history.pushState() and publishing the AppRun route event using the href link of the menu (lines 7–8).

Also, we need to change the component event handlers, for example, to handle the /Home event instead of the #Home event (Listing 7-8).

Listing 7-8. Handle /Home Event

```
1.    import app, {Component} from 'apprun';
2.    export default class extends Component {
3.        state = 'Home';
4.        view = (state) => {
5.            return <div>
6.                <h1>{state}</h1>
7.            </div>
8.        };
9.        update = {
10.            '/Home': state => state,
11.        };
12.  }
```

After changing the component event handlers, the components can handle URLs without the hash sign. The navigation menu will publish the /Home event (see Figure 7-3).

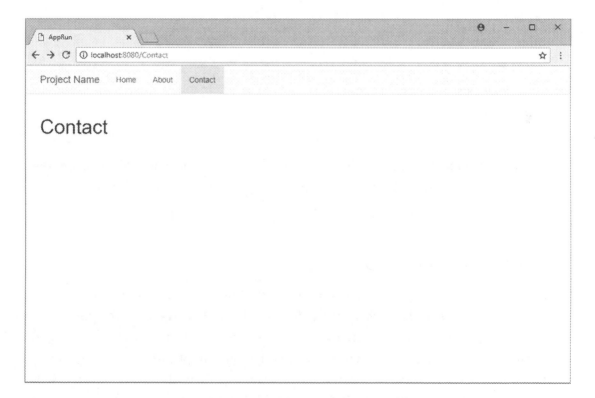

Figure 7-3. *SPA navigation without hash*

AppRun will also publish the /Home event when the browser's back and forward buttons are clicked. However, the browser refresh button does not work, because when the browser is refreshed, it will reload the web from the server. We need to implement the server-side rendering technique to solve the problem, which you will learn how to do in Chapter 9.

SPA Modules

SPA components are organized and managed using modules. Each SPA component is a JavaScript module. In complex SPAs, there could be many modules. ECMA Script 2015 (ES6) finalized the module standard in 2014, but it only started being supported by the browsers in 2018. Meanwhile, the ECMAScript module standard has been well supported by JavaScript bundlers like webpack, which can bundle modules into one script file safely and reliably to run in the browsers. We have been using webpack from the AppRun application development environment.

Static Import

We import the modules into the main program using the import expression.

```
import Home from './Home';
import About from './About';
import Contact from './Contact';
```

Webpack combines the main program code with the module code. The result of the webpack bundling is the app.js file that contains the code of the main program and three components. It is called *static import*.

Dynamic Import

The application code contains all the modules and could become a large script file. However, a larger script file takes longer to download, which slows down the initial display of the applications. We need to use some techniques to split the application code into smaller files. We want the browser to load just enough application code to get the applications displayed to the screen and started. It should import the module code only when the modules are required, which is called *dynamic import*.

ECMAScript has a proposal that defines the dynamic module import syntax using the Promise-based import function. Meanwhile, webpack can inject runtime helper functions during the module-bundling process to support dynamic module import.[1] For the AppRun components exported from a module, we can dynamically import them only when needed and then start the components in a page element.

```
import('./About').then(module => new module.default().start(element));
```

We can change the AppRun SPA main program to demonstrate the dynamic module import (Listing 7-9).

Listing 7-9. Main Program of Dynamic Module Import

```
1.    import app from 'apprun';
2.    app.on('#', _ => app.run('#Home'));
3.    app.on('//', route => { ... });   // omitted details
4.    const view = state => ... <div> // omitted details
5.    </div>
6.    app.start('main', {}, view, {});
7.    import Home from './Home';
8.    const element = 'my-app';
9.    new Home().start(element);
10.   app.on('#About', async () => {
11.       const module = await import('./About');
12.       new module.default().start(element);
13.   });
14.   app.on('#Contact', async () => {
15.       const module = await import('./Contact');
16.       new module.default().start(element);
17.   });
```

The main program has the Home component module statically imported, but it has the About component module and the Contact component module dynamically imported only when the corresponding routing events are published.

---

[1]For more information about the webpack configurations, please visit https://webpack.js.org/guides/code-splitting/#dynamic-imports.

Run the modified main program; you can see it loads the first statistically bundled code file, called `app.js` (see Figure 7-4).

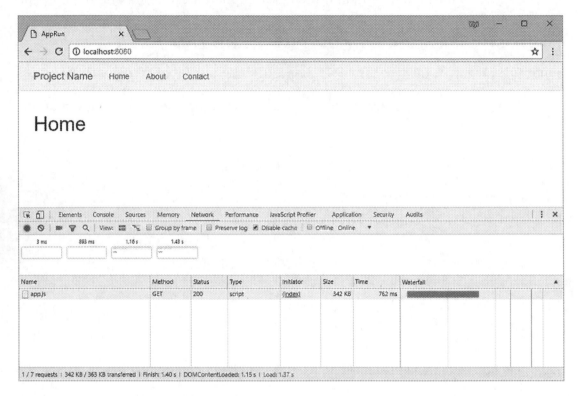

Figure 7-4. *Statistically bundled code file*

The `app.js` file contains the main program and the Home component. When the About menu is clicked, it loads the script that includes the About component (`0.js`), as shown in Figure 7-5.

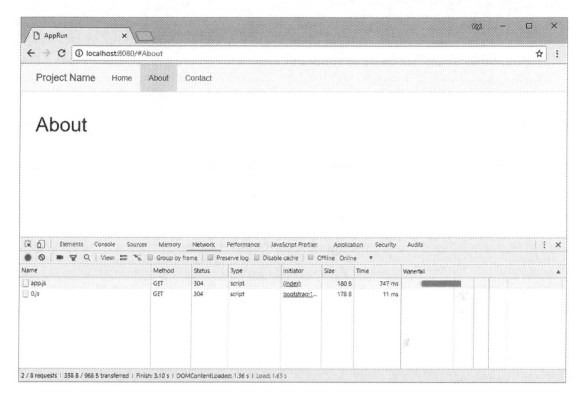

Figure 7-5. *Dynamically imported about module*

When the Contact menu is clicked, it loads the script that contains the Contact
component (1.js), as in Figure 7-6.

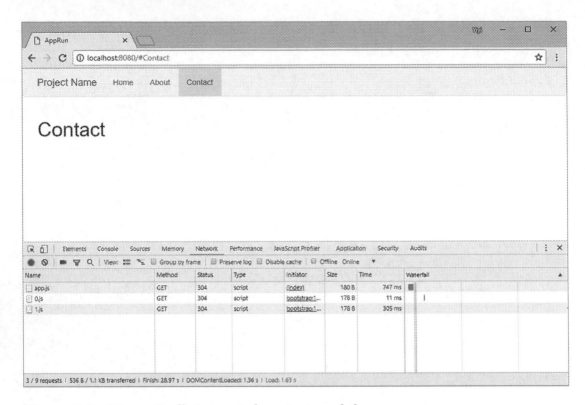

Figure 7-6. *Dynamically imported contact module*

The modules require being imported only one time. Once they are imported, there will be no more imports when the menus are clicked.

Leveraging webpack, we only made some minor changes to the main program; we can easily control which modules should be statically imported and which modules should be dynamically imported. It is a technique generally used for large SPAs.

Native Modules

In addition to dynamic module import, AppRun also supports fine-tuning modules manually. We can compile the modules into its script files and import them into HTML as native modules. Most of the latest browser versions have also added native module support.[2]

---

[2]For more information about the browser support of ES6 module, please visit https://caniuse. com/#feat=es6-module.

AppRun supports native modules. To demonstrate using native modules, we first change the HTML file (Listing 7-10).

Listing 7-10. HTML with Native Modules

```
1.   <!doctype html>
2.   <html>
3.   <head>
4.       <meta charset="utf-8">
5.       <title>AppRun * SPA * Native Modules</title>
6.       <link rel="stylesheet" href="https://maxcdn.bootstrapcdn.com/
         bootstrap/3.3.7/css/bootstrap.min.css">
7.   </head>
8.   <body>
9.       <div id="main"></div>
10.      <script src="https://unpkg.com/apprun@beta/dist/apprun-html.js">
         </script>
11.      <script src="dist/main.js"></script>
12.      <script type="module">
13.          import Home from './dist/Home.js';
14.          import About from './dist/About.js';
15.          import Contact from './dist/Contact.js';
16.          const element = 'my-app';
17.          new Home().mount(element);
18.          new About().mount(element);
19.          new Contact().mount(element);
20.      </script>
21.  </body>
22.  </html>
```

The HTML file has a mix of using a regular script file (lines 10–11) and using the `<script type="module">` syntax to import native JavaScript modules (lines 12–20).

The main program is a global AppRun application. It is the script file compiled into `main.js` and loaded into the HTML file (Listing 7-11).

Listing 7-11. Main Program of Native Modules

```
1.   declare var app: typeof import("apprun").app;
2.   app.on('#', _ => app.run('#Home'))
3.   app.on('//', route => {
4.       const menus = document.querySelectorAll('.navbar-nav li');
5.       for (let i = 0; i < menus.length; ++i) menus[i].classList.
         remove('active');
6.       const item = document.querySelector(`[href='${route}']`);
7.       item && item.parentElement.classList.add('active');
8.   })
9.   const view = () => <div>
10.      <nav className="navbar navbar-default">
11.          <div className="container">
12.              <div className="navbar-header">
13.                  <button type="button" className="navbar-
                     toggle collapsed" data-toggle="collapse" data-
                     target="#navbar" aria-expanded="false"
14.                  aria-controls="navbar">
15.                      <span className="sr-only">Toggle navigation</span>
16.                      <span className="icon-bar"></span>
17.                      <span className="icon-bar"></span>
18.                      <span className="icon-bar"></span>
19.                  </button>
20.                  <a className="navbar-brand" href="/">Project Name</a>
21.              </div>
22.              <div id="navbar" className="navbar-collapse collapse">
23.                  <ul className="nav navbar-nav">
24.                      <li className="active"><a href="#Home">Home</a></li>
25.                      <li><a href="#About">About</a></li>
26.                      <li><a href="#Contact">Contact</a></li>
27.                  </ul>
28.              </div>
```

```
29.          </div>
30.        </nav>
31.        <div className="container" id="my-app"></div>
32.    </div>;
33.    app.render(document.getElementById('main'), view());
```

The main program renders the main screen layout using AppRun's virtual DOM. The main program does not need to import other modules because the HTML file has imported them. The main program is decoupled and has no dependency on other modules. Also, it does not even import the AppRun library. Instead, it imports the type definition from the AppRun library (line 1). The HTML file loads the AppRun library from unpkg.com, which is the content delivery network (CDN) of npm packages (Listing 7-10, line 10). The AppRun library can be shared across all modules.

The technique of importing just types from the AppRun library applies to all other modules, such as the Home component module (Listing 7-12).

Listing 7-12. Home Component Module for Native Module

```
1.    declare var app: typeof import("apprun").app;
2.    declare var Component: typeof import("apprun").Component;
3.    export default class extends Component {
4.        state = 'Home';
5.        view = (state) => {
6.            return <div>
7.                <h1>{state}</h1>
8.            </div>
9.        };
10.       update = {
11.           '#Home': state => state,
12.       };
13.   }
```

The Home component module (Listing 7-12) uses the globally shared AppRun library. It only imports the types of app and components from the AppRun library. It does not import the entire AppRun library. The TypeScript compiler compiles the Home.tsx file into the JavaScript module code. Listing 7-13 shows Home.js.

Listing 7-13. Compiled Home Component Module

```
1.   export default class extends Component {
2.       constructor() {
3.           super(...arguments);
4.           this.state = 'Home';
5.           this.view = (state) => {
6.               return app.createElement("div", null,
7.                   app.createElement("h1", null, state));
8.           };
9.           this.update = {
10.              '#Home': state => state,
11.          };
12.      }
13.  }
```

The compiled JavaScript file (Listing 7-13) can be imported as the native module. We make the same changes to other components, About and Contact.

Run the modified HTML, main program, and Home, About, and Contact pages, and watch the network in the browser's DevTool. You can see that the AppRun library, the main script files, and the components are imported separately (see Figure 7-7).

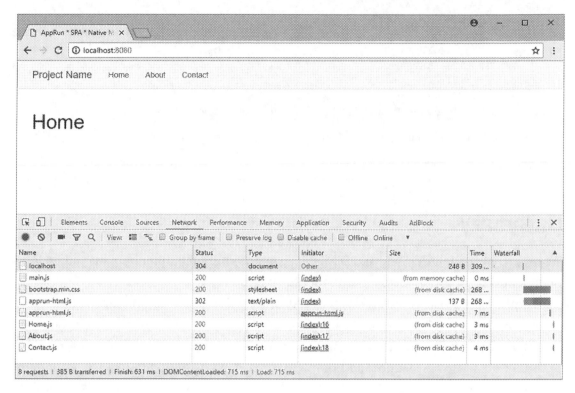

Figure 7-7. *SPA using native modules*

To summarize the technique of using native modules, we compile modules individually and import them as needed. Modules communicate with each other using events. For example, the main program publishes the #Home event to activate the Home component. AppRun event pub-sub decouples the modules. We can continue to modify the components and deploy the changed modules without impact on other modules.

Although each module has a dependency on the AppRun library, we do not need to import AppRun into each module. We include AppRun in the HTML file and share AppRun with all modules.

Source Code and Examples

You can get the source code of this chapter by cloning the GitHub project at https://github.com/yysun/apprun-apress-book. You can run the four examples of this chapter using the npm scripts in Table 7-1.

Table 7-1. *npm Scripts of This Chapter*

Example	Script
The AppRun SPA (Listings 7-1 to 7-5)	`npm run spa`
The example of routing without hash (Listings 7-6 and 7-7)	`npm run spa-non-hash`
The example of dynamic import (Listing 7-8)	`npm run spa-dynamic-import`
The example of the native module (Listings 7-9 to 7-13)	`npm run spa-es-module`

Summary

AppRun SPAs usually include an HTML file, a main program that renders the screen layout, and some components that render the pages.

AppRun SPAs use the events to route user interaction to the components. Treating routing like other web events is the smart idea of AppRun. All web events are unified under the event pub-sub pattern, which is one of the core concepts of the AppRun architecture. Routing does not require special treatment. AppRun SPAs can route with or without the hash sign in URLs.

AppRun components can be mounted to the web page elements using the code without embedding the component in HTML. It provides the flexibility to load and activate the components in code.

AppRun components are modularized using the ECMAScript module standard. We can import the modules statically and dynamically. We can also use the native module from modern browsers.

We are now equipped with many techniques and are ready for AppRun SPA development. In the next chapter, we will use the SPA template to make an administrative user interface on the home page of an SPA.

CHAPTER 8

Third-Party Library Integration

In Chapter 7, we discussed how to build the structure of single-page applications. In this chapter, we will build an administrative dashboard on the home page of the SPA boilerplate that was created by using the AppRun CLI. This will demonstrate how to use AppRun to build a complex user interface and administrative interface.

An administrative interface is for administrators to configure and manage web applications. It usually is a stand-alone web application or a restricted area of an application. The administrative interface is important because it is the management tool of the applications and systems. For a consumer-facing e-commerce web application, the administrative interface is for the owner to manage the production, prices, and orders. In a line-of-business application, the administrative interface is for managing the business processes, back-end databases, and systems.

In many cases, the administrative interface has a dashboard on its home page. The administrative, or admin, dashboard provides the overall status of the applications being managed. It is a special kind of interface that usually has a complicated layout involving a lot of visualization widgets. You should try to design one that is pleasing to view and easy to use. Often it also needs to be responsive for different devices and screen sizes. The front-end part is an important part of the administrative interface and is what we will focus on in this chapter. The back end of the administrative interface is data-driven and requires security trimming, which means it displays the content based on the user permissions. The back end is beyond the scope of this chapter.

There are many third-party libraries in the JavaScript ecosystem that have already provided excellent data visualization on the front end. In general, there are two purposes for using third-party libraries: to build the page layout and style the elements as widgets and to create the widgets from the libraries. You will learn how to use the stateless

© Yiyi Sun 2019
Y. Sun, *Practical Application Development with AppRun*, https://doi.org/10.1007/978-1-4842-4069-4_8

components introduced in Chapter 4 to build the layout and style the elements. Also, you will learn how to integrate third-party libraries into the AppRun components using the extended AppRun architecture.

Example: An Admin Dashboard

The example application we will build is a single-page application that has an administrative dashboard on the home page. First, we will create the SPA project using the AppRun CLI as discussed in Chapter 7. We will modify the code of the Home page component to make it look like Figure 8-1 (and Figures 8-2, 8-3, and 8-4 in the following sections).

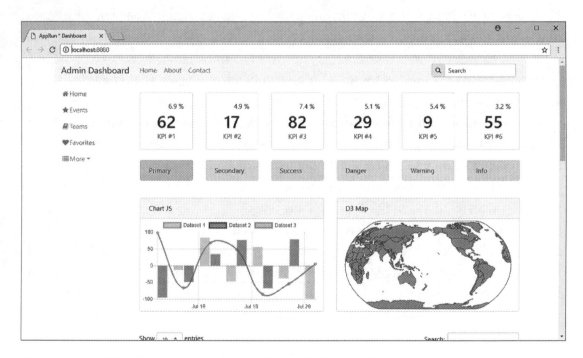

Figure 8-1. *SPA Home page as an admin dashboard*

The example admin dashboard mimics a real-world application. The top navigation is the first-level navigation that has menus to load various web pages such as the Home page, the About page, and the Contact page.

The top navigation is from the SPA boilerplate. The sidebar navigation is the second-level navigation that has the menus for the page. For example, the Home, Events, Team, and More menus are part of the Home page. We will explore more about the UI first.

Responsive UI

The example application UI is responsive to the screen size. On the computer screen, it displays all the top navigation menus and sidebar menus (see Figure 8-1). When running on mobile devices, the top navigation menus are collapsed inside the hamburger menu at the top right of the screen; the sidebar menus are also collapsed to a row of icon menus (see Figure 8-2).

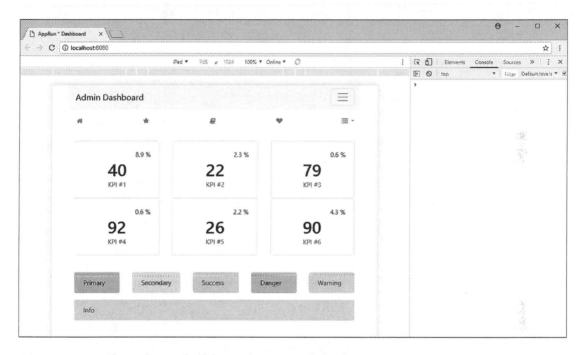

Figure 8-2. *The admin dashboard on a mobile device*

The responsive layout of the top navigation comes from the SPA boilerplate out of the box. We will create the side navigation menus in the "Sidebar Menu" section of this chapter. Also, we will create the side navigation menus based on an array contains the data that represents the menus dynamically.

Dashboard Widgets

The main content area of the home page has various kinds of widgets to visualize the data. There are widgets such as key performance indicator (KPI) cards, several types of notification/ altering messages, a chart, and a map, as you can see from Figure 8-1 and Figure 8-2. There are also a data table widget and a widget calendar in the main content area.

The data table widget displays an example of an employee list. The data is loaded dynamically from a JSON file, which includes the employee's name, position, office location, age, start date, and salary as a data table. The data table has many features commonly used in line-of-business applications, such as it is configurable to the number of rows, searchable/filterable, and sortable. It also includes the pagination for the list (see Figure 8-3).

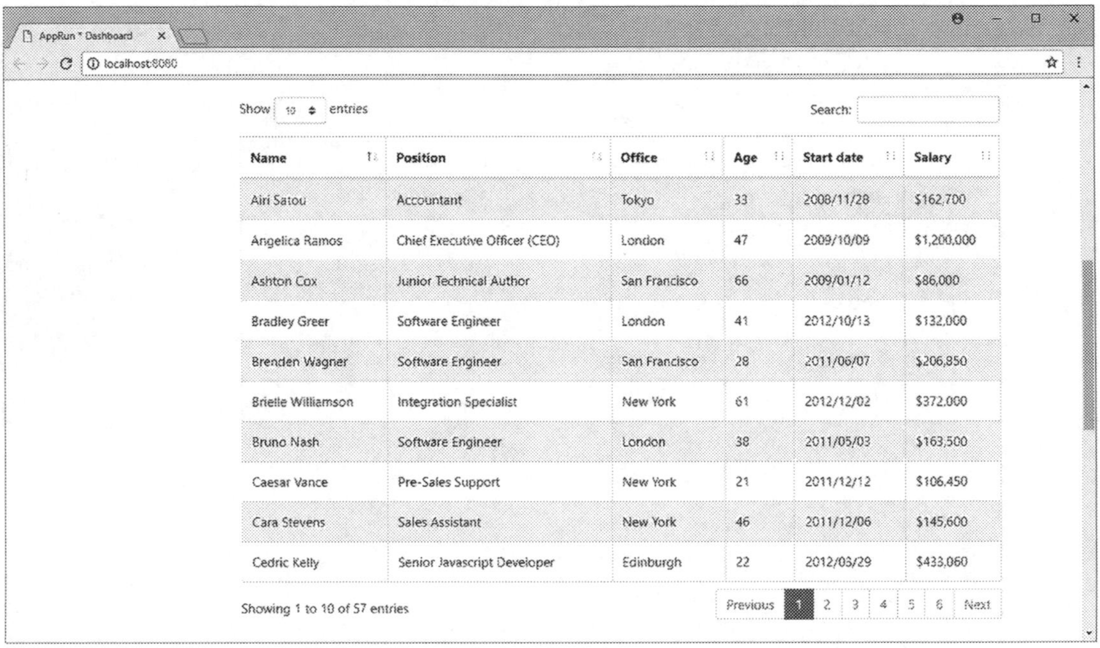

Figure 8-3. *Data table on the admin dashboard*

The calendar widget in the example application displays several events for July 2018. The event data is stored in an array. It is also a feature-rich widget. We can view the events in other years and months, and we can view the events monthly, weekly, or daily. Each event has a hyperlink that leads to the event's detail screen (see Figure 8-4).

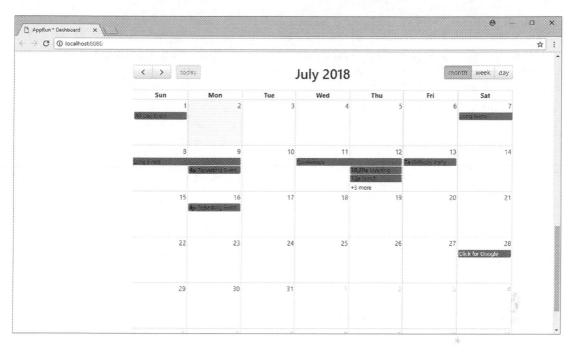

Figure 8-4. *Calendar on the admin dashboard*

Third-Party Libraries

The dashboard specification can be overwhelming the first time you look at it. The layout is complicated. The widgets are a variety of types, such as KPIs, alerts, charts, maps, data tables, and calendars. Creating all the widgets from scratch is impossible. Our plan of attack is to use the third-party libraries as much as possible.

The good news is that the development community has developed many libraries for pretty much everything, from page layout to data visualization widgets. There is probably a JavaScript library out there for anything you can think of. There is no need to re-invent the wheel. The framework we use to develop applications should always integrate easily with other libraries.

AppRun embraces open web technologies. It respects and welcomes third-party libraries. In fact, AppRun was designed to support third-party libraries. Combining the power of many third-party libraries with AppRun is the practical application development method. Table 8-1 shows the third-party libraries we will use for the admin dashboard application.

Table 8-1. *npm Scripts of This Chapter*

Feature/Widget	Third-Party Library Name	Third-Party Library URL
Responsive layout Sidebar menu KPI cards Notifications/alerts	Bootstrap	`http://getbootstrap.com/`
Chart widget	Chart.js	`https://www.chartjs.org/`
Map widget	D3.js	`https://d3js.org/`
Data table widget	DataTables (the jQuery plug-in)	`https://datatables.net/`
Calendar widget	FullCalendar	`https://fullcalendar.io/`

Extended Architecture

We will integrate the third-party libraries for more complicated dashboard widgets such as charts, maps, tables, and calendars. To do so, we will first review the extended AppRun architecture (see Figure 8-5).

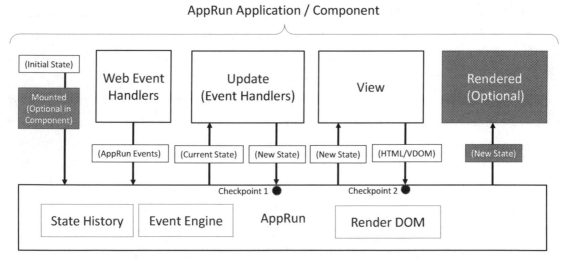

Figure 8-5. *AppRun extended architecture*

In the extended AppRun architecture, the event lifecycle has two optional functions: the mounted function and the rendered function. The mounted function is available only in the AppRun component architecture. The rendered function is available in the AppRun component architecture as well as in the AppRun global architecture.

When using stateful components in JSX, AppRun creates the component object behind the scenes. We don't have access to the constructor to initialize the state. However, AppRun will call the mounted function if presented and will pass the JSX properties as the parameters to the mounted function. By using the mounted function, we can initialize the state based on the JSX properties.

The rendered function plays a different role in the AppRun event lifecycle. Upon each AppRun event, AppRun processes the event through the event handlers to get a new state. It calls the view function to turn the new state into the virtual DOM. It then renders the virtual DOM to the real DOM. Finally, if the AppRun application or AppRun components have defined the rendered function, AppRun calls the rendered function to give us an opportunity to change the actual DOM. The rendered function is the place where we can integrate with many third-party libraries perfectly.

With the AppRun extended architecture in mind, we are ready to build the example application. We will start by creating the page layout and styles.

Layout and Styles

We usually use a CSS framework to build the page layout and style the elements. For example, we will use Bootstrap for the admin dashboard application of this chapter.

Bootstrap is a free and open source front-end framework that contains the design templates for typography, forms, buttons, navigation, and other interface components. It was initially developed at Twitter as a framework to encourage consistency across internal tools. It has become one of the most popular front-end user interface frameworks for web applications.

We start developing the admin dashboard application by using the AppRun CLI–generated SPA boilerplate, which has already included the references to Bootstrap. We will use the Bootstrap CSS classes to create the admin dashboard layout, the responsive sidebar menus, and the rows and columns of the main content on the home page.

The admin dashboard layout has the structure shown in Listing 8-1.

Listing 8-1. Bootstrap Dashboard Layout

```
1.    <div className="row h-100">
2.        <aside className="col-lg-2 p-0">
3.            <nav className="navbar navbar-expand align-items-start
              navbar-light" >
4.                <div className="collapse navbar-collapse">
5.                    {*/ menus/*}
6.                </div>
7.            </nav>
8.        </aside>
9.        <main className="col">
10.           {/* main content */}
11.       </main>
12. </div>
```

Because we start with using the Home component of the SPA, we do not need to worry about the full HTML layout and the responsive top navigation. We only need to focus on the area belonging to the home page. However, the admin dashboard page has many widgets and elements. If we put all the HTML elements and the CSS class into one place, the code will become long, complicated, and hard to read and maintain. To keep it clean, we use AppRun stateless components. The home page component is quite simple after all (Listing 8-2).

Listing 8-2. Home Page Component

```
1.    export default class extends Component {
2.        state = 'Dashboard';
3.        view = (state) => <Dashboard>
4.            <Sidebar menus={menus} />
5.            <Widgets></Widgets>
6.         </Dashboard>;
7.        update = {
8.            '#Home': state => state,
9.        }
10. }
```

The capitalized JSX tags <Dashboard>, <Sidebar>, and <Widgets> are the stateless components introduced in Chapter 4. They are the calls to the Dashboard, Sidebar, and Widgets functions (Listing 8-3).

Listing 8-3. Dashboard and Sidebar Components

```
1.    const Dashboard = (_, children) => <div className="row h-100">
2.        {children}
3.    </div>
4.    const Sidebar = (props, children) => <aside className="col-lg-2 p-0">
5.        <nav className="navbar navbar-expand align-items-start navbar-light" >
6.            <div className="collapse navbar-collapse">
7.                {props.menus ? <Menus menus={props.menus} /> : "}
8.            </div>
9.        </nav>
10.   </aside>
11.   const Widgets = () => <main className="col">
12.       <CardList />
13.       <Alerts />
14.       <Row>
15.           <Column><Chart /></Column>
16.           <Column><Map /></Column>
17.       </Row>
18.       <Row className="my-4" />
19.       <DataTable />
20.       <Row className="my-4" />
21.         <Row className="my-4">
22.         <Column className="col-md-6">
23.             <Calendar id="c1" name="My Calendar" />
24.         </Column>
25.         <Column className="col-md-6">
26.             <Calendar id="c2" name="Team Calendar" />
27.         </Column>
28.       </Row>
29.   </main>
```

Using the stateless components, we break down the complicated HTML into smaller pieces from top to bottom. This abstracts away the complexity when it is not a concern at a certain stage. For example, when building the page layout, we only need to focus on that the dashboard has a sidebar and a widgets area. The elements inside the sidebar and the widgets area are considered when developing the `Sidebar` and `Widgets` functions. One level at a time is the much easier approach. The code is also easier to understand and maintain; just compare Listing 8-2 with Listing 8-1.

Once finished with the page layout, we can move to the sidebar and then the widget area.

Sidebar Menu

The sidebar navigation is the main content of the side. The sidebar navigation menus are data-driven to mimic the real-world application scenario where the menus are dynamically created based on the logged-in user's permissions. We use a two-level menu, as shown in Listing 8-4.

Listing 8-4. Menu Data

```
1.   const menus = [
2.       { icon: 'home', text: 'Home', href: '#' },
3.       { icon: 'star', text: 'Events', href: '#' },
4.       { icon: 'book', text: 'Teams', href: '#' },
5.       { icon: 'heart', text: 'Favorites', href: '#' },
6.       { icon: 'list', text: 'More', href: '#', menus:
7.           [{ icon: 'check', text: 'Admin', href: '#' }]
8.       }
9.   ];
```

The `Sidebar` component uses the `Menu` component to create the Bootstrap menus (Listing 8-5).

Listing 8-5. Menu Component

```
1.   const Menus = ({ menus }) => <ul className="flex-lg-column flex-row
     navbar-nav w-100 justify-content-between">
2.       {menus.map(menu => menu.menus ?
```

```
3.              <li className="nav-item dropdown">
4.                  <a className="nav-link pl-0 pr-0 dropdown-toggle" data-
                    toggle="dropdown" href={menu.href} role="button" aria-
                    haspopup="true" aria-expanded="false">
5.                      <i className={`fa fa-${menu.icon} fa-fw`}></i>
6.                      <span className="d-none d-lg-inline">{menu.text}</span>
7.                  </a>
8.                  <div className="dropdown-menu border-0">
9.                      <Menus menus={menu.menus} />
10.                 </div>
11.             </li> :
12.             <li className="nav-item">
13.                 <a className="nav-link pl-0 text-nowrap" href={menu.href}>
14.                     <i className={`fa fa-${menu.icon} fa-fw`}></i>
15.                     <span className="d-none d-lg-inline">{menu.text}</span>
16.                 </a>
17.             </li>
18.         )}
19.   </ul>;
```

The Menu component supports nested child menus. It checks whether one menu item has child menus (line 2). If there are child menus, it creates the child menu structure (lines 3–11). Otherwise, it creates the regular menu item (lines 12–17).

The Bootstrap classes to make the menu responsive are flex-lg-column and flex-row (line 1). This means the menus should be displayed vertically in a column on a large screen. Otherwise, the menus should be displayed horizontally in a row. You can see that the Bootstrap classes are declarative. They clearly express our intention.

Rows and Columns

Inside the widget area, we use the Bootstrap CSS classes row and col to make the layout responsive. We create AppRun stateless components that have the row and col classes (Listing 8-6).

Listing 8-6. Row and Column

```
1.    const mergeClassName = (name, props) => {
2.        props = props || {};
3.        if (props.className) {
4.            name = `${name} ${props.className}`;
5.            delete props.className;
6.        }
7.        return name;
8.    }

9.    const Row = (props, children) =>  <div className={mergeClassName
      ('row', props)}>
10.       {children || "}
11.   </div>;

12.   const Column = (props, children) => <div className={mergeClassName
      ('col', props)}>
13.       {children || "}
14.   </div>;
```

The Row and Column components are the `<div>` elements that have Bootstrap `row` and `col` classes. Both the Row and Column components have input parameters called `props` and `children`. The `props` parameter contains the JSX tag properties. The `children` parameter contains the child JSX tags, which are called by the two components directly without modification.

By using the `props` parameter, the two components accept additional CSS classes. The `mergeClassName` function is used to merge the additional CSS classes with the basic CSS classes. For example, `<Row className="my-4" />` adds the `my-4` class to the row. By the way, `my-4` is the Bootstrap 4 spacing utility class that adds top and bottom margins to the row.[1]

Allowing the ability to add more classes to the stateless component is such a useful feature that we will demonstrate it again when discussing the notification and alert components.

---

[1]For more information about Bootstrap utility classes and spacing, please visit `https://getbootstrap.com/docs/4.1/utilities/spacing/`.

Notifications and Alerts

Notifications and alerts are messages to users. Depending on the importance of the messages, they are highlighted differently. Bootstrap has a CSS class alert for all messages and several other CSS classes for the message types, such as `alert-primary`, `alert-secondary`, `alert-success`, `alert-danger`, `alert-warning`, and `alert-info`. The class merge technique used for the rows and columns applies to the `Alert` component. The `Alert` component shown in Listing 8-7 allows us to add the CSS classes for the message types.

Listing 8-7. Alert Component

```
1.   const Alert = (props, children) => <div className={mergeClassName
     ('alert', props)} role="alert">
2.       {children || "}
3.   </div>;
```

We can add additional classes to create different types of alerts (Listing 8-8).

Listing 8-8. Different Types of Alerts

```
1.   const Alerts = () => <>
2.       <Alert className="alert-primary">Primary</Alert>
3.       <Alert className="alert-secondary">Secondary</Alert>
4.       <Alert className="alert-success">Success</Alert>
5.       <Alert className="alert-danger">Danger</Alert>
6.       <Alert className="alert-warning">Warning</Alert>
7.       <Alert className="alert-info">Info</Alert>
8.   </>;
```

It feels natural to add extra classes to the `Alert` component to define the message type by using the `props` parameter and the `mergeClassName` function.

Next, we will demonstrate another technique of using the `props` parameter in the `Card` component.

Cards

The Card component is one of the most useful Bootstrap components. It defines a rectangular area on the screen for displaying specific content. It can include a header, a body, and a footer. We will build a Card component to display the KPI and to wrap the chart and map widget. The Card component is an AppRun stateless component (Listing 8-9).

Listing 8-9. Card Component

```
1.   const Card = (props, children) => {
2.       props = props || {};
3.       return <div className={mergeClassName('card', props)}>
4.           {props.header ? <div className="card-header">{props.header}
             </div> : ''}
5.           {children || ''}
6.           {props.body ? <div className="card-body">{props.body}</div> : ''}
7.           {props.footer ? <div className="card-footer">{props.footer}
             </div> : ''}
8.   </div>
9.   }
```

The Card component is composed of the header, body, and footer, which are passed in as the properties of the props parameter and are all optional. To demonstrate the Card component, we will create the CardList component. The CardList component randomly generates six KPIs to create six cards using the Card component (Listing 8-10).

Listing 8-10. Card List

```
1.   const CardList = () => <Row className="my-4">
2.       {[1, 2, 3, 4, 5, 6].map(i => <div className="col-sm-4 col-lg-2">
3.           <Card>
4.               <div className="card-body text-center">
5.               <div className="text-right text-green">
6.                   {(Math.random() * 10).toFixed(1)} %
7.               </div>
8.               <div className="h1 m-0">{(Math.random() * 100).
                 toFixed(0)}</div>
```

```
9.                      <div className="text-muted">KPI #{i}</div>
10.                  </div>
11.              </Card>
12.          </div>)}
13.    </Row>;
```

The `CardList` component is a row in the widget area (line 2). It also organizes the KPI cards responsively using the CSS classes `col-sm-4` and `col-lg-2`. When creating the `Card` component, the contents of the card (some emphasized text and some muted text) are passed into the `Card` component as the children parameters (lines 4–10).

So far, we have created AppRun stateless components in a top-down fashion to manage the UI complexity. We have also demonstrated how to use the `props` and `children` parameters. We encourage you to visit the open source project at `https://github.com/yysun/apprun-bootstrap` to get many AppRun components for Bootstrap. There is also an open source project that has the AppRun components: Framework7 (`https://framework7.io`) is a CSS framework for developing mobile applications; see `https://github.com/yysun/apprun-f7`.

Components and Widgets

By using the AppRun stateless components, we can create some simple widgets that display only with dynamic element composition and styling such as the notification/alert widget and card widget. To create more complex widgets that have a rich user interface and user interactions, we will use the AppRun stateful components that integrate with third-party libraries. We will create four stateful components to demonstrate the approaches planned in Table 8-1.

Chart

We will follow one of the examples from the Chart.js web site that generates three random datasets and displays them as a bar chart and line chart for the admin dashboard.[2] We will also put the chart inside a card (see Figure 8-6).

---

[2]You can find out the original example from the Chart.js web site at `www.chartjs.org/samples/latest/charts/combo-bar-line.html`.

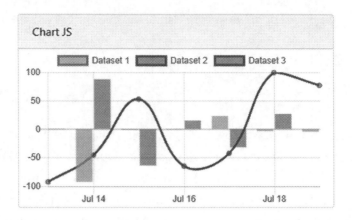

Figure 8-6. *Chart component*

Chart.js is a simple-to-use yet powerful library to build charts in web applications. It renders chart data into the <canvas> node. All it needs is a single <canvas> node. The general pattern of using Chart.js in the AppRun component is to create the <canvas> node in the view function and then create the Chart object in the rendered function, as shown in Listing 8-11.

Listing 8-11. Chart Component Pattern

```
1.   export default class extends Component {
2.       state = {
3.           data: { /* data of the chart */  }
4.       };
5.       view = _ => <canvas id="canvas"></canvas>;
6.       update = {};
7.       rendered = ({ data }) => {
8.           const ctx = (document.getElementById('canvas') as any).
             getContext('2d');
9.           new Chart(ctx, data);
10.      }
11.  };
```

The Chart component pattern renders the <canvas> node in the view function (line 5). It then creates the Chart object in the rendered function (line 9). That's all that's needed to create the structure of a Chart component. The rest of work is to follow the Chart.js document to develop the data structure to the charts.

We will use the color codes and the logic of generating the random datasets from the Chart.js example with the AppRun chart component pattern to get the complete component code (Listing 8-12).

Listing 8-12. Chart Component

```
1.    import app, { Component } from 'apprun';
2.    import { Card } from './ui';
3.    declare var Chart;
4.    declare var moment;
5.    const timeFormat = 'MM/DD/YYYY HH:mm';
6.    const color = Chart.helpers.color;
7.    const chartColors = {
8.        red: 'rgb(255, 99, 132)',
9.        orange: 'rgb(255, 159, 64)',
10.       yellow: 'rgb(255, 205, 86)',
11.       green: 'rgb(75, 192, 192)',
12.       blue: 'rgb(54, 162, 235)',
13.       purple: 'rgb(153, 102, 255)',
14.       grey: 'rgb(201, 203, 207)'
15.    };
16.    const newDateString = (days) => moment().add(days, 'd').
       format(timeFormat);
17.    const randomScalingFactor = (min = -100, max = 100) => Math.random() *
       (max - min) + min;
18.    export default class extends Component {
19.        state = {
20.            data: {
21.                type: 'bar',
22.                data: {
23.                    labels: [
24.                        newDateString(0),
25.                        newDateString(1),
26.                        newDateString(2),
27.                        newDateString(3),
28.                        newDateString(4),
```

```
29.                     newDateString(5),
30.                     newDateString(6)
31.                 ],
32.             datasets: [{
33.                 type: 'bar',
34.                 label: 'Dataset 1',
35.                 backgroundColor: color(chartColors.red).
                    alpha(0.5).rgbString(),
36.                 borderColor: chartColors.red,
37.             data: [
38.                 randomScalingFactor(),
39.                 randomScalingFactor(),
40.                 randomScalingFactor(),
41.                 randomScalingFactor(),
42.                 randomScalingFactor(),
43.                 randomScalingFactor(),
44.                 randomScalingFactor()
45.             ],
46.         }, {
47.             type: 'bar',
48.             label: 'Dataset 2',
49.             backgroundColor: color(chartColors.blue).
                alpha(0.5).rgbString(),
50.             borderColor: chartColors.blue,
51.             data: [
52.                 randomScalingFactor(),
53.                 randomScalingFactor(),
54.                 randomScalingFactor(),
55.                 randomScalingFactor(),
56.                 randomScalingFactor(),
57.                 randomScalingFactor(),
58.                 randomScalingFactor()
59.             ],
60.         }, {
61.             type: 'line',
62.             label: 'Dataset 3',
```

```
63.                    backgroundColor: color(chartColors.green).
                       alpha(0.5).rgbString(),
64.                    borderColor: chartColors.green,
65.                    fill: false,
66.                    data: [
67.                        randomScalingFactor(),
68.                        randomScalingFactor(),
69.                        randomScalingFactor(),
70.                        randomScalingFactor(),
71.                        randomScalingFactor(),
72.                        randomScalingFactor(),
73.                        randomScalingFactor()
74.                    ],
75.                }]
76.            },
77.        options: {
78.            title: {
79.            text: 'Chart.js Combo Time Scale'
80.            },
81.            scales: {
82.                xAxes: [{
83.                type: 'time',
84.                display: true,
85.                time: {
86.                    format: timeFormat,
87.                }
88.            }],
89.            },
90.            }
91.        }
92.    };
93. view = _ => <Card header="Chart JS">
94.        <canvas id="canvas"></canvas>
95. </Card>;
96. update = {};
97. rendered = ({ data }) => {
```

```
98.      const ctx = (document.getElementById('canvas') as any).
         getContext('2d');
99.      new Chart(ctx, data);
100.      }
101.  }
```

Comparing Listing 8-11 with Listing 8-10, you will notice that you can plug the Chart.js code into the AppRun component to create the state (lines 7–17 and lines 19–92). The state is used to create the chart in the rendered function (line 99). The only difference is that the `view` function wraps the `<canvas>` node with a `Card` component (lines 93–95).

Adding a `Card` component to the chart is a particular requirement of the example application of this chapter. You can use the pattern (Listing 8-10) out of the box without adding the `Card` component. On the other hand, you can follow this example to add other elements or components if needed.

D3 Map

We will use D3.js to create an interactive map using SVG, in which every country is an SVG element that can react to the mouse hovering over it to show the highlighted color. Each country graphic also has a county code attached to it. When the country graphic is clicked, we display the country code in the card header (see Figure 8-7).

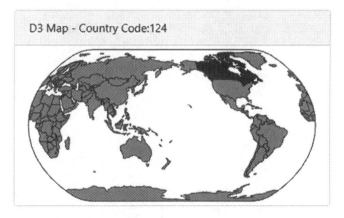

Figure 8-7. *Interactive map component*

D3.js (or just D3 for "data-driven documents") is a library for producing dynamic and interactive data visualizations. It can render complicated charts and maps into the `<svg>` node. The pattern to use D3 in the AppRun component is to create the `<svg>` node in the view function and then use D3 to create the map in the rendered function, as shown in Listing 8-13.

Listing 8-13. Map Component Pattern

```
1.    import app, { Component } from 'apprun';
2.    import { Card } from './ui';
3.    declare const d3, topojson;
4.    export default class extends Component {
5.        state = {}
6.        view = () => <svg id="svg"></svg>
7.        update = {
8.            'draw-map': (_, features) => features
9.        };
10.       rendered = (features) => { /* draw svg map using D3*/  }
11.       mounted = () => { /* load the data for the svg map*/  }
12.   }
```

The map drawing code is the typical process that creates SVG elements out of a dataset. In D3's terminology, the technique is called a *join*.[3] We load the data for drawing the map asynchronously using the d3.json function in the mounted function of the Map component and draw the map in the rendered function to the <svg> node created in the view function (Listing 8-14).

Listing 8-14. Map Component

```
1.    import app, { Component } from 'apprun';
2.    import { Card } from './ui';
3.    declare const d3, topojson;
4.    export default class extends Component {
5.        state = {}
6.        view = () => <Card header={<div id="map-text">D3 Map</div>}>
7.            <svg id="svg"></svg>
8.        </Card>;
9.        update = {
```

---

[3]The join concept is explained by the author of D3.js in the post at https://bost.ocks.org/ mike/join/.

```
10.            'draw-map': (_, features) => features
11.        };
12.      rendered = (features) => {
13.          if (!features.length) return;
14.          const sphere = { type: "Sphere" };
15.          const element = document.getElementById('svg');
16.          const width = element.clientWidth;
17.          const height = width / 2;
18.          const projection = d3.geo.naturalEarth()
19.              .scale(width / 6)
20.              .rotate([180, 0])
21.              .translate([width / 2, height / 2])
22.              .precision(.5);
23.          const path = d3.geo.path().projection(projection);
24.          const svg = d3.select(element)
25.              .attr("width", width)
26.              .attr("height", height);
27.          svg.append("path")
28.              .attr("class", "background")
29.              .attr("d", path(sphere));
30.          svg.append("g")
31.              .attr("id", "states")
32.              .selectAll("path")
33.              .data(features)
34.              .enter()
35.              .append("path")
36.              .attr("d", path)
37.              .attr("id", function (d) { return d.id; })
38.              .on('click', function () {
39.                  d3.select("#map-text").text("D3 Map - Country Code:"
                     + this.id);
40.              });
41.          }
42.          mounted = () => {
43.              const _this = this;
44.              d3.json("./world-110m.json", function (error, topo) {
```

```
45.                    if (error) throw error;
46.                    const features = topojson.feature(topo, topo.objects.
                       countries).features;
47.                    _this.run('draw-map', features);
48.              });
49.         }
50. }
```

The Map component uses the AppRun D3 pattern in Listing 8-12, which uses the rendered function and the mounted and view functions to integrate D3.js. It is quite amazing that we can draw an interactive map by using only 30 lines of code (lines 12–41).

Data Tables

HTML tables are the commonly used way to visualize tabular data, especially in business applications. We will use DataTables, a jQuery plug-in to create the HTML table that has advanced interaction such as pagination, search, and sort (see Figure 8-8).

Show [10 ◆] entries   Search: [   ]

Name ↑↓	Position ↑↓	Office ↑↓	Age ↑↓	Start date ↑↓	Salary ↑↓
Airi Satou	Accountant	Tokyo	33	2008/11/28	$162,700
Angelica Ramos	Chief Executive Officer (CEO)	London	47	2009/10/09	$1,200,000
Ashton Cox	Junior Technical Author	San Francisco	66	2009/01/12	$86,000
Bradley Greer	Software Engineer	London	41	2012/10/13	$132,000
Brenden Wagner	Software Engineer	San Francisco	28	2011/06/07	$206,850
Brielle Williamson	Integration Specialist	New York	61	2012/12/02	$372,000
Bruno Nash	Software Engineer	London	38	2011/05/03	$163,500
Caesar Vance	Pre-Sales Support	New York	21	2011/12/12	$106,450
Cara Stevens	Sales Assistant	New York	46	2011/12/06	$145,600
Cedric Kelly	Senior Javascript Developer	Edinburgh	22	2012/03/29	$433,060

Showing 1 to 10 of 57 entries   Previous 1 2 3 4 5 6 Next

Figure 8-8. *Data table component*

This is a two-step approach. First, we create regular HTML in the view function. Then, we apply the DataTables jQuery plug-in to the HTML table (Listing 8-15).

Listing 8-15. Table Component

```
1.   import app, { Component } from 'apprun';
2.   import data from './table-data';
3.   declare var $;
4.   export default class extends Component {
5.       state = { data };
6.       view = ({ data }) => <table id="table-example"
             className="table table-striped table-bordered">
7.           <thead>
8.               <tr>
9.                   <th>Name</th>
10.                  <th>Position</th>
11.                  <th>Office</th>
12.                  <th>Age</th>
13.                  <th>Start date</th>
14.                  <th>Salary</th>
15.              </tr>
16.          </thead>
17.          <tbody>
18.              {data.map(p => <tr>
19.                  <td>{p.name}</td>
20.                  <td>{p.position}</td>
21.                  <td>{p.office}</td>
22.                  <td>{p.age}</td>
23.                  <td>{p.date}</td>
24.                  <td>{p.salary}</td>
25.              </tr>)}
26.          </tbody>
27.      </table>;
28.      update = {};
29.      rendered = state => {
30.          $('#table-example').DataTable();
31.      }
32.  }
```

The Table component loads the table data from the table-data.json file (line 2). It renders the regular HTML table in the view function (lines 6–27). In the rendered function, it applies the DataTables plug-in to the HTML table (lines 28–31).

You can see it is a simple approach to add search, sort, and pagination to the HTML table by using the DataTables jQuery plug-in.

Calendar

The calendar is a UI feature that is no less complicated than the data tables. Most likely, you will not write a calendar from scratch for your applications because the FullCalendar library has implemented many calendar features for us already. Here, we will integrate FullCalendar into the AppRun application by creating a Calendar component (see Figure 8-9).

Figure 8-9. *Calendar component*

FullCalendar is also a jQuery plug-in. We can use the same two-step approach as we used for developing the DataTables component to integrate FullCalender with the AppRun component: create the HTML element in the view function and apply the jQuery plug-in to the element in the rendered function (Listing 8-16).

Listing 8-16. Calendar Component

```
1.   import app, { Component } from 'apprun';
2.   declare var $;
3.   const yyyymm = new Date().toISOString().substr(0, 7);
4.   export default class extends Component {
5.       state = {
6.           id:",
7.           name: ",
8.           events: [ /* Event Data */ ]
9.       };
10.      view = (state) => <div>
11.          <h5>{state.name}</h5>
12.          <div id={`calendar-${state.id}`}></div>
13.      </div>;
14.      update = {};
15.      mounted = ({ id, name }) => {
16.          this.setState({ ...this.state, id, name})
17.      };
18.      update = {};
19.      rendered = state => {
20.          $('#calendar').fullCalendar({
21.              header: {
22.                  left: 'prev,next today',
23.                  center: 'title',
24.                  right: 'month,basicWeek,basicDay',
25.                  title: state.name
26.              },
27.              defaultDate: `${yyyymm}-12`,
28.              navLinks: true, // can click day/week names to navigate views
29.              editable: true,
```

```
30.            eventLimit: true, // allow "more" link when too many events
31.            events: state.events
32.        });
33.    }
34. }
```

FullCalender is also a jQuery plug-in. We can use the same method used for the DataTables to create the Calendar component. The view function creates a <div> node as the placeholder for rendering the calendar (lines 2–12). The rendered function applies the FullCalendar plug-in to the <div> node created in the view function with an object that has the configurations for the calendar (lines 20–32).

It is so much fun to integrate many great third-party libraries into the AppRun components. Again, we must stop here and move on to summarize all the techniques we have used. The Chart component demonstrates the pattern that creates the <canvas> node in the view function and creates the chart object in the <canvas> node in the rendered function. The Map component demonstrates the pattern that creates the <svg> node in the view function and creates the D3 SVG map in the <svg> node in the rendered function. It also demonstrates how to load data asynchronously. The Table component demonstrates the pattern of using jQuery plug-ins. It creates the <table> node in the view function and applies the jQuery plug-in to the <table> node in the rendered function. The Calendar component follows the jQuery plug-in pattern. It is only different in that it creates a <div> node as the placeholder.

Source Code and Examples

You can get the source code of this chapter by cloning the GitHub project at https://github.com/yysun/apprun-apress-book. You can run the examples in this chapter using the npm scripts in Table 8-2.

Table 8-2. *npm Scripts of This Chapter*

Example	Script
The administrative dashboard	npm run admin
AppRun components for Bootstrap	https://github.com/yysun/apprun-bootstrap
AppRun components for Framework7	https://github.com/yysun/apprun-f7

Summary

We have seen how to use AppRun to build complex UIs in this chapter. AppRun was designed to support third-party libraries. The virtual DOM is resilient to allow other libraries to change to the DOM. Also, the extended AppRun architecture event lifecycle has the `mounted` and `rendered` functions to makes it easy to use other libraries in AppRun applications.

Using jQuery and the jQuery plug-ins is not an anti-pattern. It is welcomed and encouraged. We embrace third-party libraries and recommend you use them because it is an important AppRun application development technique.

In the next chapter, we will introduce another important technique, server-side rendering.

CHAPTER 9

Server-Side Rendering

The single-page application (SPA) has become popular because it has a smooth and fluent user experience more like a native desktop application or even a native mobile app. This approach solves the problem of being interrupted by a white/blank screen caused by reloading the full page on the server side. However, an SPA comes with its own problems. It tends to be slow on startup because the application code is compiled into client-side scripts. The scripts usually are large files that require some time to download and parse. When the browser is downloading and parsing the scripts, the screen is blank when the application is starting. Users have to wait. Besides, the JavaScript rendered content is not search-engine-friendly.

Now, *server-side rendering* (SSR) takes client-side templates of SPAs and renders them on the server side. Most of the front-end frameworks have specific SSR libraries to render the client-side templates on the server side. Examples include Next.js for React, Angular Universal for the Angular framework, and Nuxt.js for the Vue framework.

AppRun is a front-end library for developing SPAs. It also supports the rendering of SPAs on the server side just like other frameworks. Furthermore, it allows us to turn existing traditional server-side rendered applications into SPAs. AppRun can make it easy to convert many applications built using the server-side Model-View-Control (MVC) architecture into SPAs.

This chapter introduces the AppRun features that support SSR. You will learn about the project structure and techniques of building SSR AppRun applications, as well as the methods of converting traditional SSR applications into SPAs.

AppRun SSR

We will start by analyzing the SPA architecture. Then we will discuss the AppRun SSR architecture and create an example AppRun SSR/SPA.

© Yiyi Sun 2019
Y. Sun, *Practical Application Development with AppRun*, https://doi.org/10.1007/978-1-4842-4069-4_9

SPA Architecture

SPAs usually load an HTML skeleton and application code from the server. The application code then loads the page content and renders the content to the screen dynamically upon user interaction (see Figure 9-1).

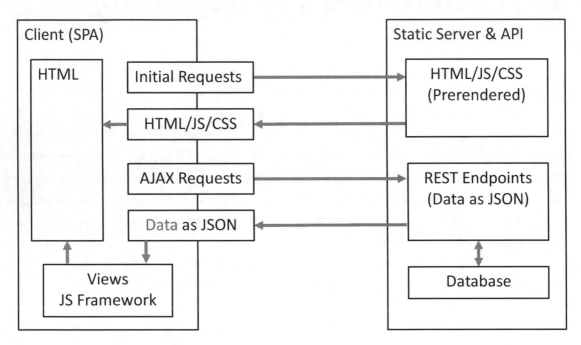

Figure 9-1. *SPA architecture*

When the SPA starts, the HTML is empty. The screen is blank until the browser finishes downloading and parsing application code and then retrieves the page data. The page content usually is the JSON format and is rendered using the client-side templates/views.

One of the techniques to improve the startup experience is to prerender the home page. The prerendering technique is to create the home page and some important pages as static HTML files.[1] The initial requests to the Home page and those important pages get the HTML content on the screen immediately. Users can view the pages while application code is downloading and parsing in the background.

---

[1] For example, there is a webpack plug-in for prerendering pages at `https://github.com/ chrisvfritz/prerender-spa-plugin`.

AppRun SSR Architecture

The prerendering technique is limited and does not scale. When applications have many pages and routes or when they have dynamic content, such as when page content is based on user privileges, it is impossible to prerender the dynamic content into HTML files. A better approach is the so-called isomorphic JavaScript approach or universal JavaScript, which renders the same application code on both the client and server sides. AppRun is isomorphic/universal. AppRun components can render on the client side, as well as on the server side using the AppRun server-side view engine (see Figure 9-2).

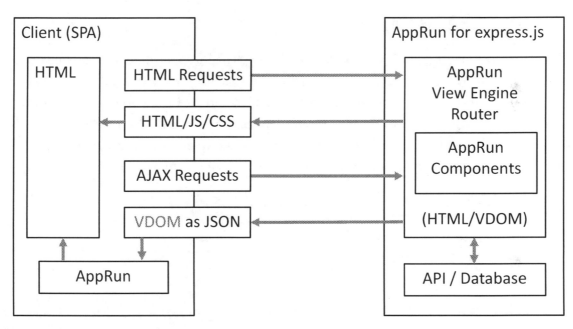

Figure 9-2. *AppRun SSR architecture*

AppRun components are event-driven. We can handle the server-side routing to publish AppRun events to drive AppRun components to produce the virtual DOM on the server side.

The AppRun server-side view engine performs the content negotiation. When accessing the pages directly, for example, the get /About page, the view engine returns server-rendered HTML based on the virtual DOM produced by the components. When accessing the pages with the HTTP Accept header to be application/json, the view engine returns the virtual DOM in JSON format. AppRun on the client side can render the virtual DOM to the screen directly.

The content negotiation and the virtual DOM as JSON make the client side of AppRun SSR/SPA small and effective. Unlike a regular SPA that gets data as JSON from the server and then applies the client-side templates/views to the data, AppRun SSR/SPA does not need to have client-side templates anymore. The client-side scripts only need to request pages from the server by setting the HTTP Accept header to be application/json. It then gets the virtual DOM to render the screen right away.

Getting the virtual DOM from the server is a unique feature of AppRun.

An SSR/SPA Example

We'll develop an example AppRun SSR/SPA. The pages of the application are rendered on the server side. When the application starts, the Home page is the server-rendered full-page HTML. It has the same timestamp in the navigation bar and the Home page (see Figure 9-3). We can click the Home menu after the application starts to reload the Home page. The screen is partially updated to have a different timestamp than the timestamp in the navigation bar. The JSON data returned from the server is the virtual DOM (see Figure 9-4).

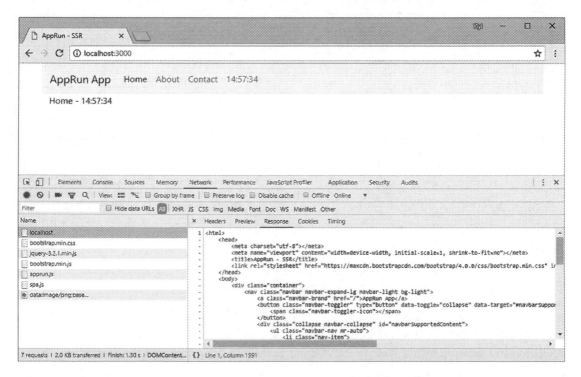

Figure 9-3. *Server-rendered Home page*

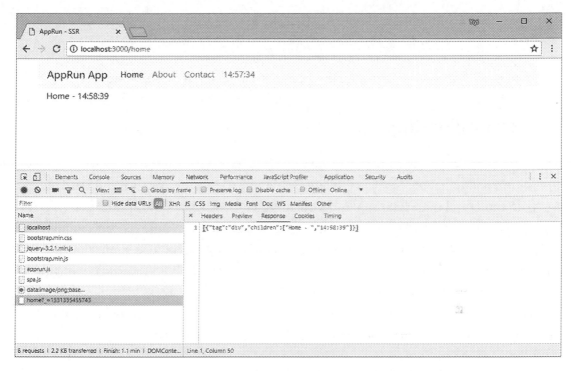

Figure 9-4. *Client-rendered Home page*

The page links of the top navigation menu are links without using the hash. They are /, /home, /about, and /contact. The client-side script (spa.js) changes these page links to send Ajax requests that have an HTTP Accept header as application/json. The client-side script switches the application into the SPA mode.

To summarize, when users type the page links into the browser address bar or when users hit the browser's refresh button, the pages are rendered on the server side. When users click the page links or users hit the browser's back or forward button, the pages are rendered on the client side using the virtual DOM JSON retrieved from the server by the Ajax requests.

The SSR for SPA

To build the SSR AppRun application, we will develop the following:

- The server application (server.ts)

- The site layout (components/layout.tsx)

- The components (components/*.tsx)

- The client-side application (/public/spa.js)

In this section, we walk through the development of all of these elements.

Server Application

The server application is an Express.js application. Express.js (https://expressjs.com) is a minimal and flexible Node.js web application framework. Express.js implements the MVC architectural pattern. It separates the different concerns of the application (input logic, business logic, and UI logic). The objects and components are loosely coupled.

Express.js applications route user requests to the controllers. The controllers invoke the model, process the business logic, and then render the HTML using a view engine. The view engine is configurable; it can be Pug, Mustache, and EJS.

The AppRun server application (server.ts) routes the user requests to AppRun components and uses the AppRun view engine for rendering (Listing 9-1).

Listing 9-1. The Server Application

```
1.    import * as viewEngine from 'apprun/viewEngine';
2.    import * as express from 'express';
3.    const app = express();
4.    app.use(express.static('public'));
5.    app.engine('js', viewEngine());
6.    app.set('view engine', 'js');
7.    app.set('views', __dirname + '/components');
8.    const route = async (Component, req, res) => {
9.        const ssr = req.headers.accept.indexOf('application/json') < 0;
10.       const getState = (component) => new Promise((resolve, reject) => {
11.           const state = component._state;
12.           if (state instanceof Promise)
13.               state.then(s => resolve(s))
14.                    .catch(r => reject(r));
15.           else
16.               resolve(state);
17.       });
```

```
18.        const component = new Component();
19.        try {
20.            const event = (req.path === '/' ? '/home' : req.path);
21.            component.mount();
22.            component.run(event);
23.            const state = await getState(component);
24.            const vdom = component.view(state);
25.            res.render('layout', { ssr, vdom });
26.        } catch (ex) {
27.            res.render('layout', { ssr, vdom: { Error: ex.message || ex } });
28.        } finally {
29.            component.unmount();
30.        }
31.    }
32.    import Home from './components/Home';
33.    import About from './components/About';
34.    import Contact from './components/Contact';
35.    app.get(/^\/(home)?$/, async (req, res) => {
36.        route(Home, req, res);
37.    });
38.    app.get('/about', async (req, res) => {
39.        route(About, req, res);
40.    });
41.    app.get('/contact', async (req, res) => {
42.        route(Contact, req, res);
43.    });
44.    const listener = app.listen(process.env.PORT || 3000, function () {
45.        console.log('Your app is listening on port ' + listener.address().
           port);
46.    });
```

The server application in the listing has four parts. It imports and sets the AppRun view engine as the view engine for Express.js (lines 3–7). It has a route function to route user requests to components (lines 8–31). It then imports the components and does the routing (lines 32–43). Finally, it starts the web server (lines 44–46). We will explain each of these parts.

View Engine

AppRun includes a view engine for Express.js. We can import and use it to replace the default view engine (Listing 9-2).

Listing 9-2. Use AppRun View Engine

```
1.  import * as viewEngine from 'apprun/viewEngine';
2.  app.engine('js', viewEngine());
3.  app.set('view engine', 'js');
4.  app.set('views', __dirname + '/components');
```

The AppRun view engine takes in the virtual DOM from the components and outputs the HTML or JSON of the virtual DOM based on the ssr flag. We use the render function to invoke the view and the AppRun view engine.

```
res.render('layout', { ssr, vdom });
```

By default, Express.js loads views from the views folder. We configure Express.js to load the view from the components folder instead (line 4). It loads layout.js, the compiled file of layout.tsx from the components folder.

Site Layout

The layout.js file has a view function to be loaded by the AppRun view engine, which processes the virtual DOM of each page based on the ssr flag (Listing 9-3). When the ssr flag is true, it combines the page and layout to form the full-page structure. Otherwise, it just uses the virtual DOM of the page content. At this stage, regardless of whether the layout and the page content are combined, the output of the view function is also the virtual DOM.

The AppRun view engine renders the output of the view function. It checks the ssr flag again. When the ssr flag is true, it renders the virtual DOM as HTML. Otherwise, it renders the virtual DOM as JSON.

Listing 9-3. The Site Layout

```
1.  import app from 'apprun';
2.  export default ({ ssr, vdom }) => !ssr ? vdom :
3.  <html>
```

198

```
4.    <head>
5.        <meta charset="utf-8" />
6.        <meta name="viewport" content="width=device-width, initial-
          scale=1, shrink-to-fit=no" />
7.        <title>AppRun - SSR</title>
8.        <link rel="stylesheet" href="https://maxcdn.bootstrapcdn.com/
          bootstrap/4.0.0/css/bootstrap.min.css"/>
9.        </head>
10.       <body>
11.           <div className="container">
12.               <nav className="navbar navbar-expand-lg navbar-light
                  bg-light">
13.                   <a className="navbar-brand" href="/">AppRun App</a>
14.                   <button className="navbar-toggler" type="button"
                          data-toggle="collapse" data-target="#navbar
                          SupportedContent"
                          aria-controls="navbarSupportedContent"
                          aria-expanded = "false"
                          aria-label="Toggle navigation">
15.                       <span className="navbar-toggler-icon"></span>
16.                   </button>
17.                   <div className="collapse navbar-collapse"
                       id="navbarSupportedContent">
18.                   <ul className="navbar-nav mr-auto">
19.                       <li className="nav-item">
20.                           <a className="nav-link active"
                              href="/home">Home</a>
21.                       </li>
22.                       <li className="nav-item">
23.                           <a className="nav-link" href="/about">
                              About</a>
24.                       </li>
25.                       <li className="nav-item">
26.                           <a className="nav-link" href="/contact">
                              Contact</a>
27.                       </li>
```

```
28.                        <li>
29.                            <a className="nav-link">{new Date().
                               toLocaleTimeString()}</a>
30.                        </li>
31.                    </ul>
32.                </div>
33.            </nav>
34.            <div className="container" id="my-app">
35.                {vdom || "}
36.            </div>
37.        </div>
38.        <script src="https://code.jquery.com/jquery-3.2.1.min.js">
           </script>
39.        <script src="https://maxcdn.bootstrapcdn.com/bootstrap/4.0.0/
           js/bootstrap.min.js"></script>
40.        <script src="https://unpkg.com/apprun@latest/dist/apprun.js">
           </script>
41.        <script src="spa.js"></script>
42.    </body>
43.    </html>
```

The layout function creates the layout of the web application, including the HTML structure, the navigation menus including a timestamp (line 29), and the <div> element that can embed other pages (lines 34–36). The layout uses the jQuery library (line 38), the Bootstrap framework (line 39), AppRun (line 40), and the client-side code of the spa.js application (line 41).

Both the layout function and the AppRun view engine require the input of the ssr flag and the virtual DOM. They are produced by the route function.

Routing

The route function does four steps including setting the ssr flag, routing the user requests to components, retrieving the virtual DOM output from the components, and invoking the layout view (Listing 9-4).

Listing 9-4. The route Function

```
1.    const route = async (Component, req, res) => {
2.        const ssr = req.headers.accept.indexOf('application/json') < 0;
3.        const getState = (component) => new Promise((resolve, reject) => {
4.            const state = component._state;
5.            if (state instanceof Promise)
6.                state.then(s => resolve(s))
7.                    .catch(r => reject(r));
8.            else
9.                resolve(state);
10.        });
11.       const component = new Component();
12.       try {
13.           component.mount();
14.           const event = (req.path === '/' ? '/home' : req.path);
15.           component.run(event);
16.           const state = await getState(component);
17.           const vdom = component.view(state);
18.           res.render('layout', { ssr, vdom });
19.       } catch (ex) {
20.           res.render('layout', { ssr, vdom: { Error: ex.message || ex }
});
21.       } finally {
22.           component.unmount();
23.       }
24.   }
```

The route function sets the ssr flag based on the accept parameter of the request HTTP header (line 2). Regular HTTP requests have the accept parameter of */*, which means they require SSR. The Ajax requests have the accept parameter of application/json, which means they do not need SSR.

Routing requests to the components is relatively easy. We create a new instance of the component and mount it. The component mounts to nothing and becomes the hidden component that does not render to real DOM elements. It can react to the events to create states (line 12).

Then we publish the path of the requests as the AppRun events to the components using the component.run function (line 14).

Getting the state out of the component after the event publication is a little tricky because if the AppRun event handler is asynchronous, we don't know when the event handling is completed. The asynchronous event handlers return Promise. The good news is that the AppRun component saves the output of the asynchronous event handlers to an internal property called _state. The _state property could be a value or a Promise object. Therefore, we create a helper function called getState to watch the _state property (line 6). If the _state property is a Promise, we wait for Promise to resolve or reject (lines 5–7). Otherwise, we return the _state right away (line 9).

With the getState Promise, the route function waits for the state and then invokes the view of the component to produce the virtual DOM and renders the virtual DOM (Listing 9-5).

Listing 9-5. Component Routing

```
1.    const event = (req.path === '/' ? '/home' : req.path);
2.    component.mount();
3.    component.run(event);
4.    const state = await getState(component);
5.    const vdom = component.view(_state);
6.    res.render('layout', { ssr, vdom });
7.    component.unmount();
```

At the end of the process, we unmount the component to clean up event handlers to prevent memory leak.

Finally, we connect the Express.js route to the route function and components (Listing 9-6).

Listing 9-6. Express Routing

```
1.    import Home from './components/Home';
2.    import About from './components/About';
3.    import Contact from './components/Contact';
4.    app.get(/^\/(home)?$/, (req, res) => {
5.        route(Home, req, res);
6.    });
```

```
7.   app.get('/about', (req, res) => {
8.       route(About, req, res);
9.   });
10.  app.get('/contact', (req, res) => {
11.      route(Contact, req, res);
12.  });
```

To summarize, for the requests coming to Express.js, we call the route function, which waits for the component state. Once the AppRun components create the state, it calls the view function of the component to create the virtual DOM. Then, the route function passes the virtual DOM into the layout view along with the SSR flag. Finally, the AppRun view engine renders the virtual DOM into HTML or JSON.

Components

The components of SSR applications are regular AppRun components, covered in Chapter 7. We are making some modifications to them. The Home component sets a timestamp to the state in the event handler (Listing 9-7).

Listing 9-7. The Home Component

```
1.   import app, {Component} from 'apprun';
2.   export default class extends Component {
3.       state = '';
4.       view = (state) => <div>
5.           Home - {state}
6.       </div>;
7.       update = {
8.           '/home': _ => new Date().toLocaleTimeString()
9.       }
10.  }
```

The Home component displays the timestamp (see Figure 9-3 and Figure 9-4).

Also, we make the Contact component return the state as a Promise (Listing 9-8) to demonstrate asynchronous event handlers.

Listing 9-8. The Contact Component

```
1.   import app, {Component} from 'apprun';
2.   export class Contact extends Component {
3.       state = '';
4.       view = (state) => <div>
5.         Contact - {state}
6.       </div>;
7.       update = {
8.           '/contact': async _ => new Promise(resolve =>
9.           setTimeout(() => resolve(new Date().toLocaleTimeString() +
               ' - delayed'), 200))
10.      }
11.  }
```

The Contact component has a delay to mimic the long-running operations
(see Figure 9-5).

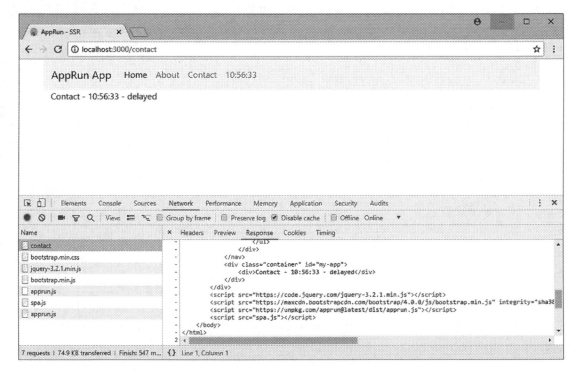

Figure 9-5. *Component async event handler*

Also, we make the About component throw an error (Listing 9-9) to demonstrate the error handling (see Figure 9-6).

Listing 9-9. The About Component

```
1.   import app, {Component} from 'apprun';
2.   export class About extends Component {
3.       state = ";
4.       view = (state) => <div>
5.           About  - {state}
6.       </div>;
7.       update = {
8.           '/about': _ => {
9.               throw new Error('test');
10.          }
11.      }
12.  }
```

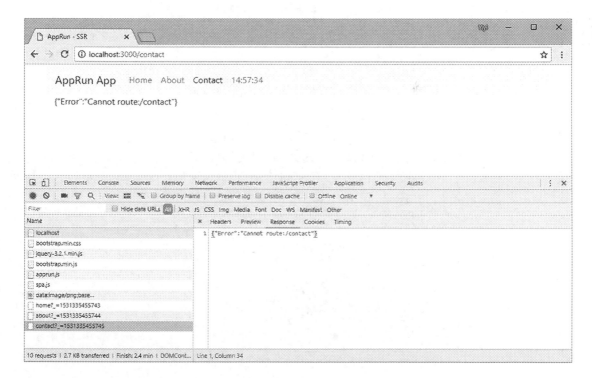

Figure 9-6. *Component error message*

The error thrown from the component event handler is displayed correctly. That's all for the server side. The server-side code is ready for the client to request HTML or the virtual DOM.

Client-Side Script

On the client side, there is a global AppRun application, spa.js, that can switch from the SSR pages into an SPA (Listing 9-10).

Listing 9-10. Client-Side Script

```
1.   $.ajaxSetup({ cache: false });
2.   const get = url => new Promise((resolve, reject) => {
3.       $.getJSON(url)
4.           .then(d => resolve(d))
5.           .fail(e => reject(e))
6.   });
7.   window.addEventListener('popstate', (e) => {
8.       const path = document.location.pathname;
9.       app.run('/', path);
10.  });
11.  $('.navbar-nav li a').on('click', function (event) {
12.      event.preventDefault();
13.      $('.navbar-nav li a').removeClass('active');
14.      const menu = $(this).addClass('active')[0];
15.      history.pushState(null, '', menu.href);
16.      app.run('/', menu.pathname);
17.  });
18.  const view = (state) => state;
19.  const update = {
20.      '/': async (_, path) => {
21.          const json = await get(path);
22.          return json;
23.      }
24.  };
25.  app.start('my-app', null, view, update);
```

The client-side application modifies the menu link behavior. It stops the browser from loading a new page and instead publishes the AppRun / event when the menu is clicked (lines 11–17).

The event handler makes an Ajax call to the server to get the virtual DOM as the state (lines 20–22). The view function returns the virtual DOM directly without the client-side rendering of JSON data (line 20). AppRun renders the virtual DOM to the screen. Because of it communicating with the server using the virtual DOM, the client-side application is simple. The components and their JSX code reside on the server side only.

This is a brilliant solution that simplifies not only the client-side logic but also the server-side logic. It does not increase the server-side load because the server needs to pull data from the databases or API calls and serialize the data into JSON. Now the server serializes the data into the virtual DOM instead. No big deal.

The SPA for SSR

Because AppRun can handle the virtual DOM from the server, we can develop middleware that outputs the virtual DOM to turn many traditional SSR applications into SPAs (see Figure 9-7). It is not limited to JavaScript and node.js. It applies to all back-end server technologies.

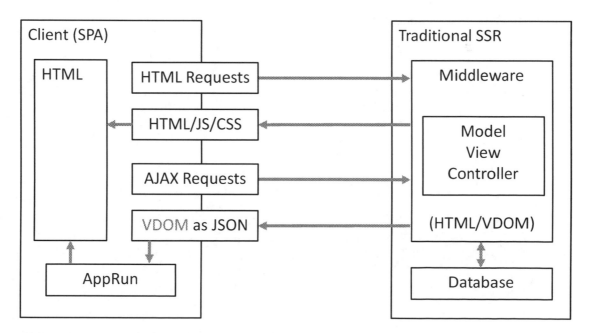

Figure 9-7. *SPA for traditional SSR*

The middleware is the web server technology that allows us to add extra logic to the web request process pipeline before and after the application code. It makes the application clean and has no dependence on infrastructure-related configurations and implementations. Most of the server-side technology supports middleware.

Once the server has middleware to output the virtual DOM, we can alter the client-side menu behavior to get the virtual DOM. The application can become an SPA immediately.

We will modify an application developed using the ASP.NET MVC framework (`https://www.asp.net/mvc`) and turn it into an SPA.

ASP.NET MVC

The ASP.NET MVC framework is the server-side technology for building dynamic web applications on the .NET platform. ASP.NET MVC applications are traditional SSR applications where each page is fully rendered HTML on the server side. ASP.NET MVC applications have the same problems as traditional SSR. By adding AppRun to the traditional SSR applications, we can make them SPAs to solve the user experience problem. At the same time, we can continue to get the benefits of SSR.

The SPA starts with the server-rendered page (see Figure 9-8). When users navigate to other pages, it gets the virtual DOM from the server. AppRun renders the screen using the virtual DOM (see Figure 9-9).

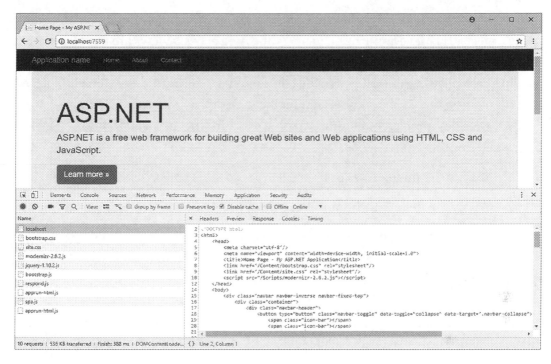

Figure 9-8. *ASP.NET MVC application*

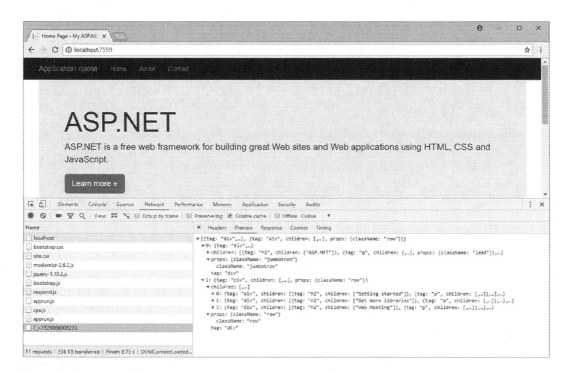

Figure 9-9. *Virtual DOM of the ASP.NET MVC application*

ASP.NET MVC applications also implement the MVC architectural pattern. Models are the objects that have application logic for the data access. Views are the components that render the HTML. The views use the Razor syntax for embedding server-based code into web pages.[2] Controllers are the components that route user interaction to the models and then invoke the views to render the data of the models to HTML.

It is a well-designed architecture. We can easily turn the application into an SPA. To do so, we follow these three steps:

1. Create the middleware or filter (`VirtualDomAttribute.cs`).

2. Apply the filter to the controller.

3. Add the client-side script to make it SPA.

Virtual DOM Filter

The middleware in the ASP.NET MVC framework is the `filter` attribute that can attach to a route in the controller (Listing 9-11) .

Listing 9-11. Virtual DOM Filter

```
1.   public class VirtualDomAttribute : FilterAttribute, IResultFilter
2.   {
3.       StringWriter textWriter;
4.       TextWriter originalWriter;
5.       bool isSSR;
     public VirtualDomAttribute()
6.       {
7.       }
     public void OnResultExecuting(ResultExecutingContext filterContext)
8.       {
9.           var accept = filterContext.HttpContext.Request.Headers["accept"];
10.          this.isSSR = accept.IndexOf("application/json") < 0;
11.          originalWriter = filterContext.HttpContext.Response.Output;
12.          textWriter = new StringWriter(CultureInfo.InvariantCulture);
```

---

[2]For more information about the Razor syntax, please visit https://docs.microsoft.com/en-us/
aspnet/core/mvc/views/razor?view=aspnetcore-2.1.

```
13.            filterContext.HttpContext.Response.Output = textWriter;
14.        }
15.    public void OnResultExecuted(ResultExecutedContext filterContext)
16.        {
17.            var capturedText = textWriter.ToString();
18.            var vdom = capturedText;
19.            if (!this.isSSR)
20.            {
21.                var doc = new HtmlDocument();
22.                doc.LoadHtml(capturedText);
23.                var root = doc.DocumentNode.SelectSingleNode("//div[@
                   id='apprun-app']");
24.                if (root == null) root = doc.DocumentNode.
                   SelectSingleNode("/div");
25.                vdom = RemoveWhiteSpace(Convert(root).
                   GetValue("children").ToString(Formatting.None));
26.            }
27.            filterContext.HttpContext.Response.Output = originalWriter;
28.            filterContext.HttpContext.Response.Write(vdom);
29.        }
30.    string RemoveWhiteSpace(string s)
31.        {
32.            return s.Replace("\\r", "").Replace("\\n", "").Trim();
33.        }
34.    public JObject Convert(HtmlNode documentNode)
35.        {
36.            if (documentNode.Name == "#comment") return null;
37.            if (documentNode.Name == "#document") documentNode.Name = "div";
38.            var children = new JArray();
39.            foreach (var child in documentNode.ChildNodes)
40.            {
41.                if (child.Name == "#text")
42.                {
```

```
43.                     if (RemoveWhiteSpace(child.InnerText).Length > 0)
44.                     {
45.                         children.Add(new JValue(HtmlEntity.
                            DeEntitize(child.InnerText)));
46.                     }
47.                 }
48.             else
49.             {
50.                 var ch = Convert(child);
51.                 if (ch != null) children.Add(ch);
52.             }
53.         }
54.         var vdom = JObject.FromObject(new
55.         {
56.             tag = documentNode.Name,
57.             children = children
58.         });
59.         var props = JObject.FromObject(new {});
60.         documentNode.Attributes.ToList().ForEach(attr =>
61.         {
62.             var name = attr.Name;
63.             if (name == "class") name = "className";
64.             props.Add(name, attr.Value);
65.         });
66.         if (props.HasValues) vdom.Add("props", props);
67.         return vdom;
68.     }
69. }
```

There are major functions in the virtual DOM filter.

- The OnResultExecuting function (lines 9–16) checks the request
  HTTP header for the accept parameter to decide whether it is an SSR
  request. If yes, it sets the isSSR flag (line 10).

- The `OnResultExecuted` function (lines 17–32) outputs the HTML when the request is SSR. Otherwise, it parses the HTML using the HTML Agility Pack (`http://html-agility-pack.net`) and then uses the `Convert` function to create the virtual DOM (line 19–26). Notice that it searches the element for the main content of the SPA, an element that has an `id` of `apprun-app` in this example. By converting the HTML inside the main content element, the virtual DOM only has the page content. The page header, navigation, and footer are not included in the virtual DOM.

- The `Convert` function (lines 36–71) walks through the HTML recursively and collects the elements and properties into the virtual DOM.

The virtual DOM `filter` attribute is a generic utility that you can use in other ASP. NET MVC applications.

The Controller

In the three-page example application, the controller is a class that has three routes for the Home page, the About page, and the Contact page. We add the virtual DOM filter to each route (Listing 9-12).

Listing 9-12. Controller of the MVC Application

```
1.   public class HomeController : Controller
2.   {
3.       [VirtualDom]
4.       public ActionResult Index()
5.       {
6.           return View();
7.       }
8.       [VirtualDom]
9.       public ActionResult About()
10.      {
11.          ViewBag.Message = "Your application description page.";
12.          return View();
13.      }
```

```
14.     [VirtualDom]
15.     public ActionResult Contact()
16.     {
17.         ViewBag.Message = "Your contact page.";
18.         return View();
19.     }
20. }
```

Adding the `filter` attribute to the routes of the controller does not require modification of the regular application logic. It has no impact on the existing application logic of the controller. It can be turned on and off as needed.

With the `filter` attribute, the routers and views have no knowledge and relationship to the final output format. The output is the result of the content negotiation.

The Layout

The layout provides the overall page structure including the top navigation menu, the area for each page, and the footer (Listing 9-13).

Listing 9-13. Layout of the MVC SPA

```
1.  <!DOCTYPE html>
2.  <html>
3.  <head>
4.      <meta charset="utf-8" />
5.      <meta name="viewport" content="width=device-width, initial-scale=1.0">
6.      <title>@ViewBag.Title - My ASP.NET Application</title>
7.      @Styles.Render("~/Content/css")
8.      @Scripts.Render("~/bundles/modernizr")
9.  </head>
10. <body>
11.     <div class="navbar navbar-inverse navbar-fixed-top">
12.     <div class="container">
13.     <div class="navbar-header">
14.         <button type="button" class="navbar-toggle" data-
            toggle="collapse" data-target=".navbar-collapse">
15.             <span class="icon-bar"></span>
```

```
16.                <span class="icon-bar"></span>
17.                <span class="icon-bar"></span>
18.        </button>
19.        @Html.ActionLink("Application name", "Index", "Home", new
           { area = "" }, new { @class = "navbar-brand" })
20.        </div>
21.        <div class="navbar-collapse collapse">
22.            <ul class="nav navbar-nav">
23.                <li>@Html.ActionLink("Home", "Index", "Home")</li>
24.                <li><a href="/Home/About">About</a></li>
25.                <li><a href="/Home/Contact">Contact</a></li>
26.            </ul>
27.        </div>
28.        </div>
29.        </div>
30.        <div class="container body-content" id="my-app">
31.            @RenderBody()
32.        </div>
33.        <div class="container">
34.            <hr />
35.            <footer>
36.                <p>&copy; @DateTime.Now.Year - My ASP.NET Application</p>
37.        </footer>
38.        </div>
39.    @Scripts.Render("~/bundles/jquery")
40.    @Scripts.Render("~/bundles/bootstrap")
41.    @RenderSection("scripts", required: false)
42.    <script src="https://unpkg.com/apprun@latest/dist/apprun.js"></script>
43.    <!-- AppRun application for SPA -->
44.        <script>
45.            $.ajaxSetup({ cache: false });
46.            const get = url => new Promise((resolve, reject) => {
47.                $.getJSON(url)
48.                    .then(d => resolve(d))
49.                    .fail(e => reject(e))
50.            })
```

```
51.          window.addEventListener('popstate', (e) => {
52.              const path = document.location.pathname;
53.              app.run('/', path);
54.          });
55.          $('.navbar-nav li a').on('click', function (event) {
56.              event.preventDefault();
57.              $('.navbar-nav li a').removeClass('active');
58.              const menu = $(this).addClass('active')[0] ;
59.              history.pushState(null, ", menu.href);
60.              app.run('/', menu.pathname);
61.          });
62.          const view = (state) => state;
63.          const update = {
64.              '/': async (_, path) => {
65.                  const json = await get(path);
66.                  return json;
67.              }
68.          };
69.          app.start('my-app', null, view, update);
70.      </script>
71.  </body>
72.  </html>
```

The change to the layout is minimal. The original site structure has no difference. We only add a reference to AppRun (line 42) and an AppRun application for switching SSR to an SPA (lines 44–69). You can see the AppRun application is the same as the one (spa.js) in Listing 9-10.

To summarize, we have successfully changed a traditional SSR application developed with ASP.NET MVC into an SPA by using the virtual DOM filter and the client-side AppRun application (spa.js). The virtual DOM filter and the spa.js file are reusable for your projects.

We can apply the same technology to change an ASP.NET Core MVC application into an SPA. We have listed the GitHub project of an ASP.NET Core MVC SPA in the next section.

Source Code and Examples

You can get the source code of this chapter by cloning the GitHub project at `https://github.com/yysun/apprun-apress-book`. You can find the examples of this chapter using the `npm` scripts in Table 9-1.

Table 9-1. *npm Scripts of This Chapter*

Example	Script
The server-side rendering example	`npm run ssr`
The ASP.NET MVC middleware	`https://github.com/yysun/apprun-ssr-aspnet`
The ASP.NET Core MVC middleware	`https://github.com/yysun/apprun-ssr-aspnet-core`
The node/express middleware	`https://github.com/yysun/apprun-ssr-express`

Summary

AppRun is isomorphic/universal. The client-side AppRun components can render on the server side using the AppRun server-side view engine. The server-side application routes the requests to the AppRun events. The AppRun components handle the events and create the virtual DOM. The server-side application performs the content negotiation. In the case of SSR requests, the AppRun view engine outputs the fully rendered HTML. In the case of Ajax requests, the AppRun view engine outputs the virtual DOM as JSON. On the client side, a simple AppRun application alters the menu links and switches the application to the SPA mode.

To convert the traditional server-side rendered application into SPAs, we develop the middleware for the application platform. The middleware does the content negotiation to decide whether to output HTML or the virtual DOM on the server side. The same client-side application can turn traditional server-side rendered applications into SPAs.

The original application can be on any platform including but not limited to node.js, ASP.NET, and ASP.NET Core. You are welcome to use the techniques introduced in this chapter for other frameworks and platforms.

Starting from the SPA boilerplate (Chapter 7), we have developed the admin dashboard SPA (Chapter 8) and the SSR/SPA (this chapter). In the next chapter, we will develop an AppRun SPA that mimics a real-world line-of-business application that has authentication and full create, retrieve, update, and delete (CRUD) functionality.

CHAPTER 10

A Real-World SPA

RealWorld (`https://github.com/gothinkster/realworld`) is a project that demonstrates how to build a full-stack application by developing a blog application—a clone of medium.com, called Conduit.[1] Conduit has the following general functionality:

- Authenticate users via JWT (login/signup pages and logout button)

- CRU* users (sign-up and settings pages—no deleting required)

- CRUD articles

- CR*D comments on articles (no updating required)

- GET and display paginated lists of articles

- Mark articles as favorites

- Follow other users

RealWorld is meant to be the new TodoMVC. Its specifications include more functions than a to-do application. The RealWorld/Conduit back-end specification includes the following features: querying and persisting data to a database; an authentication system; session management; and full create, retrieve, update, and delete (CRUD) for resources. For the RealWorld/Conduit front-end specification, we'll build an API-based single-page web application. By implementing RealWorld, not only will we learn how to develop the application with AppRun, but we also can compare the AppRun application architecture frameworks and libraries such as React/Redux, React/MobX, Angular, Elm, Vue, and others.

In this chapter, we will use all the techniques introduced in the previous chapters to develop the RealWorld blogging application. In addition, you will learn about authentication and authorization, which is a commonly needed feature in the real-world

---

[1]You can see the live demo of Conduit at `https://demo.realworld.io`.

© Yiyi Sun 2019
Y. Sun, *Practical Application Development with AppRun*, https://doi.org/10.1007/978-1-4842-4069-4_10

application. You will also learn about using the state pattern of editing the data, using modal dialog for confirmation, and implementing error handling. Also, we will develop the application using statically typed data models and use the event decorator for event handlers.

Single-Page Application

The RealWorld project has published a standard design, which includes Ioncoin icons, Google fonts, and the Bootstrap 4 base theme CSS. The CSS produces the user interface's look and feel for all Conduit applications.

Conduit is a single-page application. The page has a page header, a main content area, and a page footer (see Figure 10-1). The front-end application runs inside the page. The footer content is static and contains the copyright information.

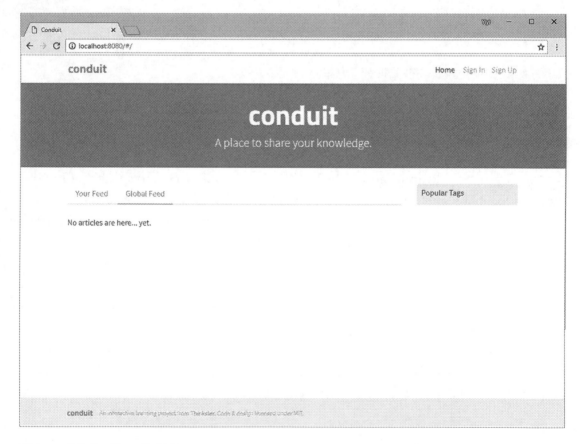

Figure 10-1. *Conduit home page*

There is only one HTML file, the index.html file (Listing 10-1).

Listing 10-1. index.html

```
1.   <!DOCTYPE html>
2.   <html>
3.   <head>
4.       <meta charset="utf-8">
5.       <title>Conduit</title>
6.       <!-- Import Ionicon icons & Google Fonts our Bootstrap theme
         relies on -->
7.       <link href="//code.ionicframework.com/ionicons/2.0.1/css/ionicons.
         min.css"
         rel="stylesheet" type="text/css">
8.       <link href="//fonts.googleapis.com/css?family=Titillium+Web:700
         |Source+Serif+Pro:400,700|Merriweather+Sans:400,700|Source+San
         s+Pro:400,300,600,700,300italic,400italic,600italic,700italic"
         rel="stylesheet" type="text/css">
9.       <!-- Import the custom Bootstrap 4 theme from our hosted CDN -->
10.      <link rel="stylesheet" href="//demo.productionready.io/main.css">
11.      <style>
12.          .modal-backdrop.show { opacity: 0.5;  z-index: 1040 !important; }
13.          .modal-open { position: absolute; width: 100% }
14.          .modal-dialog { z-index: 1100 !important; }
15.      </style>
16.  </head>
17.  <body>
18.      <nav class="navbar navbar-light">
19.          <div class="container">
20.              <a class="navbar-brand" href="#">conduit</a>
21.              <div id="header" />
22.          </div>
23.      </nav>
24.      <div id='my-app'></div>
25.      <script src='app.js'></script>
```

```
26.        <footer>
27.          <div class="container">
28.              <a href="#" class="logo-font">conduit</a>
29.              <span class="attribution">
30.                  An interactive learning project from <a
                     href="https://thinkster.io">Thinkster</a>.
                     Code & design licensed under MIT.
31.              </span>
32.          </div>
33.        </footer>
34.    </body>
35.    </html>
```

The `<div id="header">` node is the page header (line 21). The `<div id='my-app'>` node is the main section (line 24). The front-end application (line 25) updates the content of the header section and main section dynamically.

Page Header

The page header is the section on the top of the page. It displays the logo of Conduit. It also shows menu options in the top-right corner. The menu options are different for visitors versus registered users. The menus for visitors are Sign In and Sign Up (see Figure 10-2). The menus for the registered and signed-in users are New Post, Settings, Profile (shown as the username), and Sign Out (see Figure 10-3).

conduit   Home   Sign in   Sign Up

Figure 10-2. *The Home page menus for visitors*

conduit   Home   ☑ New Post   ⚙ Settings   user 1   Sign Out

Figure 10-3. *The Home page menus for signed-in users*

We will develop the HeaderComponent component and mount it to `<div id = "header">`.

Main Section

The main section displays all the functional pages of the applications. The pages are the Home page (see Figure 10-4), Sign In page (see Figure 10-5), Sign Up page (see Figure 10-6), Settings page (see Figure 10-7), Profile page (see Figure 10-8), Article page (see Figure 10-9), and Article Editor page (see Figure 10-10).

We will develop AppRun components and mount them to `<div id='my-app'>`. Every component is a mini-application that has the state, view, and update. If the view is complicated, we use a stateless component to break down the view into smaller and more manageable pieces.

The components are `HomeComponent`, `SigninComponent`, `RegisterComponent`, `SettingsComponent`, `ProfileComponent`, `ArticleComponent`, and `EditorComponent`.

Components

Each component implements client-side routing and standard user interaction functions as per the Conduit functional specification.

Home Page

The Home page (see Figure 10-4) displays all the articles or the articles by feed and by tag as a paginated list. Each article on the list has the hyperlink to the Article page and a hyperlink to the author's Profile page. It also has a button displaying how many times the article has being favorited. A button is enabled for the signed-in user to favorite or unfavorite the article.

The routes of the home page are as follows:

- All articles: `/#/`

- User article feed: `/#/feed`

- Articles by tag: `/#/tag/:name`

- Pagination for list of articles: `/#/(feed|tag)?/:page`

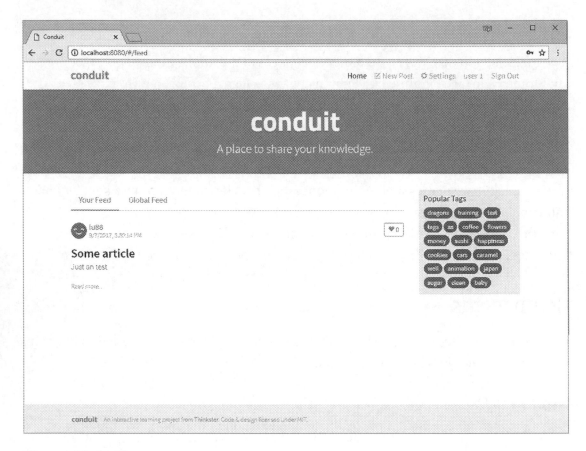

Figure 10-4. *Home page*

Sign In Page

The Sign In page (see Figure 10-5) allows the user to sign in using the back-end API. If the back-end authentication succeeds, it stores the security token returned from the server to the local storage. It then redirects to the original page. Otherwise, it displays an error message.

The route of the Sign In page is /#/login.

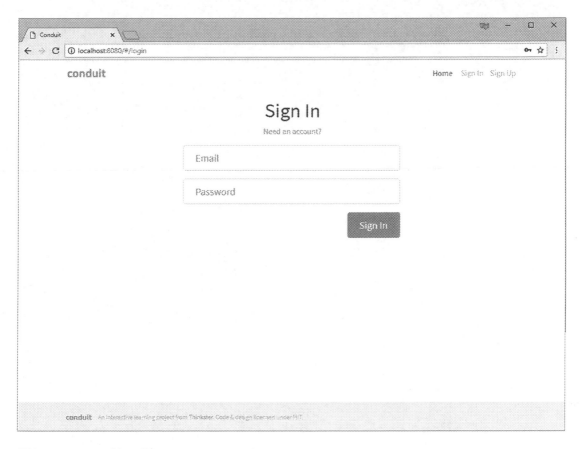

Figure 10-5.   *Sign In page*

Sign Up Page

The Sign Up page (see Figure 10-6) allows the user to register a user account. It redirects to the home page when the API call succeeds. Otherwise, it displays an error message.

The route of the Sign Up page is /#/register.

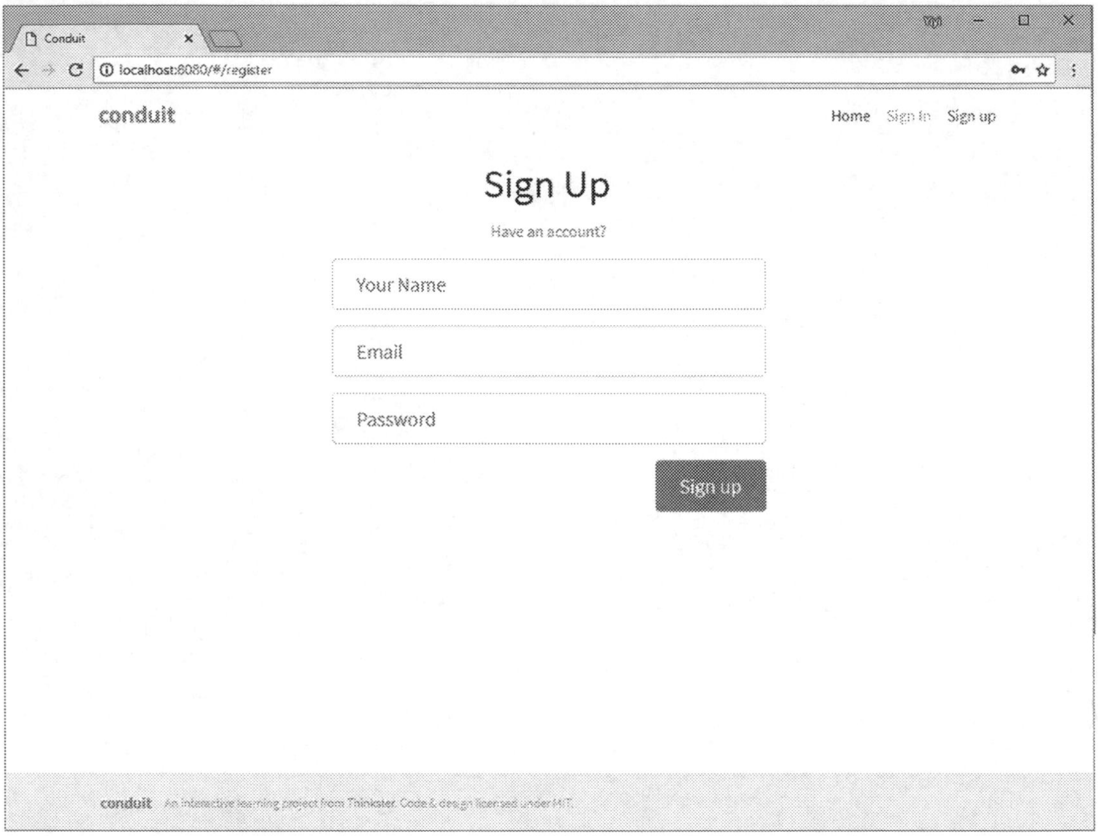

Figure 10-6. *Sign Up page*

Settings Page

The Settings page (see Figure 10-7) allows the user to set up a picture, e-mail, bio, and password. It redirects to the Home page when the API call succeeds. Otherwise, it displays an error message.

The route of the Settings page is /#/settings.

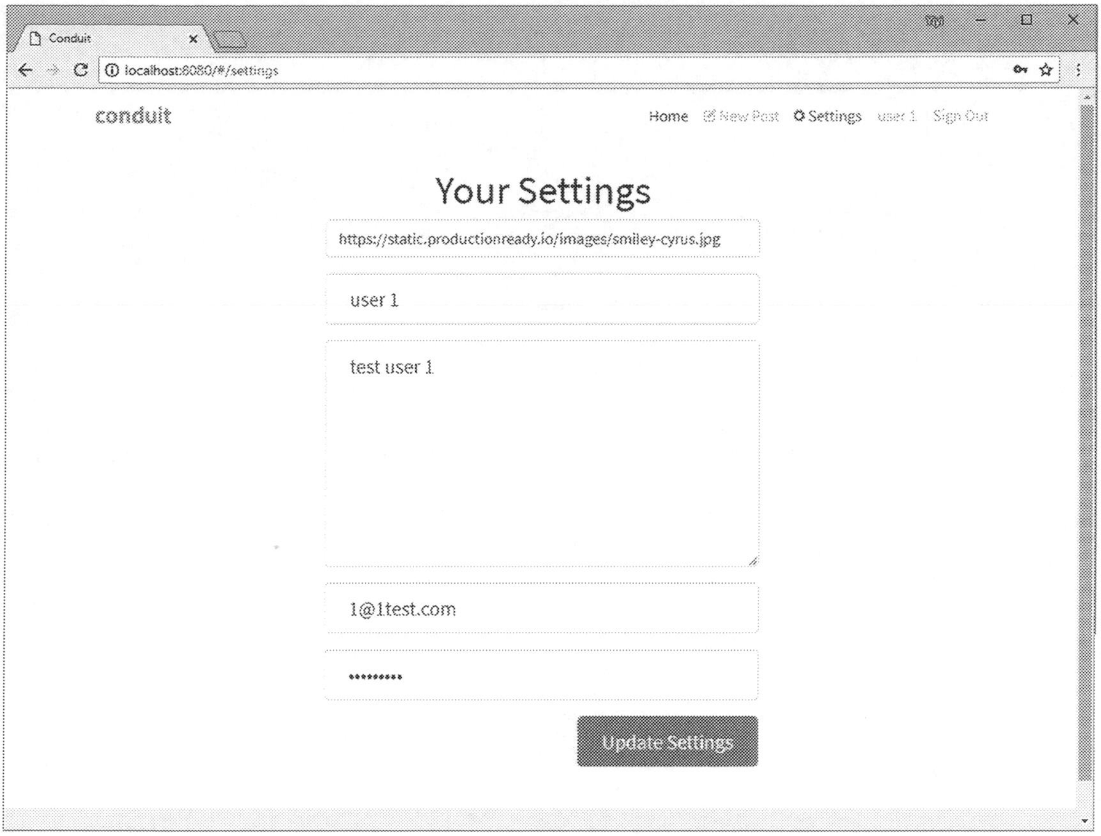

Figure 10-7. *Settings page*

Profile Page

The Profile page (see Figure 10-8) displays necessary information about the user. It also shows the articles authored and favorited by the user. For the signed-in user, it enables a button to follow the user.

The route of the Profile page is /#/profile/:username.

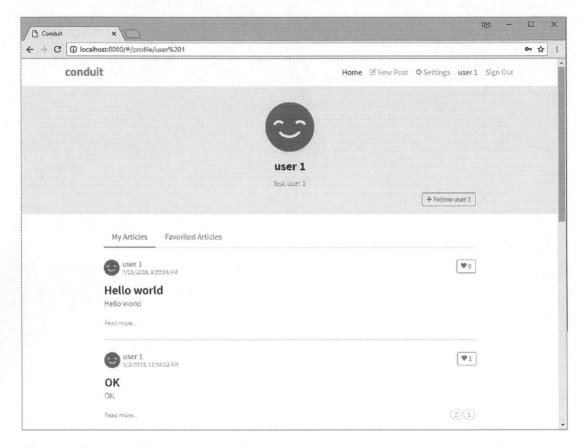

Figure 10-8. *Profile page*

Article Page

The Article page (see Figure 10-9) displays the selected article from the article lists including My articles, Favorited Articles on the Profile page, and My Feed and Global Feed on the Home page. It can render the Markdown format for the article body. It has many interaction functions, as follows:

- Edit and Delete article buttons for the article author

- Follow the author button for signed-in user, but not the article's author

- Favorite the article button for signed-in user, but not the article's author

- Display the comments of the article

- Add a new comment to the article

- Delete the comment button for the comment's author

The route of the Article page is /#/article/:article-slug.

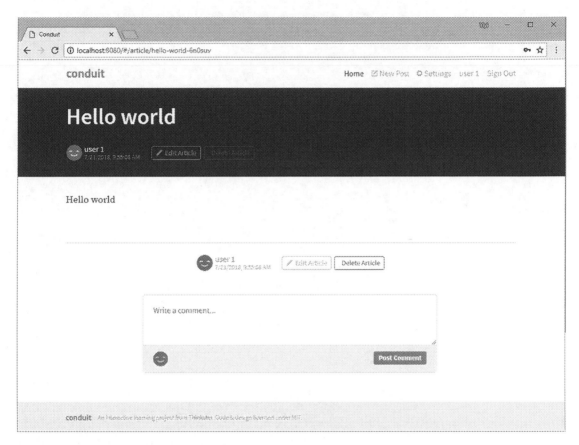

Figure 10-9. *Article page*

Editor Page

The editor (see Figure 10-10) page is used for creating new articles as well as editing articles. You get to this page when you click New Post and also when you click Edit Article on an article page. It has the HTML form to collect the article's title, description, body, and tags (separated by commas). It has a button to create or update the article. If the API call fails, it displays an error message.

The routes of the Editor page are as follows:

- *New article page*: /#/editor

- *Article editor page*: /#/editor/:article-slug

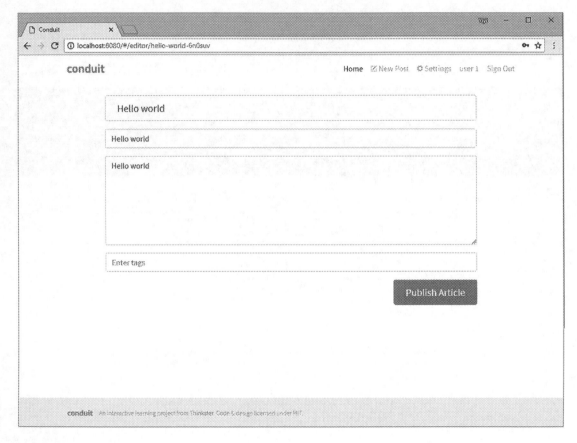

Figure 10-10. *Editor page*

The Main Program

Each of the application pages is an AppRun component. The main program imports all components and routes the AppRun routing events to the components (Listing 10-2).

Listing 10-2. The Main Program

```
1.    import app from 'apprun';
2.    import './components/header';
3.    import './components/home';
```

```
4.    import './components/signin';
5.    import './components/register';
6.    import './components/profile';
7.    import './components/settings';
8.    import './components/editor';
9.    import './components/article';
10.   app.on('#', async (route, ...p) => {
11.       app.run(`#/${route || "}`, ...p);
12.   })
13.   app.run('/get-user');
```

The default AppRun routing event convention is to support the routes with a hash sign, as in #/, #/article, #profile, and so on. This is different from the Conduit convention. The Conduit convention has an extra slash sign, as in /#/, /#/article, /#/ profile, and so on. We can easily translate AppRun routing events into the Conduit convention (line 11).

After importing all the components, the main program publishes the /get-user event to load the current user.

Back-End API

The RealWorld project has more than 20 back-end servers implementing the RealWorld specification, which includes the standardized data models and API.

Core Data Models

The data models of the RealWorld specification include User, Profile, Article, Comment, and Tag. We define them using the TypeScript interface (Listing 10-3).

Listing 10-3. Data Models

```
1.    export interface IUser {
2.        username: string;
3.        bio: string;
4.        image: string;
5.        following: boolean;
6.    }
```

```
7.   export interface IProfile extends IUser {
8.       email: string;
9.       token: string;
10.  }

11.  export interface IArticle {
12.      slug: string;
13.      title: string;
14.      description: string;
15.      body: string;
16.      createdAt: Date;
17.      updatedAt: Date;
18.      favorited: boolean;
19.      favoritesCount: number;
20.      author: IAuthor;
21.      tagList: Array<string>;
22.  }

23.  export interface IComment {
24.      id: number;
25.      body: string;
26.      createdAt: string;
27.      author: IAuthor;
28.  }

29.  export type ITag = string;
```

API Data Models

The RealWorld API specification uses the request-response pattern. We need a few more data types to model the API (Listing 10-4).

Listing 10-4. API Data Models

```
1.   export interface IAuthResponse {
2.       user: IUser
3.   }
```

```
4.    export interface ITags {
5.        tags: Array<string>;
6.    }

7.    export interface IFeed {
8.        articles: Array<IArticle>;
9.        articlesCount: number;
10.   }

11.   export interface IArticlesRequest {
12.       tag?: string;
13.       author?: string;
14.       favorited?: string;
15.       limit: number;
16.       offset: number;
17.   }

18.   export interface INewArticle {
19.       title: string,
20.       description: string,
21.       body: string,
22.       tagList: Array<string>;
23.   }

24.   export interface IArticlesResponse {
25.       article: IArticle
26.   }

27.   export interface ICommentsResponse {
28.       comments: Array<IComment>
29.   }

30.   export interface IProfileResponse {
31.       profile: IProfile
32.   }
```

API Layer

We have introduced the technique of breaking the API access logic into the API layer and fetch wrappers introduced in Chapter 6.

We create an API layer where we group the Conduit API functions into several API namespaces such as auth, articles, comments, profile, and tags. Also, we make the API namespaces static typing by using the core data models and the API data models (Listing 10-5).

Listing 10-5. API Namespaces

```
1.   export const auth = {
2.       current: () => getToken() ? get<IUser>('/user') : null,
3.       signIn: (user: { email: string, password: string }) =>
4.           post< IUser >('/users/login', { user }),
5.       register: (user: { username: string, email: string, password:
         string }) =>
6.           post< IUser >('/users', { user }),
7.       save: user => put('/user', { user }),
8.       authorized: () => {
9.           return app['user'] ? true : app.run('#/login');
10.      }
11.  }

12.  export const articles = {
13.      search: (request: IArticlesRequest) =>
14.          get<IFeed>(`/articles?${toQueryString(request)}`),
15.      feed: (request: {limit: number, offset: number}) =>
16.          get<IFeed>(`/articles/feed?${toQueryString(request)}`),
17.      get: (slug: string) =>
18.          get<IArticlesResponse>(`/articles/${slug}`),
19.      delete: (slug: string) =>
20.          del(`/articles/${slug}`),
21.      favorite: (slug: string) =>
22.          post(`/articles/${slug}/favorite`),
23.      unfavorite: (slug: string) =>
24.          del(`/articles/${slug}/favorite`),
```

```
25.      update: (article: IArticle) =>
26.          put(`/articles/${article.slug}`, { article }),
27.      create: (article: INewArticle) =>
28.          post<IArticlesResponse>('/articles', { article })
29.  }

30.  export const comments = {
31.      create: (slug: string, comment: { body: string }) =>
32.          post(`/articles/${slug}/comments`, { comment }),
33.      delete: (slug: string, commentId: string) =>
34.          del(`/articles/${slug}/comments/${commentId}`),
35.      forArticle: (slug: string) =>
36.          get<ICommentsResponse>(`/articles/${slug}/comments`)
37.  };

38.  export const profile = {
39.      get: (username: string) =>
40.          get<IProfileResponse>(`/profiles/${username}`),
41.      follow: (username: string) =>
42.          post<IProfileResponse>(`/profiles/${username}/follow`),
43.      unfollow: (username: string) =>
44.          del(`/profiles/${username}/follow`)
45.  };

46.  export const tags = {
47.      all: () => get<ITags>('/tags')
48.  }
```

The API functions use the functions get<T>, post<T>, del<T>, and put<T>. They are the statically typed wrappers of the browser fetch function (Listing 10-6).

Listing 10-6. Fetch Wrappers

```
1.   export async function fetchAsync(method: 'GET' | 'POST' | 'DELETE' |
     'PUT', url: string, body?: any) {
2.       const headers = { 'Content-Type': 'application/json; charset=utf-8' };
3.       if (access_token) headers['Authorization'] = `Token ${access_token}`;
```

```
4.          const response = await window['fetch'](`${defaultBasePath}${url}`, {
5.              method,
6.              headers,
7.              body: body && JSON.stringify(body)
8.          });
9.          if (response.status === 401) throw new Error('401');
10.         const result = await response.json();
11.         if (!response.ok) throw result;
12.         return result;
13.     }

14.     export function get<T>(url: string): Promise<T> {
15.         return fetchAsync('GET', url);
16.     }

17.     export function post<T>(url: string, body?: any): Promise<T> {
18.         return fetchAsync('POST', url, body);
19.     }

20.     export function del(url: string) {
21.         return fetchAsync('DELETE', url);
22.     }

23.     export function put(url: string, body?: any) {
24.         return fetchAsync('PUT', url, body);
25.     }
```

The fetchAsync function wrapper sets the content type in the HTTP header to application/json; charset=utf-8 to let the back-end server send back the data in JSON format (line 2). It also sets the authorization in the HTTP header using the security token obtained after the successful user sign-in (line 3).

Authentication

Conduit allows anonymous access for reading articles, and authenticated users can submit and edit articles. The API authorizes a user's permission by verifying the security token in the HTTP header. The security token is issued from the server when the user is signed in using the sign-in page. The security token is saved to local storage.

Get User

Because the security token is saved to local storage, when the application starts, the main program publishes the /get-user event to reload the signed-in user information. The event is handled in api.ts as one of the global events (Listing 10-7).

Listing 10-7. Getting the Current User

```
1.   app.on('/get-user', async () => {
2.       try {
3.           const current = await auth.current();
4.           if (current) app.run('/set-user', current.user);
5.       } catch {
6.           setToken(null);
7.           document.location.reload(true);
8.       }
9.   });
```

The event handler calls the auth.current() function to retrieve the user. If it successfully gets the user, it publishes another global event, /set-user. If the saved token is not valid and the auth.current() API call fails, it clears the token and reloads the page.

Set User

The /set-user event is handled in two places. First, it is handled in HeaderComponent, where the component displays the menus accordingly (Listing 10-8).

Listing 10-8. Setting the User in the Page Header

```
1.   view = state => {
2.       {user && <a>New Post</a>}
3.       {user && <a>Settings</a>}
4.       {user ? ": <a>Sign In</a>}
5.       {user ? " : <a>Register</a>}
6.       {user && <a>{state.user.username}</a>}
7.   }
```

The /set-user event is handled in api.ts, where the event handler stores the user globally and sets the security token to the fetch module and local storage (Listings 10-9 and 10-10).

Listing 10-9. Setting the User in the API Module

```
1.    app.on('/set-user', user => {
2.    app['user'] = user;
3.    setToken(user ? user.token : null);
4.    });
```

Listing 10-10. Setting the User in the Fetch Module

```
1.    export function setToken(token: string) {
2.        access_token = token;
3.        if (!window.localStorage) return;
4.        if (token)
5.            window.localStorage.setItem('jwt', token);
6.        else
7.            window.localStorage.removeItem('jwt');
8.    }
```

Authorization

The /set-user event stores the authenticated user globally in the app object. The globally saved user is used for authorization. The auth.authorized() function verifies the global user (Listing 10-11).

Listing 10-11. Authorization Function

```
1.    export const auth = {
2.        authorized: () => {
3.            return app['user'] ? true : app.run('#/login');
4.        }
5.    }
```

Whenever we need authorization, we call the `auth.authorized()` function. For example, on the home page, the personal feed is available only to the signed-in user. It requires authorization (Listing 10-12).

Listing 10-12. Authorization of Personal Feed

```
1.    switch (type) {
2.        case 'feed':
3.            if (!auth.authorized()) return { ...state, articles: [], max: 0};
4.            feed = await articles.feed({ limit, offset });
5.            break;
6.        case 'tag':
7.            feed = await articles.search({ tag, limit, offset });
8.            break;
9.        default:
10.           feed = await articles.search({ limit, offset });
11.           break;
12.   }
```

The authorization function publishes the #/login event to bring out the Sign In page in case the user fails to sign in.

Sign-In

The #/login event activates SigninComponent. It saves the return-to route and calls the API function auth.signIn with the username and password (Listing 10-13).

Listing 10-13. Sign-in Component

```
1.    import app, { Component, on } from 'apprun';
2.    import { auth, serializeObject } from '../api'
3.    import Errors from './error-list';

4.    class SigninComponent extends Component {
5.        state = {}
6.        view = (state) => {
7.            return <div className="auth-page">
8.                <div className="container page">
```

```
9.                  <div className="row">
10.                 <div className="col-md-6 offset-md-3 col-xs-12">
11.                 <h1 className="text-xs-center">Sign In</h1>
12.                 <p className="text-xs-center">
13.                     <a href="#/register">Need an account?</a>
14.                 </p>
15.                 {state.errors && <Errors errors={state.errors} />}
16.                 <form onsubmit={e => this.run('sign-in', e)}>
17.                     <fieldset className="form-group">
18.                         <input className="form-control form-control-lg"
                            type="text"
                              placeholder="Email" name="email" />
19.                     </fieldset>
20.                     <fieldset className="form-group">
21.                     <input className="form-control form-control-lg"
                        type="password"
                                placeholder="Password" name="password" />
22.                     </fieldset>
23.                     <button className="btn btn-lg btn-primary pull-xs-
                        right">
24.                         Sign In
25.                     </button>
26.                 </form>
27.                 </div>
28.                 </div>
29.         </div>
30.         </div>
31.     }

32.     @on('#/login')
33.     login = state => ({ ...state, messages: [], returnTo: document.
        location.hash })

34.     @on('sign-in')
35.     signIn = async (state, e) => {
```

```
36.          try {
37.              e.preventDefault();
38.              const session = await auth.signIn(serializeObject(e.target));
39.              app.run('/set-user', session.user);
40.              const returnTo: string = (state.returnTo || "").replace
                 (/\#\/login\/?/, ")
41.              if (!returnTo)
42.                  document.location.hash = '#/feed';
43.              else {
44.                  app.run('route', returnTo);
45.                  history.pushState(null, null, returnTo);
46.              }
47.          } catch ({ errors }) {
48.              return { ...state, errors }
49.          }
50.      }

51.      @on('#/logout')
52.      logout = state => {
53.          app.run('/set-user', null);
54.          document.location.hash = '#/';
55.      }
56.  }

57.  export default new SigninComponent().mount('my-app')
```

When the user sign-in succeeds, SigninComponent publishes the /set-user event to update the menu in HeaderComponent and the security token in the API module (line 39). It also reroutes to the return-to route. If the user sign-in fails, it sets the error messages into the state (line 48), which will be displayed in the view function (line 15).

Sign-Out

The SigninComponent component also has the #/logout event handler (lines 51–55). It sets the current user to null and redirects the user to the home page.

Event Decorator

The event handlers in SigninComponent use the on decorators. A decorator is an ECMAScript 2018 feature that is already supported by the TypeScript compiler. You need to enable the experimentalDecorators flag in the tsconfig.json file for using the decorators.

The decorator is the syntax sugar that makes the code easier to read. The event handlers using the decorators (Listing 10-14) are the same as those that use the update object (Listing 10-15).

Listing 10-14. Event Handlers Using Decorators

```
1.   the class extends Component {
2.       @('/#login') login = ()=> {}
3.       @('/#logout'): logout = ()=> {}
4.       @('sign-in'):  signout=()=> {}
5.   }
```

Listing 10-15. Event Handlers in Update

```
1.   class extends Component {
2.       update = {
3.           '/#login': ()=> {},
4.           '/#logout': ()=> {},
5.           'sign-in': ()=> {}
6.       }
7.   }
```

Modal Dialog

Applications often require a modal dialog to confirm a user interaction and notify the user of the result of the interaction. We can create a generic model component using the Bootstrap classes (Listing 10-16).

Listing 10-16. Modal Dialog

```
1.    import app from 'apprun';
2.    export default function ({ title, body, ok, cancel, onOK, onCancel }) {
3.        return <div className="modal-open">
4.            <div className="modal-dialog" role="document">
5.                <div className="modal-content">
6.                    <div className="modal-header">
7.                        <h5 className="modal-title">{title}
8.                            <button type="button" className="close"
                             data-dismiss="modal"
                                 aria-label="Close" onclick={e =>
                                 onCancel(e)}>
9.                                <span aria-hidden="true">×</span>
10.                           </button>
11.                       </h5>
12.                   </div>
13.                   <div className="modal-body">
14.                       <p>{body}</p>
15.                   </div>
16.                   <div className="modal-footer">
17.                       {cancel && <button type="button"
                          className="btn btn-secondary"
                              data-dismiss="modal" onclick={e =>
                              onCancel(e)}>
18.                           {cancel}
19.                       </button>}  
20.                       <button type="button" className="btn btn-primary"
                             onclick={e => onOK(e)}>
21.                           {ok}
22.                       </button>
23.                   </div>
24.               </div>
25.           </div>
```

```
26.              <div className="modal-backdrop show" onclick={e =>
             onCancel(e)}></div>
27.      </div>
28.  }
```

ModalComponent is a stateless component. It accepts the dialog title, the dialog body, the OK button caption, and the Cancel button caption. It also takes two callback functions: onOK and onCancel. The onOK and onCancel functions are called when the user clicks the OK or Cancel button.

We use ArticleComponent as the example to demonstrate the Modal component (Listing 10-17). The application prompts a modal dialog to confirm with the user when the user clicks the button to delete an article (see Figure 10-11).

Listing 10-17. Article Component (Simplified)

```
1.   class ArticleComponent extends Component {
2.       state = { /* article */ }
3.       view = (state) => {
4.           return <div className="article-page">
5.           {
6.               state.deleting ? <Modal title='Delete Article'
7.               body='Are you sure you want to delete this article?'
8.               ok='Delete' cancel='No'
9.               onOK={e => this.run('ok-delete-article', e)}
10.              onCancel={e => this.run('cancel-delete-article', e)} /> : "
11.          }
12.              <div className="banner">
13.                  <div className="container">
14.                      {/* code to display the article */}
15.                  </div>
16.          </div>
17.      }

18.      @on('#/article')
19.      root = async (state, slug) => { /* load article */}

20.      @on('delete-article')
21.      deleteArticle = (state, article) => ({ ...state, deleting: true })
```

```
22.      @on('ok-delete-article')
23.      okDelete = (state, e) => {
24.          articles.delete(state.article.slug);
25.          document.location.hash = '#/';
26.      }

27.      @on('cancel-delete-article')
28.      cancelDelete = (state, article) => ({ ...state, deleting: false })
29. }

30. export default new ArticleComponent().mount('my-app')
```

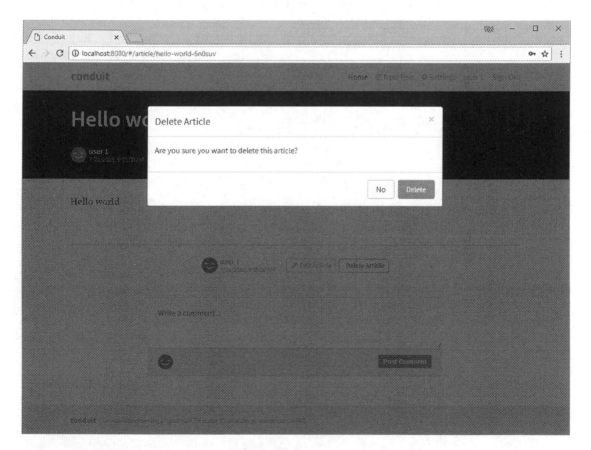

Figure 10-11. *Article deletion confirmation*

To display the modal dialog, `ArticleComponent` sets the deleting property to true in the state when the user clicked the delete button (line 21). The view function displays the `Modal` component when the deleting property is true (lines 5–11). When the user clicks the OK button, the `Modal` component calls the `onOK` callback function, which then publishes the `ok-delete-article` event to do the deletion.

Similarly, when the user clicks the Cancel button, the `Modal` component calls the `onCancel` callback function, which then publishes the `cancel-delete-article` event. In the cancellation case, `ArticleComponent` sets the deletion property to false. The `view` function does not display the modal dialog.

To summarize, we do not delete the article right away when the user clicks the delete button. We add a confirmation step by using a deletion property to display the modal dialog. It is easy to implement the deletion confirmation using `ModalComponent`.

`ModalComponent` is used in other components of the example application. You can use it in your applications too.

Live Demo and Source Code

The AppRun RealWorld example application is live at `https://gothinkster.github.io/apprun-realworld-example-app`.

You can get the source code from the GitHub project at `https://github.com/gothinkster/apprun-realworld-example-app`.

Summary

In this chapter, we discussed several important design concepts used in developing the AppRun RealWorld example application, including the project structure, components, routes of the components, and back-end API data model. We demonstrated the authentication/authorization and modal dialog features. We only explained `SigninComponent` and `ModalComponent` in detail, because other components use the patterns and techniques introduced in the previous chapter. Combining the knowledge of this chapter and previous chapters, you can build a line-of-business application in the real world.

The RealWorld example applications is a complicated application. In addition to building the application, we will test the application and verify it in the next two chapters.

CHAPTER 11

Unit Testing

Unit testing is a software development process in which the smallest testable parts of an application, called *units*, are individually and independently scrutinized for proper operation.[1] Many companies and teams apply the test-driven development (TDD) process. Unit testing is important to these companies and teams.

The AppRun architecture is unit test–oriented. The three architectural parts—the state, view, and update (event handlers)—are decoupled and easy to test. In AppRun application development, there are two types of unit test. The first type is the white-box test, which is to test the events and the states. The testing process can be generalized as publishing the events and asserting the states. The second type of unit testing is the black-box test, which is to set the states and assert the virtual DOM output of the `view` function.

We will use the AppRun RealWorld example application developed in Chapter 10 to demonstrate unit testing techniques. Let's start with the testing framework and a few patterns of writing unit tests that are useful for testing AppRun applications.

Jest Framework

The AppRun development environment includes the Jest framework (`https://jestjs.io`). The convention to run the tests is to use the `npm` script.

```
npm run jest
```

We can also run the Jest testing interactive mode using the `npm` script.

```
npm test
```

Jest watches for file changes and runs the test files only on changed files. Jest quickly executes the tests in parallel. The interactive way for us to define which tests to be executed is during the watch mode. Listing 11-1 shows the available Jest usage options.

---

[1]`https://searchsoftwarequality.techtarget.com/definition/unit-testing`

© Yiyi Sun 2019
Y. Sun, *Practical Application Development with AppRun*, https://doi.org/10.1007/978-1-4842-4069-4_11

Listing 11-1. Jest Usage

```
Watch Usage
 › Press a to run all tests.
 › Press f to run only failed tests.
 › Press p to filter by a filename regex pattern.
 › Press t to filter by a test name regex pattern.
 › Press u to update failing snapshots.
 › Press i to update failing snapshots interactively.
 › Press q to quit watch mode.
 › Press Enter to trigger a test run.
```

By typing only one character, we can choose to run all tests, failed tests, tests in files matching a regex pattern, or tests that have names matching a regex pattern. It is a pleasure to write and run tests using Jest.

We can open the component file being tested, the unit test file, and the integrated terminal side by side in Visual Studio Code (see Figure 11-1).

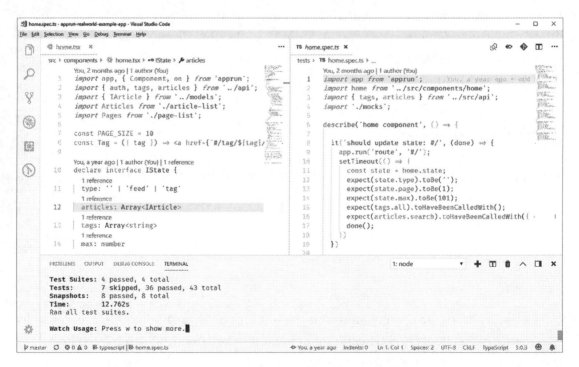

Figure 11-1. *Interactive unit testing in Visual Studio Code*

The home component source file is in the left panel. The unit test code file is in the middle panel. The terminal window is in the right panel. We run Jest in the terminal window, where Jest monitors the file changes and executes the relevant tests automatically.

Test Suites and Tests

The default folder to store the source code of the tests is named __tests__. JavaScript and TypeScript files are treated as the source code of tests. Also, JavaScript and TypeScript files that are named as *.spec.js, *.spec.jsx, *.spec.ts, or *.spec.tsx in any other folders are treated as the source code of the tests.

We write unit tests using syntax like the Jasmine unit testing framework and organize them into test suites (Listing 11-2).

Listing 11-2. Test Suites and Tests

```
1.   describe('home component', () => {
2.       it('should update state: #/', () => {
3.       /* unit test code*/
4.       });
5.   });
```

The describe() function defines the test suites. The it() function defines the test. Usually we group the tests by AppRun component. Each test suite is for one AppRun component. We do not mix tests for different components into one test suite. Jest reports the testing results by component (Listing 11-3).

Listing 11-3. Jest Testing Results

```
HeaderComponent
    √ should handle the event: /set-user (13ms)
  HomeComponent
    √ should handle the event: #/ (5ms)
    √ should handle the event: #/feed (4ms)
    √ should handle the event: #/tag (2ms)
    √ should handle the event: update-article (1ms)
```

SigninComponent
  √ should handle the event: #/login (3ms)
  √ should handle the event: #/logout (3ms)
  √ should handle the event: sign-in (2ms)
RegisterComponent
  √ should handle the event: #/register (2ms)
  √ should handle the event: register (2ms)
ProfileComponent
  √ should handle the event: #/profile (2ms)
  √ should handle the event: update-article
  √ should handle the event: update-follow (1ms)
SettingsComponent
  √ should handle event: #/settings (1ms)
  √ should handle event: submit-settings (1ms)
  ○ skipped 2 tests
EditorComponent
  √ should handle event: #/editor (1ms)
  √ should handle event: submit-article (1ms)
ArticleComponent
  √ should handle event: #/article (4ms)
  √ should handle event: /new-comment (3ms)
  √ should handle event: update-article (2ms)
  √ should handle event: delete-article
  ○ skipped 5 tests

Test Coverage

We can have Jest report the test coverage by adding the --coverage option to the npm script (Listing 11-4).

```
npm run jest -- --coverage
```

Listing 11-4. Jest Testing Coverage

```
-------------------|----------|----------|----------|----------|-------------------|
File               | % Stmts  | % Branch | % Funcs  | % Lines  | Uncovered Line #s |
-------------------|----------|----------|----------|----------|-------------------|
All files          |   62.85  |   51.74  |   42.65  |   62.72  |                   |
 src               |   28.18  |   13.46  |    9.09  |   29.17  |                   |
  api.ts           |   32.73  |      25  |    8.33  |   34.04  |... 31,132,133,134 |
  fetch.ts         |   23.64  |      10  |   11.11  |   24.49  |... 74,76,78,79,84 |
 src/components     |   70.51  |   64.63  |   59.04  |   70.98  |                   |
  article-list.tsx |   90.91  |     100  |      80  |   88.89  |                17 |
  article-meta.tsx |   63.64  |      50  |      20  |      60  |      20,24,30,37  |
  article.tsx      |    62.5  |   63.64  |   42.86  |   64.71  |... 97,103,104,105 |
  comment-list.tsx |   54.55  |    12.5  |      20  |      50  |       5,6,25,39,54 |
  editor.tsx       |   54.29  |      40  |      80  |   51.72  |... 64,65,66,67,68 |
  error-list.tsx   |      40  |     100  |       0  |      50  |               4,5 |
  header.tsx       |     100  |      60  |     100  |     100  | 11,17,23,27,31,35 |
  home.tsx         |   94.55  |      88  |      90  |   93.02  |       102,103,115 |
  modal.tsx        |   15.38  |       0  |       0  |   28.57  |       4,9,19,21,25 |
  page-list.tsx    |     100  |     100  |     100  |     100  |                   |
  profile.tsx      |   72.09  |   77.27  |      75  |   72.22  |... 78,79,80,81,94 |
  register.tsx     |      75  |   77.78  |      80  |   78.95  |       23,49,50,51 |
  settings.tsx     |    69.7  |   72.73  |      50  |   67.86  |... 68,69,70,71,78 |
  signin.tsx       |   67.74  |   53.85  |   83.33  |   69.23  |... 53,54,55,57,58 |
 tests             |   96.88  |     100  |      30  |     100  |                   |
  mocks.ts         |   96.88  |     100  |      30  |     100  |                   |
-------------------|----------|----------|----------|----------|-------------------|
```

Asynchronous Tests

When testing the asynchronous code, such as AppRun asynchronous event handlers, we use the done function callback (Listing 11-5).

Listing 11-5. done Callback

```
1.   it('should update state: #//2', (done) => {
2.       setTimeout(() => {
3.           /* unit test code */
4.           done();
5.       });
6.   });
```

We use setTimeout to schedule the test code execution. Jest waits until we call the done function.

Mock API

During the testing, we don't want to call the back-end server. We need to mock the API functions (Listing 11-6).

Listing 11-6. Mocking the API Functions

```
1.    import { auth, tags, articles, comments, profile } from '../src/api';
2.    auth.current = jest.fn(() => null);
3.    auth.signIn = jest.fn(() => { });
4.    auth.register = jest.fn(() => { });
5.    auth.save = jest.fn(() => { });
6.    tags.all = jest.fn(() => ({ tags: [1, 2, 3] }));
7.    articles.search = jest.fn(() => ({ articles: [], articlesCount: 10 }));
8.    articles.feed = jest.fn(() => ({ articles: [], articlesCount: 5 }));
9.    articles.get = jest.fn((slug) => ({
10.       article: {
11.           slug,
12.           author: {},
13.           title: ",
14.           body: ",
15.           tagList: []
16.       },
17.   }));
```

```
18.   articles.delete = jest.fn(() => { });
19.   articles.favorite = jest.fn(() => { });
20.   articles.unfavorite = jest.fn(() => { });
21.   articles.update = jest.fn(() => { });
22.   articles.create = jest.fn(() => { });
23.   comments.create = jest.fn(() => { });
24.   comments.delete = jest.fn(() => { });
25.   comments.forArticle = jest.fn(() => ({ comments: [] }));
26.   profile.get = jest.fn(() => { });
27.   profile.follow = jest.fn(() => { });
28.   profile.unfollow = jest.fn(() => { });
```

Mock functions[2] replace the actual implementation of functions. The mocked API functions will not call the back-end server. Also, the mocked functions can capture calls to the functions (and the parameters passed in those calls) and can return values. For example, `tags.all` (line 6), `articles.search` (line 7), `articles.feed` (line 8), and `articles.get` (lines 9–17) return the data values to the caller functions.

In Chapter 6, we recommended building the data access logic using an API layer that has the API namespaces on top of the `fetch` module. Now, we can reveal the reason is that we can mock the API functions.

Building the data access logic using the API layer and the API namespaces lets us mock the API functions for unit testing.

Testing Events

To demonstrate the patterns of writing Jest unit tests, we will test the event handling of the home component.

The home component displays the article list of three types: all articles, personal feed, or articles of a tag. It also displays the list of tags and the list of pages for pagination. Listing 11-7 shows the data model of the state.

---

[2]https://jestjs.io/docs/en/mock-functions

Listing 11-7. Data Model of the Home Component State

```
declare interface IState {
  type: " | 'feed' | 'tag'
  articles: Array<IArticle>
  tags: Array<string>
  max: number
  page: number
}
```

We define the testing plan shown in Table 12-1.

Table 12-1. *Home Component Route Test Plan*

Route	Expectations
#/	The default route of the home page should display the first ten articles. It is an asynchronous event. • The component state should have a type property of " (an empty string). • The component should call `tags.all` to retrieve tags. • The component should call `articles.search` to retrieve tags in order to retrieve ten articles for the first page. • The component state should have a page property of 1. • The component state should have `max` set to 101 (returned by the mock function).
#//2	This route should display the second ten articles. It is also an asynchronous event. • The component state should have a type property of ". • The component should call `tags.all` to retrieve tags. • The component should call `articles.search` to find ten articles for the second page (offset 10). • The component state should have a page property of 2. • The component state should have `max` set to 101 (returned by the mock function).
#/feed	This route is available only for the signed-in user. • It should publish the #/login event. • It should not call the `articles.feed` function.

(continued)

Table 12-1. (*continued*)

Route	Expectations
#/feed/3	Assuming the user is signed in, this route displays the third page of the user's feed. • The component state should have the type of property be `'feed'`. • The component should call `tags.all` to retrieve tags. • The component should call `articles.feed` to retrieve ten articles for the third page (offset 20). • The component state should have a `page` property of 1 (the last page of the total five articles). • The component state should have `max` set to 5 (returned by the mock function).
/#/tag	This route displays the first page of articles with no tags. • The component state should have a type property of `'tag'`. • The component state should have the `tag` property be undefined. • The component should call `tags.all` to retrieve tags. • The component should call `articles.search` to retrieve ten articles without tags. • The component state should have `page` be 1. • The component state should have `max` be 100 (returned by the mock function).
/#/tag/t2	This route displays the first page of articles that have a tag of `'t2'`. • The component state should have the type property be `'tag'`. • The component state should have the tag property be `'t2'`. • The component should call `tags.all` to retrieve tags. • The component should call `articles.search` to retrieve ten articles that have the tag `'t2'`. • The component state should have the `page` property be 1. • The component state should have `max` be 101 (returned by the mock function).
/#/tag/t3/20	This route displays the 20th page of articles that have the tag `'t3'`. • The component state should have a type property of `'tag'`. • The component state should have a tag property of `'t3'`. • The component should call `tags.all` to retrieve tags. • The component should call `articles.search` to retrieve ten articles that have the tag `'t3'`. • The component state should have the `page` property be 11 (the last page of the total 101 articles). • The component state should have `max` be 101 (returned by the mock function).

We can develop the tests for the home components as shown in Listing 11-8.

Listing 11-8. Home Component Test

```
1.    import app from 'apprun';
2.    import home from '../src/components/home';
3.    import { tags, articles } from '../src/api';
4.    import './mocks';
5.    describe('home component', () => {
6.        it('should update state: #/', (done) => {
7.            app.run('route', '#/');
8.            setTimeout(() => {
9.                const state = home.state;
10.               expect(state.type).toBe('');
11.               expect(state.page).toBe(1);
12.               expect(state.max).toBe(101);
13.               expect(tags.all).toHaveBeenCalledWith();
14.               expect(articles.search).toHaveBeenCalledWith({ offset: 0,
                  limit: 10 });
15.               done();
16.           })
17.       })

18.       it('should update state: #//2', (done) => {
19.           app.run('route', '#//2');
20.           setTimeout(() => {
21.               const state = home.state;
22.               expect(state.type).toBe('');
23.               expect(state.page).toBe(2);
24.               expect(state.max).toBe(101);
25.               expect(tags.all).toHaveBeenCalledWith();
26.               expect(articles.search).toHaveBeenCalledWith({ offset: 10,
                  limit: 10 });
27.               done();
28.           })
29. })
```

```
30.      it('should not call #/feed w/o user', () => {
31.          const login = jest.fn();
32.          app.on('#/login', login);
33.          app.run('route', '#/feed');
34.          expect(login).toHaveBeenCalled();
35.          expect(articles.feed).not.toHaveBeenCalled();
36.      })

37.      it('should update state: #/feed/3', (done) => {
38.          app['user'] = {};
39.          app.run('route', '#/feed/3');
40.          setTimeout(() => {
41.              const state = home.state;
42.              expect(state.type).toBe('feed');
43.              expect(state.page).toBe(1);
44.              expect(state.max).toBe(5);
45.              expect(tags.all).toHaveBeenCalledWith();
46.              expect(articles.feed).toHaveBeenCalledWith({ offset: 20,
                 limit: 10 });
47.              done();
48.          })
49.      })

50.      it('should update state: #/tag', (done) => {
51.          app.run('route', '#/tag');
52.          setTimeout(() => {
53.              const state = home.state;
54.              expect(state.type).toBe('tag');
55.              expect(state.tag).toBeUndefined();
56.              expect(state.page).toBe(1);
57.              expect(state.max).toBe(101);
58.              expect(tags.all).toHaveBeenCalledWith();
59.              expect(articles.search).toHaveBeenCalledWith(
                 { tag:undefined, offset: 0, limit: 10 });
60.              done();
61.          })
62.      })
```

```
63.      it('should update state: #/tag/t2', (done) => {
64.          app.run('route', '#/tag/t2');
65.          setTimeout(() => {
66.              const state = home.state;
67.              expect(state.type).toBe('tag');
68.              expect(state.max).toBe(101);
69.              expect(state.tag).toBe('t2');
70.              expect(state.page).toBe(1);
71.              expect(tags.all).toHaveBeenCalledWith();
72.              expect(articles.search).toHaveBeenCalledWith(
                      { tag: 't2', offset: 0, limit: 10 });
73.              done();
74.          })
75.      })

76.      it('should update state: #/tag/t3/20', (done) => {
77.          app.run('route', '#/tag/t3/20');
78.          setTimeout(() => {
79.              const state = home.state;
80.              expect(state.type).toBe('tag');
81.              expect(state.tag).toBe('t3');
82.              expect(state.page).toBe(11);
83.              expect(tags.all).toHaveBeenCalledWith();
84.              expect(articles.search).toHaveBeenCalledWith(
                      { tag: 't3', offset: 190, limit: 10 });
85.              done();
86.          })
87.      })
88.  })
```

The testing code is expressive. It matches exactly the test plan in Table 12-1. We can develop similar unit test plans and test code for other components.

Testing Views

Besides testing the events and routes, we can also test the `view` function. Testing the AppRun function is easy because the `view` function is a pure function. The output of the `view` function depends only on the state parameter that is passed into the `view` function.

The `view` function testing process is to set the state value and assert the virtual DOM output of the `view` function. The process itself is simple, but writing the assertions of the virtual DOM is tedious and time-consuming. The good news is that we can leverage a particular type of test call snapshot test provided by the Jest testing framework.

We convert the virtual DOM into JSON format and tell Jest to save it as a snapshot. Jest saves the first snapshot as a new snapshot. Jest then compares the further snapshots with the saved snapshot. It reports an error if the snapshots are different.

If the snapshots are different, then obviously either the saved one is wrong or the new one is wrong. If the saved snapshot is wrong, it means that we have developed something new. We need to update the saved snapshot to be the new one. If the new snapshot is wrong, it means that we have introduced an issue and have broken the test. We need to fix our code to match the saved snapshot.

Take the home component as an example again; we can develop a snapshot test of its `view` function (Listing 11-9).

Listing 11-9. Snapshot Test

```
1.    import home from '../src/components/home';
2.    describe('home component', () => {
3.        it('view test', () => {
4.            const state = {
5.                type: 'feed',
6.                articles: [],
7.                tags: ['1', '2', '3'],
8.                max: 10,
9.                page: 1
10.            }
11.            const vdom = home['view'](state);
12.            expect(JSON.stringify(vdom, undefined, 2)).toMatchSnapshot();
13.        })
14.    });
```

In the test, we don't need to write many assertions to verify the virtual DOM. Instead, we create snapshots of the virtual DOM. Jest saves the snapshot the first time it runs the test (Listing 11-10).

Listing 11-10. Saving the Snapshot

```
PASS  tests/home.view.spec.ts
  home component view
    √ view test (11ms)

  › 1 snapshot written.
Snapshot Summary
  › 1 snapshot written from 1 test suite.

Test Suites: 1 passed, 1 total
Tests:       1 passed, 1 total
Snapshots:   1 written, 1 total
Time:        7.12s
Ran all test suites matching /home.view/i.
```

We can make a change to the test code by changing the tag from 3 to 3x.

```
tags: ['1', '2', '3x']
```

When we run the test again, Jest detects the differences in the virtual DOM (Listing 11-11).

Listing 11-11. Snapshot Differences

```
FAIL  tests/home.view.spec.ts
  home component view
    × view test (28ms)
   * home component view › view test
     expect(value).toMatchSnapshot()
     Received value does not match stored snapshot "home component view test 1".

     - Snapshot
     + Received
```

```
     @@ -195,15 +195,15 @@
                                       ]
                                     },
                                     {
                                       "tag": "a",
                                       "props": {
-                                        "href": "#/tag/3/1",
+                                        "href": "#/tag/3x/1",
                                         "className": "tag-pill tag-default"
                                       },
                                       "children": [
-                                        "3"
+                                        "3x"
                                       ]
                                     }
                                   ]
                                 }
                               ]

    11 |     }
    12 |     const vdom = home['view'](state);
  > 13 |     expect(JSON.stringify(vdom, undefined, 2)).
             toMatchSnapshot();
       |                                                      ^
    14 |   })
    15 | });
    16 |
    at Object.<anonymous> (tests/home.view.spec.ts:13:48)

› 1 snapshot failed.
Snapshot Summary
› 1 snapshot failed from 1 test suite. Inspect your code changes or press
`u` to update them.
```

```
Test Suites: 1 failed, 1 total
Tests:       1 failed, 1 total
Snapshots:   1 failed, 1 total
Time:        8.018s
Ran all test suites matching /home.view/i.
Watch Usage: Press w to show more.
```

Jest has successfully found the changes in the virtual DOM. It recommends the following: Inspect your code change or press `u` to update them. If we have broken the test, we need to fix the code. If we have updated the virtual DOM, we press **u** to update the snapshot. It is a smart way of testing the user interfaces.

Debugging the Unit Tests

Although an error message can show us a stack trace when unit tests fail, sometimes we also need to go through the code execution to find the data context that is causing the problems. Many developers use console.log to print the values of variables. However, we can debug unit tests in Visual Studio Code.

To configure Visual Studio Code for debugging the Jest tests, open the file .vscod/ launch.json (create it if it does not exist). We can add the debug configurations as shown in Listing 11-12.

Listing 11-12. Visual Studio Code Jest Debug Configuration

```
1.   {
2.       // Use IntelliSense to learn about possible attributes.
3.       // Hover to view descriptions of existing attributes.
4.       // For more information, visit: https://go.microsoft.com/
             fwlink/?linkid=830387
5.       "version": "0.2.0",
6.       "configurations": [
7.       {
8.           "type": "node",
9.           "request": "launch",
10.          "name": "Launch Jest",
```

```
11.         "program": "${workspaceFolder}/node_modules/jest/bin/jest.js",
12.         "args": [
13.             "${relativeFile}"
14.         ],
15.         "console": "integratedTerminal",
16.         "internalConsoleOptions": "neverOpen"
17.     }
18.     ]
19. }
```

The debug configuration makes Visual Studio Code start the debug process and runs Jest against the current file in the editor. We can open the unit test file to be debugged in Visual Studio Code and set breakpoints. Then we press F5 to start the debugging (see Figure 11-2).

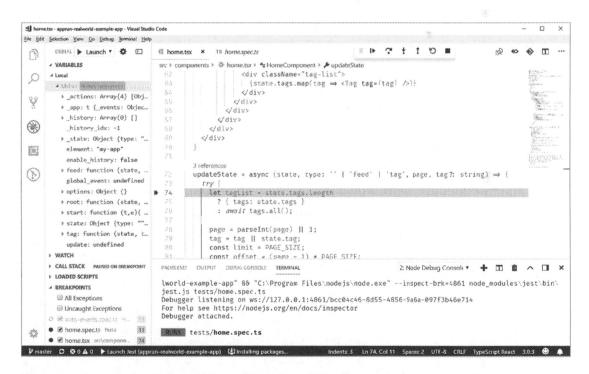

Figure 11-2. *Debugging unit tests in Visual Studio*

Live App and Source Code

The RealWorld example application is live at `https://gothinkster.github.io/apprun-realworld-example-app`.

You can get the source code from the GitHub project at `https://github.com/gothinkster/apprun-realworld-example-app`.

After getting the source code, run `npm install` and `npm test` to watch the unit tests described in this chapter.

Summary

Unit testing makes you sleep well. Whether you or your team has decided to enforce the TDD practice or not, unit tests should be part of the codebase. A well-developed unit test is as important as the application code.

The white-box type of testing is how we test the AppRun events. We use mock functions and assertions to verify the exact behavior of the event handlers. The tests can even serve as documentation. Reading the event testing example, you can see it is a code version of the event test plan.

The black-box type of testing is how we test the `view` functions. By leveraging the Jest snapshot testing feature, we can save time. Once we have developed the screens, we always look to see if they display correctly. We take advantage of this visual checking and automate the testing against the initial snapshot.

The unit tests should cover the happy path as well as the corner cases. Write a test while you are developing new features. Write a test while you are fixing bugs. The unit tests should have good coverage. In the next chapter, we will introduce the AppRun DevTools to automatically generate the event tests and the snapshot tests that help to achieve excellent testing coverage.

CHAPTER 12

AppRun DevTools

After we have developed the unit tests for the AppRun applications, there is one more thing to do. We must make sure the events and states in the AppRun applications work as expected. AppRun comes with handy tools for developers to fine-tune the events and states.

In this chapter, we will use the AppRun RealWorld example application to demonstrate the AppRun DevTools. You will learn how to verify the registered components and events and how to monitor the events and state changes of the running application.

Use AppRun DevTools

AppRun exposes the app instance globally to the window object. AppRun event publication and subscription allows us to attach the DevTools to examine and monitor the components, states, and events of the AppRun applications. There is no need to set any debug flag or compile the code into debug mode. The application code remains the same.

The AppRun DevTools script is distributed with the AppRun package. To use the AppRun DevTools, we include the script in the HTML file, as shown here:

```
<script src="https://unpkg.com/apprun@latest/dist/apprun-dev-tools.js">
</script>
```

Once we finish using the AppRun DevTools, we remove the AppRun DevTools script from the HTML file.

© Yiyi Sun 2019
Y. Sun, *Practical Application Development with AppRun*, https://doi.org/10.1007/978-1-4842-4069-4_12

Command Line in the Console

The AppRun DevTools script adds a command-line interface (CLI) to the JavaScript console. The CLI provides a few commands that we can type in the JavaScript console. To run the commands, type the following:

```
_apprun `<command> [options]`
```

The help command lists the available commands (see Figure 12-1).

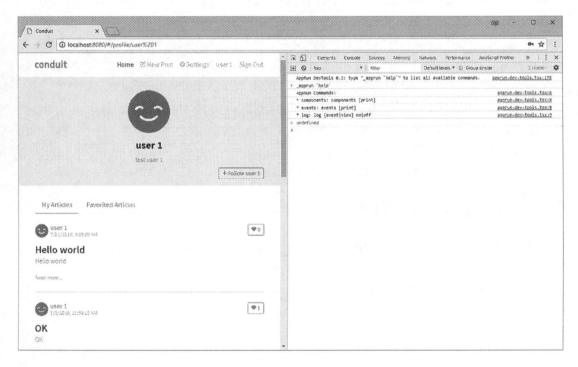

Figure 12-1. *AppRun CLI in the console*

The AppRun DevTools CLI has the following commands:

- components: Lists registered components

- events: Lists registered events

- log: Configures the logging of the AppRun debug events

We can use the CLI commands to verify the components, events, and debug events of the AppRun RealWorld example application.

Components

When we developed the AppRun RealWorld example application in Chapter 10, we planned the components and their events, as shown in Table 12-1.

Table 12-1. *Components and Events*

Element	Component	Events
#my-app	HomeComponent	• #/
		• #/feed
		• #/tag
		• update-article
	SigninComponent	• #/login
		• #/logout
		• sign-in
	RegisterComponent	• #/register
		• register
	SettingsComponent	• #/settings
		• submit-settings
		• ok
		• cancel
	ProfileComponent	• #/profile
		• update-article
		• update-follow
	ArticleComponent	• #/article
		• /new-comment
		• /delete-comment
		• edit-article
		• update-article
		• update-follow
		• delete-article
		• cancel-delete-article
		• ok-delete-article
	EditorComponent	• #/editor
		• submit-article
#header	HeaderComponent	• /set-user

In Table 12-1 the events that have names starting with #/ are the routing events. The events that have names starting with / are global events. The other events are local events.

We can use the AppRun DevTools CLI to verify whether the components are registered as planned. To do so, we can run the `components` command in the console (see Figure 12-2).

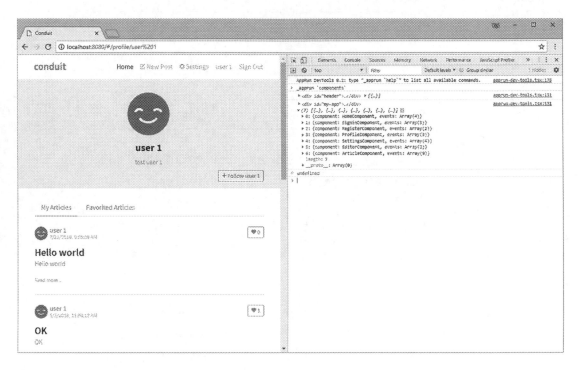

Figure 12-2. *The components command*

You can see that the running components and the events match the design. There is one component mounted to the header `#element`. There are seven components mounted to the `#my-app` elements.

The benefit of using the browser's JavaScript console is that it prints the objects nicely and allows us to drill down to the properties. We can further drill down to see the events subscribed to by each component (see Figure 12-3).

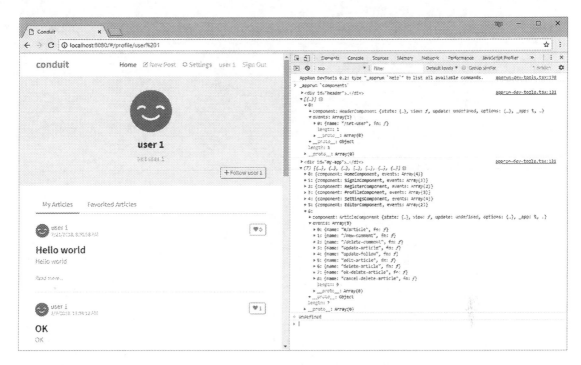

Figure 12-3. *Elements, components, and events*

The components command has a print option.

_apprun `components print`

The print option makes the AppRun DevTools CLI print the elements, components, and events in a new window (see Figure 12-4).

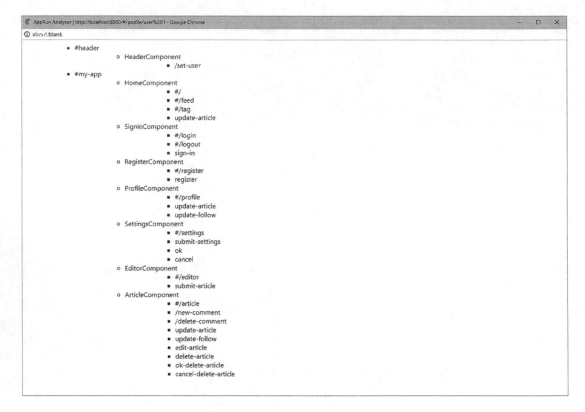

Figure 12-4. *Printing the elements, components, and events*

We can print to a printer to get a hard copy of the elements, components, and events of our applications.

Events

Besides verifying the components, we want to verify the events subscribed to by the components globally and locally. It is important to use the events only when they are necessary. Unnecessary events could cause memory leak and performance issues.

We run the `events` command in the console. The `events` command lists all event subscriptions grouped by global and local events in the console (see Figure 12-5).

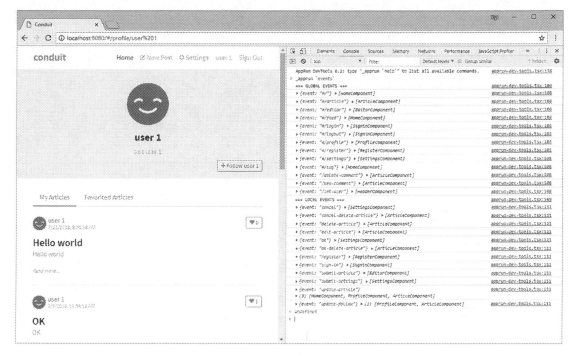

Figure 12-5. *The events command*

We can also use the print option with the events command.

```
_apprun `events print`
```

The print option prints the events and the components in a new window
(see Figure 12-6).

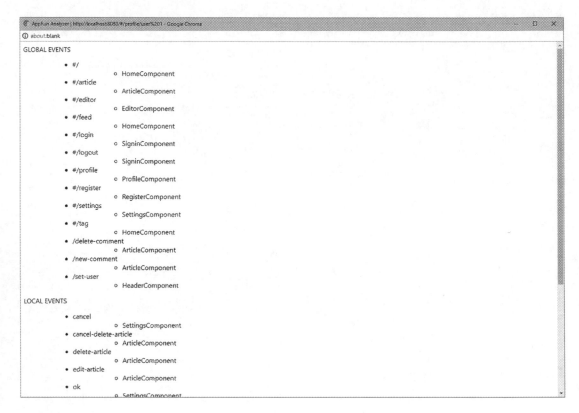

Figure 12-6. *Printing events*

By verifying the components and events, we have confirmed the AppRun RealWorld example application has been developed as per the design (see Table 12-1). Next, we will see whether the events are published and handled as expected.

Debug Events

AppRun publishes the debug events at the two AppRun event lifecycle checkpoints: when AppRun components complete handling the events and when AppRun components complete the `view` function. Using the AppRun DevTools CLI, we can turn on and off the logging of the debug events.

- `log on`: Starts logging the event handling and `view` function

- `log off`: Stops logging the event handling and `view` function

- `log event on`: Starts logging the event handling

- `log event off`: Stops logging the event handling

- `log view on`: Starts logging the `view` function

- `log view off`: Stops logging the `view` function

We can turn on logging the event handlers and view functions of the AppRun RealWorld example application (see Figure 12-7).

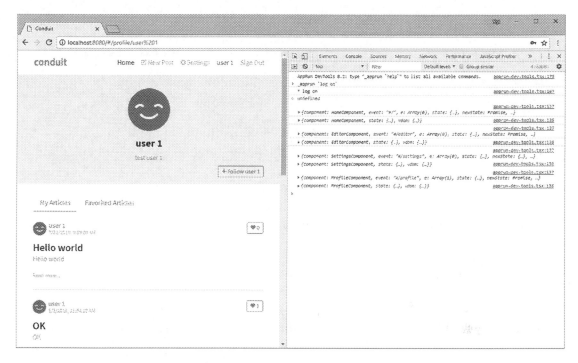

Figure 12-7. *Debugging events*

We can also drill down to examine the details of the events, the state, the new state, and the virtual DOM (see Figure 12-8).

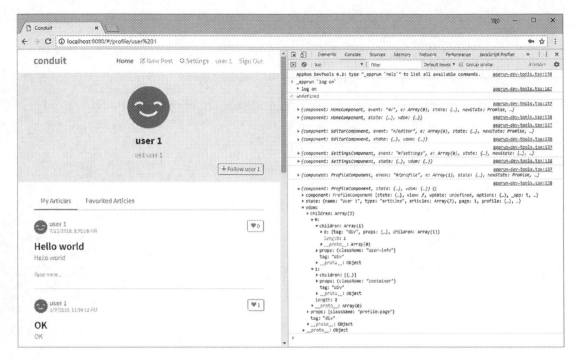

Figure 12-8. *Debug event, state, and virtual DOM*

Extend the Command Line

The AppRun DevTools CLI in the console is extensible. You can create your commands to enhance the CLI by registering your command function in the window object.

Register the Command

The AppRun DevTools CLI uses the following naming convention:

```
window['_apprun-<command>'] = [
    'command brief description]',
    (p) => { /* command implementation*/},
`[command long description]`
]
```

The AppRun CLI command is like a tuple that has three fields: the brief description, the function implementation, and the optional long description of the command.

When users type _apprun `command` in the browser's DevTools console, the AppRun CLI searches the window object for _apprun-command. If it finds the command tuple, it executes the command function.

In the command function, we use the two AppRun built-in events to retrieve the components and monitor the checkpoints of the AppRun event lifecycle. To demonstrate the AppRun DevTools CLI's extensibility, we will develop two commands to generate unit tests and to generate snapshot tests.

Generate Unit Tests

The built-in AppRun event get-components returns the mounted components grouped by the elements that the components mount to. We can iterate through the components to do many interesting things. For example, we can develop a command to generate unit tests of the components and events (Listing 12-1).

Listing 12-1. Generating Unit Tests

```
1.   let win;
2.   function openWin(name) {
3.       win = window.open(", name);
4.       win.document.write(`<html>
5.           <title>AppRun Analyzer | ${document.location.href}</title>
6.           <style>
7.               body { font-family: -apple-system, BlinkMacSystemFont,
                   "Segoe UI" }
8.           </style>
9.       <body><pre>`);
10.  }
11.  function write(text) {
12.    win.document.write(text + '\n');
13.  }
14.  function closeWin() {
15.    win.document.write(`</pre>
16.    </body>
17.    </html>`);
18.    win.document.close();
19.  }
```

```
20.  const _createEventTests = () => {
21.      const o = { components: {} };
22.      app.run('get-components', o);
23.      const { components } = o;
24.      openWin(");
25.      Object.keys(components).forEach(el => {
26.          components[el].forEach(component => {
27.              write(`const component = ${component.constructor.name};`);
28.              write(`describe('${component.constructor.name}', ()=>{`);
29.              component._actions.forEach(action => {
30.                  write(`  it ('should handle event: ${action.name}',
                     ()=>{`);
31.                  write(`component.run('${action.name}');`);
32.                  write(`expect(component.state).toBeTruthy();`);
33.                  write(`})`);
34.              });
35.              write(`});`);
36.          });
37.      });
38.      closeWin();
39.  }
40.  window['_apprun-create-event-tests'] = ['create-event-tests',
41.    () => _createEventTests()
42.  ]
```

If we print the generated result in the console, it would be difficult to copy from the console. We want to print the results into a new window instead. The three functions—openWin, write, and closeWin—are the helper functions that let us write text to a new window (lines 2–19).

The _createEventTests function generates the unit tests (lines 20–39). It is registered as an AppRun DevTools command (lines 40–42).

The _createEventTests function uses the get-component event to retrieve the mounted components from AppRun (lines 20–23). It then iterates through the results and prints the unit tests.

Include the script (Listing 12-1) into the HTML and run the command `_apprun` `create-event-tests` in the console (see Figure 12-9). This generates the unit tests for components and events in a new window (see Figure 12-10).

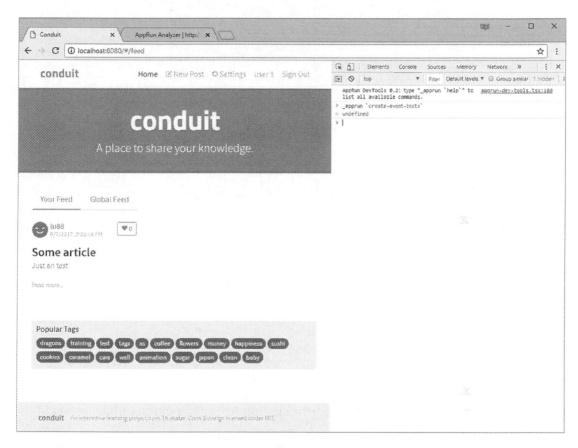

Figure 12-9. *Command create-event-tests*

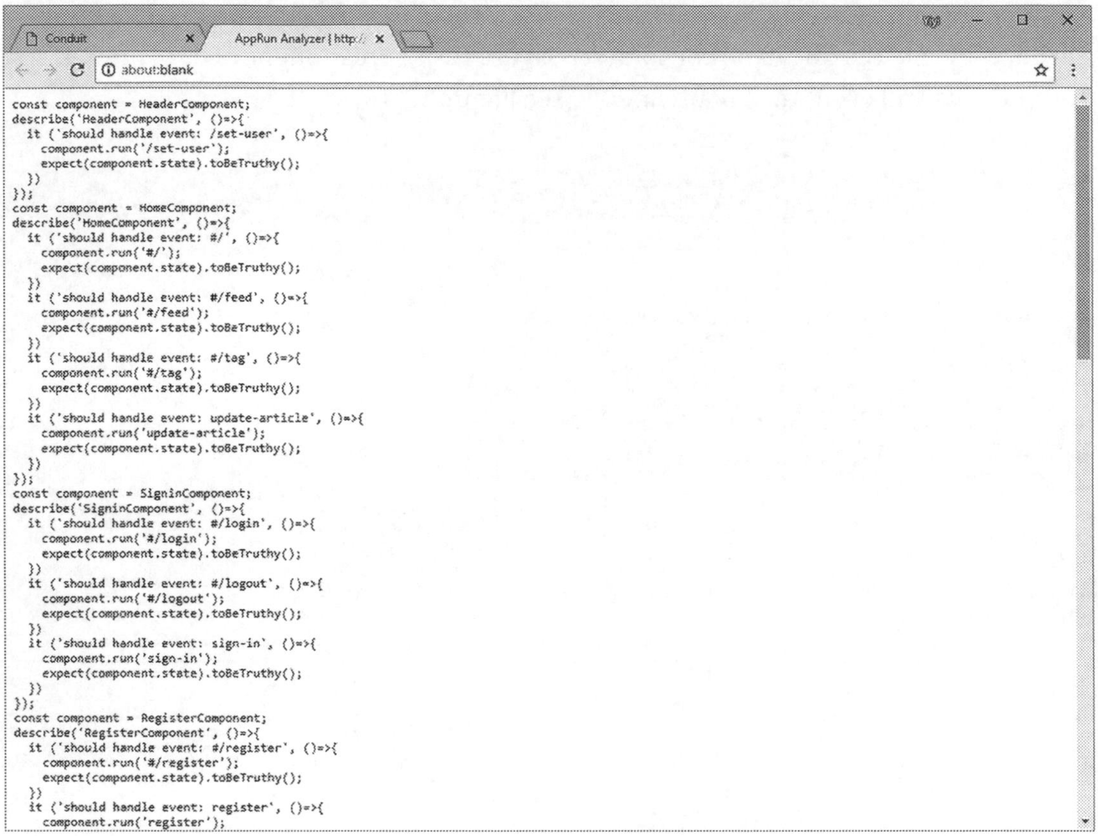

Figure 12-10. *Generated event tests*

We can copy the generated unit tests into the project and continue to add mock functions and assertions.

Generate Snapshot Tests

Besides getting components out of AppRun, we can also create an AppRun CLI command to monitor the AppRun events at application runtime using the debug event that AppRun publishes at the two checkpoints of the event lifecycle.

For example, we can develop an AppRun DevTools command, `create-state-tests` (Listing 12-2) to record the states and generate snapshot tests.

Listing 12-2. create-state-tests

```
1.   let recording = false;
2.   let events = [];

3.   app.on('debug', p => {
4.       if (recording && p.vdom) {
5.           events.push(p);
6.           console.log(`* ${events.length} state(s) recorded.`);
7.       }
8.   });

9.   const _createStateTests = (s) => {
10.      const printTests = () => {
11.          if (events.length === 0) {
12.              console.log('* No state recorded.');
13.              return;
14.          }
15.          openWin('');
16.          events.forEach((event, idx) => {
17.              write(`it ('view snapshot: #${idx+1}', ()=>{`);
18.              write(`const component = ${event.component.constructor.
                     name};`);
19.              write(`const state = ${JSON.stringify(event.state,
                     undefined, 2)};`);
20.              write(`const vdom = component['view'](state);`);
21.              write(`expect(JSON.stringify(vdom)).toMatchSnapshot();`);
22.              write(`})`);
23.          });
24.          closeWin();
25.      }
26.      if (s === 'start') {
27.          events = [];
28.          recording = true;
29.          console.log('* State logging started.');
30.      } else if (s === 'stop') {
31.          printTests();
```

```
32.            recording = false;
33.            events = [];
34.            console.log('* State logging stopped.');
35.        } else {
36.            console.log('create-state-tests <start|stop>');
37.        }
38.    }
39.    window['_apprun-create-state-tests'] = ['create-state-tests <start|stop>',
40.        (p?) => _createStateTests(p)
41.    ]
```

The create-state-tests command accepts a parameter. When we run _apprun
`create-state-tests start`, it starts recording the states (see Figure 12-11).

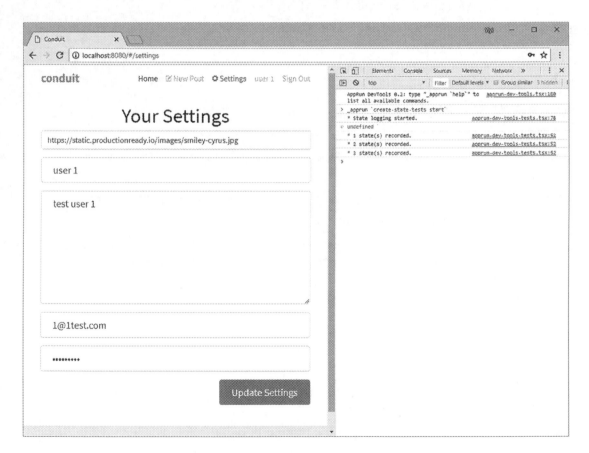

Figure 12-11. *create-state-tests start*

When we run _apprun `create-state-tests stop`, it stops recording the states and generates the snapshot tests (see Figure 12-12).

Figure 12-12. *create-state-tests stop*

Using the create-state-tests command, we can click through pages and let it record the states into the snapshot tests to be copied into the project.

The create-events-tests command and the create-state-tests command are included in a script file and released with the AppRun package. You can reference the script file in the HTML when you need to generate the tests.

```
<script src="https://unpkg.com/apprun@latest/dist/apprun-dev-tools-tests.
js"></script>
```

You can remove the script reference from the HTML when you no longer need the commands.

Browser DevTools Extension

The AppRun debug event has another great benefit. We can connect AppRun events to the Redux DevTools Extension (https://github.com/zalmoxisus/redux-devtools-extension). Redux DevTools Extension is a browser extension for monitoring Redux applications. Ever since the version 2.0 release, it allows other non-Redux applications to communicate with the extension directly.

It is simple and straightforward to connect to the extension (Listing 12-3).

Listing 12-3. Connecting to the Redux DevTools Extension

```
1.  let devTools_running = false;
2.  const devTools = window['__REDUX_DEVTOOLS_EXTENSION__'].connect();
3.  devTools.subscribe((message) => {
4.      if (message.type === 'START') devTools_running = true;
5.      else if (message.type === 'STOP') devTools_running = false;
6.  });
7.  app.on('debug', p => {
8.      if (devTools_running && p.event) {
9.          const state = p.newState;
10.         const type = p.event;
11.         const payload = p.e;
12.         const action = { type, payload };
13.         if (state instanceof Promise) {
14.             state.then(s => devTools.send(action, s));
15.         } else {
16.             devTools.send(action, state);
17.         }
18.     }
19. });
```

We can turn on and off monitoring the AppRun debug event based on the extensions' start and stop messages (lines 3–6). In the AppRun debug event handler, we send the AppRun event and state of the AppRun event handler to the extension (lines 7–19).

We can install the Redux DevTools Extension from the Chrome Web Store or the Firefox add-ons. Then we can run the AppRun RealWorld example application and see AppRun events (see Figure 12-13) and application states on the Redux tab inside the browser's DevTools (see Figure 12-14).

Figure 12-13. *Events in Redux DevTools Extension*

The AppRun events are logged and displayed in the Redux extension in the sequence of the events being published. Each of the events is displayed as an action using the Redux terminology. The AppRun event name becomes the action type. The AppRun event parameters become the action payload.

Figure 12-14. *States in Redux DevTools Extension*

The states of each AppRun component are logged and displayed with the associated AppRun event. If the AppRun events are asynchronous events, the state is a `Promise` object. The AppRun DevTools wait for the `Promise` object to resolve and then send the state to the DevTools Redux Extension. The extension can display the state on the Chart tab in a tree view.

The AppRun connection to the Redux DevTools Extension is included in the file that has the AppRun DevTools CLI engine and commands.

```
<script src="https://unpkg.com/apprun@latest/dist/apprun-dev-tools.js">
</script>
```

Summary

Developing applications involves more than just coding. We need tools to explore, verify, measure, and monitor the applications to confirm the code was developed according to the design specifications. AppRun has provided the DevTools to assist us in achieving that goal.

The AppRun DevTools are nondestructive to the application codebase. We attach the AppRun DevTools when they are needed and detach them when they are not needed. The application does not require recompiling to use DevTools.

The AppRun DevTools introduced in this chapter are part of the AppRun package in two files.

```
<script src="https://unpkg.com/apprun@latest/dist/apprun-dev-tools.js">
</script>
<script src="https://unpkg.com/apprun@latest/dist/apprun-dev-tools-tests.
js"></script>
```

You can use the commands and the Redux extension out of the box. You can also use the code in this chapter as a demonstration and reference to extend the AppRun DevTools.

Index

A

Administrative dashboard
  calendar, 166–167
  data table, 165–166
  home page, 164
  layout and styles
      (*see* Layout and styles)
  npm scripts, 168
  responsive UI, 165
Application programming interface
      (API), 141
app.render function, 73
AppRun
  application state, 18
  app.start function, 6
  architecture, 168–169
  async event handler, component, 204
  CLI (*see* Command-line
      interface (CLI))
  command registration, 274–275
  component, 9–10
  counter application, 11–12
  create-event-tests command, 277
  DevTools, 265
  Elm architecture, 5–7
  event pub-sub, 7–9
  event-tests generating, 278
  generating unit tests, 275–276
  mounting components, 275

MVC architecture, 5–6
  rendered function, 8–9
  static typed counter application, 20–21
  unit testing (*see* Unit testing)
  update type, 19–21
  view function, 7–8, 19
AppRun event handlers, 122–123
AppRun events, 94–95
AppRun SSR
  SPA, 194–195
      architecture, 192–193
      client-rendered home page, 195
      client side, 206
      components, 203
      layout function, 198
      route function, 200
      server application, 196
      server-rendered Home page, 194
      view engine, 198
Article component modal dialog, 244–246
async/await, 121
async functions, 137
Asynchronous events
  operations (*see* Asynchronous
      operations)
  pulling data, weather application
      (*see* Weather application)
  server requests
      Fetch API, 125–126
      XHR, 124–125

287

© Yiyi Sun 2019
Y. Sun, *Practical Application Development with AppRun*, https://doi.org/10.1007/978-1-4842-4069-4

Printed in the United States
By Bookmasters